국내여행 안내영어

김도영(Do-Young Kim) 저

최유진(Yoo-Jin Choi)
제임스 로라드 포스컷
(James, Ronald Forscut) 감수

Domestic Tour Guide English

기문사
www.kimoonsa.co.kr

머리말

여행은 인간에게 가장 새로운 경험과 지식을 가져다주는 다양한 객체들과의 만남의 행위 중의 하나입니다. 우리는 여행을 통하여 아름다운 추억과 사랑을 나눌 수 있으며 사색의 즐거움을 간직할 수 있고, 정신적 · 신체적 건강을 추구할 수 있습니다.

또한 교류를 통하여 교육 · 문화 · 경제적 혜택의 함께하는 공유를 통하여 인간의 삶을 보다 더 윤택하게 할 수 있으며, 참 '나'를 찾는 시간일 수 있습니다. 그 중심에 현지 안내가이드(Local Guide)와 인솔자(Tour Escort)가 있습니다. 국내여행안내영어서는 영어권 외국인의 국내 안내 시 다양한 주제를 어떻게 짧은 시간에 효율적으로 전해주고 표현할 수 있을까를 생각하며 발간하게 되었습니다. 그리고 저자의 현장 경험에 기초하여 '국내여행안내 NCS 직무수행' 능력개발과 제고를 위한 지침서로 자리매김할 수 있도록 자료를 정리하고 보완하였습니다.

아울러 영어권 외국인들을 국내에 유치하기 위해 관광통역안내사 자격증과 외국인 문화해설사 자격증을 취득하고자 하는 분들에게 실무적으로 이해의 폭을 넓혀주고자 노력하였습니다. 교재 공부 중 '수행 Tips'과 'Tourism Guide Quiz'를 적극적으로 해결한다면 교재 효과를 배가시킬 수 있다고 사료합니다.

우리나라 정부와 정부기관 및 각 지자체의 정확하고 충실한 관광정보가 없었더라면 이 책은 나오지 못했을 것입니다. 자료를 수집하고 정리하면서 각 지방자치정부 및 관련기관에서 단체와 개별 외국인관광객(FIT) 유치를 위하여 노력하고 있는 모습에 감탄과 경의를 표하지 않을 수 없었습니다. 이 저서가 그들의 노력도 함께하고 있으며 인정받기를 바랍니다. 혹 기준에 미치지 못하거나 미흡한 부분이 있다면 그것은 전적으로 저자의 책임입니다.

외국관광객을 국내에 유치하기 위해서는 관광콘텐츠 기획이 무엇보다도 중요합니다. K-Culture 등을 바탕으로 국내여행 상품을 개발하고 기획하며, 이를 알리기 위해 다양한 홍보활동을 펼칩니다. 그러나 보다 더 중요한 것은 국내여행안내를 담당하는 안내자들의 이탈 관광고객 방지 노력입니다. 기존 관광고객을 유지하는 것보다 이탈한 관광고객을 다시 충성고객, 재방문고객으로 유치하기 위해서는 10배 이상의 에너지가 소비되기 때문입니다. 여행안내자는 1명의 관광고객 뒤에 100명의 잠재 관광고객이 있다는 점을 인지하고, 한 명의 관광고객이라도 이탈하지 않도록 노력해야 합니다.

유창한 외국어 능력과 함께 우리문화 및 방문자 나라의 문화에 대한 이해도 필수입니다. 국내여행영어 안내자의 영어를 기본으로 안전하고 편안하며 섬세히 관광지식을 알려주고 배려할 줄 아는 서비스정신은 재방문고객 창출과 관광고객 이탈을 방지할 수 있을 것입니다. 그리고 문제발생 시에는 반드시 관계기관과 협력하여 어떻게 대처하는 것이 고객의 불만을 최소화할 수 있는 방법인지에 대해 논의하고 신속 · 정확하게 행동하여 신뢰를 잃지 않도록 해야 합니다.

본서가 출간됨에 있어 지면의 제한과 편집에 대한 시간의 분주함에 의하여 미흡한 부분도 있을 것입니다. 지속적으로 수정 보완할 것을 약속드리며 많은 성원과 편달부탁 드립니다. 아무쪼록 이 책을 보는 모든 독자들에게 행복하고 풍요로운 삶이 더욱 더 확장될 수 있기를 기원합니다. 끝으로 이 책이 출간되기까지 처음부터 끝까지 꼼꼼히 체크하며 쉽게 이해할 수 있도록 감수를 해주신 최유진 교수님과 제임스 교수께 감사를 드립니다. 아울러 출판을 맡아 협력해주신 도서출판 기문사 사장님과 편집을 맡아 애써준 편집부 여러분께도 감사드립니다.

2017년 7월 27일 대한민국 서울에서

저자 씀.

C·o·n·t·e·n·t·s

차례

관광통역안내사 자격시험 안내

1. 개요

관광도 하나의 산업으로서 국가경제에 미치는 영향이 크다고 판단되어 문화체육관광부에서 실시하는 통역분야의 유일한 국가공인자격증으로서 외국인 관광객의 국내여행안내와 한국의 문화를 소개한다.

1) 자격명　관광통역 안내사(영어)
2) 영문명　Tourist Guide
3) 관련부처　문화체육관광부 관광사업과
4) 시행기관　한국 산업인력 공단

2. 변천과정

- 관광통역안내원에서 관광통역안내사로 명칭 변경(2004년)
- 외국어시험이 공인어학 성적증명서로 대체 (2007년)
- 한국관광공사에서 한국산업인력공단으로 자격시험 시행기관 변경(2009년)

3. 수행직무

관광통역안내사는 국내를 여행하는 외국인에게 외국어를 사용하여 관광지 및 관광대상물을 설명하거나 여행을 안내하는 등 여행의 편의를 제공

4. 진로 및 전망

- 여행사, 호텔, 항공사, 해외여행업계, 프리랜서, 무역회사, 통역사 등 경제, 사회적

발전과 더불어 교통수단의 발전문화교류의 증대, 여가시간의 증가에 따라 관광산업은 인류 전체에 공통적으로 해당되는 유망직종임.

- 외국인 관광객을 대상으로 하는 여행업자는 관광통역안내사 자격을 가진 사람을 관광안내에 종사하도록 관광진흥법이 개정 되었습니다.(동법 제38조제1항 단서 신설, 2009. 3. 2 일부개정)

5. 응시자격

- 제한 없음

※ 단, 「관광진흥법」 제38조제5항(동법 제7조 준용)에 해당하는 결격사유가 없는 자

6. 결격사유

관광통역안내사 결격사유자

1. 금치산자, 한정치산자
2. 파산선고를 받고 복권되지 아니한 자
3. 이 법을 위반하여 징역 이상의 실형을 선고받고 그 집행이 끝나거나 집행을 받지 아니하기로 확정된 후 2년이 지나지 아니한 자 또는 형의 집행유예 기간 중에 있는 자

7. 시험과목 및 방법(배점)

구 분	교시	시 험 과 목	문항수	배점	시험시간	시험방법
제1차 시험	1	1. 국사(근현대사 포함) 2. 관광자원해설	25	40% 20%	50분 (09:30~10:20)	객 관 식 4지택일형
	2	3. 관광법규 4. 관광학개론	25	20% 20%	50분 (10:50~11:40)	
제2차 시험	1. 국가관, 사명감 등 정신자세 2. 전문지식과 응용능력 3. 예의, 품행 및 성실성 4. 의사발표의 정확성과 논리성				1인당 10~15분 내외	면 접

※ 외국어시험은 공인외국어성적으로 대체

8. 합격기준

구 분	합 격 결 정 기 준
1차 시험	매 과목 4할 이상이고 전 과목 점수가 배점 비율로 환산하여 6할 이상
2차 시험	총점의 6할 이상을 득점한 자

9. 취득 방법

〈관광진흥법 제38조〉

관광종사원의 자격을 취득하려는 자는 문화체육부장관이 실시하는 시험에 합격한 후 문화체육부장관에게 등록하여야 한다.

10. 공인어학성적기준

	TOEIC	TEPS	TOEFL		G-TELP (Level 2)	FLEX	PELX (main)
			CBT	IBT			
영어	760점 이상	677점 이상	217점 이상	81점 이상	74점 이상	776점 이상	345점 이상

	JPT	일검(NIKKEN)	FLEX	JLPT
일본어	740점 이상	750점 이상	776점 이상	N1 이상

	HSK	FLEX	BCT			CPT	TOP(TOCFL)
중국어	5급 이상	776점 이상	4급 이상	듣기/읽기 601점 이상	듣기/읽기/쓰기 181점 이상	750점 이상	고급 5급 이상 (Lv. 4 이상)

	불어		독일어		스페인어		러시아어		이탈리아어		그 외
	FLEX	DELF	FLEX	독일어 능력 검정시험	FLEX	DELF	FLEX	TORFL	CILS	CELI	
기타	776점 이상	DELF B2 이상	776점 이상	Goethe-Zertifikat 1 B1(ZD) 이상	776점 이상	Diploma Intermedia 이상	776점 이상	1단계 이상	Livello Due-B2 이상	CELI B 이상	625점 이상

※ 시험은 정기시험만 인정하며 응시원서접수 마감일 기준 2년 이내에 시행된 시험에서 취득한 점수에 한함

※ FLEX는 듣기, 읽기 영역만 포함

11. 면제 대상자

■ **외국어시험, 일부과목, 필기시험 면제 근거**

- 필기시험 및 외국어시험에 합격하고 면접시험에 불합격한 자에 대하여는 다음 회의 시험에만 필기시험 및 외국어 시험을 면제
- 「고등교육법」에 따른 전문대학 이상의 학교 또는 다른 법령에서 이와 동등 이상의 학력이 인정되는 교육기관에서 해당 외국어를 3년 이상 계속하여 강의한 자에 대하여 해당 외국어시험을 면제
- 4년 이상 해당 언어권의 외국에서 근무하거나 유학을 한 경력이 있는 자 및 「초 · 중등교육법」에 따른 중 · 고등학교 또는 고등기술학교에서 해당 외국어를 5년 이상 계속하여 강의한 자에 대하여 해당 외국어 시험을 면제
- 「고등교육법」에 따른 전문대학 이상의 학교에서 관광분야를 전공하고 졸업한 자(졸업예정자 및 관광분야 과목을 이수하여 다른 법령에서 이와 동등한 학력을 취득한 자를 포함한다)에 대하여 필기시험 중 관광법규 및 관광학개론 과목을 면제
- 관광통역안내사 자격증을 소지한 자가 다른 외국어를 사용하여 관광안내를 하기 위하여 시험에 응시하는 경우 필기시험을 면제
- 문화체육관광부장관이 정하여 고시하는 교육기관에서 실시하는 60시간 이상의 실무교육과정을 이수한 사람에 대하여 필기시험 중 관광법규 및 관광학개론 과목을 면제.

※ 이 경우 실무교육과정의 교육과목 및 그 비중은 다음과 같다.

1) 관광법규 및 관광학개론 : 30%
2) 관광안내실무 : 20%
3) 관광자원안내실습 : 50%

■통계자료(최근 5년)

구 분		2011	2012	2013	2014	2015
1차	대상	2,930	6,083	9,423	11,465	14,680
	응시	2,618	5,466	8,278	10,418	13,096
	응시률(%)	89.4%	89.9%	87.8%	90.9%	89.2%
	합격	1,214	1,503	2,476	4,260	3,481
	합격률(%)	46.4%	27.5%	29.9%	40.9%	27.0%
2차	대상	1,530	2,014	3,123	6,233	5,441
	응시	1,404	1,862	2,902	5,730	4,879
	응시률(%)	91.8%	92.5%	92.9%	91.9%	90.0%
	합격	899	1,164	1,674	3,198	2,522
	합격률(%)	64.0%	62.5%	57.7%	55.8%	52.0%

국내여행 안내영어(Domestic Tour Guide English) NCS 직무 개요

1. 직무 개요 및 정의

국내여행안내는 우리나라를 여행하는 외래관광객을 대상으로 안전하고 즐겁게 여행할 수 있도록 편의를 제공하고 국내여행안내 행사지시서 확인, 국내여행안내 행사준비, 영접(meeting), 교통편 탑승 후 오리엔테이션, 관광자원 해설, 국내여행안내 행사진행, 국내여행안내 안전관리, 국내여행안내 고객만족관리, 환송(Sending), 국내여행안내 정산 · 보고를 하는 일이다.

2. 능력단위

순번	능 력 단 위	
1	국내여행안내 행사지시서 확인	
2	국내여행안내 행사준비	
3	영접(meeting)	
4	교통편 탑승 후 오리엔테이션	
5	관광자원 해설	
6	국내여행안내 행사진행	
7	국내여행안내 시 안전관리	
8	국내여행고객 만족관리	
9	환송(Sending)	
10	국내여행안내 정산 · 보고	
11	영접(meeting) 지원	
12	환송(Sending) 지원	

3. 능력단위 사례

분류번호 : 1203010305_16v2

능력단위 명칭 : 관광자원 해설

능력단위 정의 : 관광자원 해설이란 스토리를 발굴하고, 차내에서 사전 안내 및 현장에서 자원을 안내하고, 질의에 응답하는 능력이다.

<table>
<tr><th>능력단위요소</th><th>수 행 준 거</th></tr>
<tr><td rowspan="4">1203010305_
16v2.1
스토리 발굴하기</td><td>1.1 해설 관광자원에 따라 관련정보를 수집할 수 있다.
1.2 해설 관광자원에 따라 고객들에게 전달할 핵심 스토리를 발굴할 수 있다.
1.3 해설 관광자원에 따라 고객들에게 전달할 부가정보를 고안할 수 있다.</td></tr>
<tr><td>【지 식】
• 역사, 문화, 지리에 대한 상식 • 여행사 업무
• 소비자 심리 • 관광자원</td></tr>
<tr><td>【기 술】
• 정보수집 능력 • 컴퓨터활용 능력
• 언어능력</td></tr>
<tr><td>【태 도】
• 적극적, 능동적 태도 • 여행사지침 준수
• 예의바르고 친절한 태도</td></tr>
<tr><td rowspan="4">1203010305_
16v2.2
차내에서 사전
안내하기</td><td>2.1 고객들에게 관광지에서의 활동시간을 안내할 수 있다.
2.2 차량에서 하차 전, 고객들에게 차량정보에 대해 안내할 수 있다.
2.3 차량에서 해설하게 될 관광자원에 대한 기본 안내를 할 수 있다.</td></tr>
<tr><td>【지 식】
• 역사, 문화, 지리에 대한 상식 • 여행사 업무
• 소비자 심리 • 관광자원</td></tr>
<tr><td>【기 술】
• 정보수집 능력 • 컴퓨터활용 능력 • 언어능력</td></tr>
<tr><td>【태 도】
• 적극적, 능동적 태도 • 여행사지침 준수
• 예의바르고 친절한 태도</td></tr>
<tr><td rowspan="4">1203010305_
16v2.3
현장에서 자원
안내하기</td><td>3.1 관광자원을 해설할 안내장소를 선정할 수 있다.
3.2 해설 관광자원에 따라 고객들에게 핵심스토리를 안내할 수 있다.
3.3 해설 관광자원에 따라 전달할 부가정보를 안내할 수 있다.</td></tr>
<tr><td>【지 식】
• 역사, 문화, 지리에 대한 상식 • 여행사 업무
• 소비자 심리 • 관광자원</td></tr>
<tr><td>【기 술】
• 정보수집 능력 • 컴퓨터활용 능력 • 언어능력</td></tr>
<tr><td>【태 도】
• 적극적, 능동적 태도 • 여행사지침 준수
• 예의바르고 친절한 태도</td></tr>
</table>

능력단위요소	수 행 준 거
1203010305_16v2.4 질의 · 응답하기	4.1 관광대상에 대해 해설과 연관된 질문을 유도할 수 있다. 4.2 관광대상에 대해 고객들의 질문에 응답할 수 있다. 4.3 관광 대상에 대해 고객들의 예상 외 질문에 대처할 수 있다.
	【지 식】 • 역사, 문화, 지리에 대한 상식 • 여행사 업무 • 고객관리에 대한 지식 • 여행일정 • 관광자원
	【기 술】 • 정보수집 능력 • 의사소통 능력 • 대인관계기술 • 언어능력
	【태 도】 • 복장, 용모 등 자기관리 노력 • 긍정적인 사고와 태도 • 경어사용 태도 • 예의바르고 친절한 태도

4. 평가 시 고려사항

- 수행준거에 제시되어 있는 내용을 성공적으로 수행할 수 있는지를 평가해야 한다.
- 평가자는 다음 사항을 평가해야 한다.
  - 여행상품에 대한 이해
  - 관광자원에 대한 이해
  - 행사 지시서 이해 능력
  - 정보수집 능력(해설 관광자원에 정보 수집, 스토리 발굴 등)
  - 의사소통 능력(해설 · 질의응답 등)
  - 대인관계 능력

5. 직업기초능력

순번	직업기초능력	
	주요영역	하위영역
1	의사소통능력	문서이해 능력, 문서작성 능력, 경청능력, 의사표현 능력, 기초외국어 능력
2	대인관계능력	팀워크능력, 리더십능력, 갈등관리 능력, 협상능력, 고객서비스능력
3	자원관리능력	시간자원관리능력, 예산자원관리 능력, 물적자원관리능력, 인적자원관리능력
4	직업윤리	근로윤리, 공동체 윤리
5	문제해결능력	사고력, 문제처리 능력

Part 1

Korea and Seoul To Begin With

Unit 1

Meeting

Domestic Tour Guide English

Unit 1

Meeting

- ♣ 가이드 미팅 후 대기하시는 동안 휴대품 정리와 음료준비, 관광중에 필요한 물건은 트렁크에서 손가방에 미리 챙겨주세요. 큰 짐은 버스 아래 칸에 넣겠습니다. 관광도중에 꺼내기 어렵습니다.
- ♣ 서로 원활한 일정을 위해 대기하시는 동안 미리 준비해주시기 바랍니다. 한국의 버스 드라이버는 물을 판매하지 않습니다. 근처 자판기 또는 편의점을 이용하시기 바랍니다. 1,000원 지폐도 가능합니다.
- ♣ 협조의 말씀; 버스의 맨 앞쪽 좌석은 가이드 전용석이므로 비워둡니다. 안전상의 이유로 사고시 여행자 보험이 적용되지 않습니다.-세계 공통-
- ♣ 여행 중 아침식사는 대부분 호텔식이며 점심, 저녁은 관광 중 한식이나 현지식입니다. (혹 소지하고 계신 주류를 식당에서 드시는 것은 결례가 됩니다. 특히 뷔페식사시 적당량을 가져다 드시고, 음식이나 음료수등 반출하지 않도록 합니다).
- ♣ 여행 중 식당에서 음료 및 알코올 종류는 별도의 요금을 지불합니다.
- ♣ 호텔 욕실사용 시 욕실문을 반드시 닫고 샤워커튼을 안쪽으로 치고 사용하십시오.
- ♣ 버스 안에서는 관자 등 음식물을 반입하여 드시는 경우 의자나 바닥에 흘리지 않도록 주의하셔야 하며 특히 아이스크림, 탄산음료의 종류는 차내에서 드시지 않도록 부탁 드립니다.
- ♣ 관광지에서는 크게 떠들거나 예의에 어긋나는 일이 없도록 서로 주의하시고, 품위를 지켜주시기 바랍니다.
- ♣ 여행 시 서로 배려하는 마음을 가지고 즐거운 여행이 되시길 바랍니다.
- ♣ 공항 미팅 후 가이드는 간단한 자기소개 및 인사와 함께 여행 중 고객들이 여행 안전을 지켜야 할 주의 사항과 일정 소개를 합니다. 또한 도착 공항 및 교통안내, 숙박호텔, 당일 일정 등을 안내 후 호텔도착 시까지의 안내를 진행합니다. 특히 안전여행을 위한 관광지 및 호텔외출시 주의 사항, 주의해야 할 교통안전, 다양한 교통편 이용, 안전하고 재미있게 즐길 수 있는 밤문화 등에 대하여 다음과 같이 안내합니다.

My name is James Kim. I'd like to welcome you all to korea. On behalf of Korea Tour Agency. I am your guide and will support you during the tour.

I'll tell you all about the things you will see. If you have any questions, please ask. It's my job to answer them. All my time is free to talk to you, sightseers.

Photo 1-1 Incheon Airport (Credit: Incheon Airport)

♣ 인천공항에 대한 간단한 소개

We arrived to the Incheon international Airport at noon, opened in March 2001, It is the largest airport in Korea and serves as the main arrivals gate for travelers visiting Korea.

In particular, the Incheon International Airport was ranked No.1 by Airport Service Quality (ASQ) for operating transportation services to 186 cities, carrying 49 million passengers, its ability to handle 2.6 million tons of freight.

There are several different ways to travel from Incheon International Airport to downtown Seoul.

The most popular ways include taking the Airport Railroad Express (AREX), Seoul Metropolitan Subway, airport limousine buses, and taxis. Among these, the Airport Railroad has the benefit of avoiding traffic on the roads, allowing tourists to arrive at their destination at a specific time.

The Airport Railroad Express runs directly from Incheon International Airport to Seoul Station, with no stops along the way.

On the other hand, the airport buses make it easy to reach a variety of tourist attractions and hotels throughout Seoul. For tourists who spent a long time on the airplane, the spacious seats of the airport limousines are well sought after.

If the train and bus are too confusing, visitors can also pay more and take a taxi from the airport directly to their destination.

There are six arrival gates named A, B, C, D, E, and F at Incheon Airport. Welcoming parties should always check the monitor and go to the designated gates to meet arriving passengers. After checking the arrival gate on the flight information monitor, you may wait at the appropriate arrival gate or stay at the meeting area located between gates A and B (east) or between gates E and F (west).

♣ 공항에서 호텔까지의 일정 중 한강 및 국회의사당 소개

The bus ride to you hotel takes you about 1hour 10minutes. Right now I'd like to take a minute to familiarize you with the area and tell a brief safety precaution. You have to fasten safety belts and remain seated until we reach your respective hotels.

I promise you are going to enjoy your stay here in Korea. This is a beautiful, capital city in Korea where you can relax, enjoy great meals and feel very safe.

At this time we are passing by The Han River. It is the 2nd longest river in Korea and provides the main water supply to the citizens of Seoul. The comprehensive development plan of the Han River has begun this and will be completed by 2021.

It has played very important role in the history of Korea from the ancient time.

Photo 1-2 The Han River Park

The domed structure over there is the national assembly building of korea. It is regarded as the largest among its counterparts in Asia.

The national assembly building was constructed in 1975 and was specially designed to accommodate all the representatives of the northern part as well as the southern part of our country.

It is modeled of this renaissance. The national assembly of Korea adopts a unicameral legislature system and the tenure of office of the members is 4 years.

The building stands as a symbol of parliamentarianism, public census. civil rights and the national solidarity for the essential reunification of our divided country.

Photo 1-3 The national assembly of korea

Tourism Guide Quiz

1. Introduce yourself briefly.
2. Explain Incheon International Airport.
3. Explain the Han River.

4. Introduce the national assembly building.

5. Can you tell me about the definition of being a good tour guide.

수행 Tips : The ability to raise

Table 1-1 고객 현장안전 지침서

관광지에서	• 모이는 장소, 시간 잘 기억해주시고 가이드 인솔에 협조 부탁드립니다. • 일행과 떨어지거나 길을 잃었을 땐 당황하지 마시고 가이드 및 인솔자에게 연락해 주세요(가이드 및 인솔자 연락처는 안내문 첫장에 기록되어 있으며 여행중 꼭 기록하여 소지해주세요).
버스에서	• 버스 맨 앞쪽 좌석은 비워주세요.(안전상의 이유) • 버스 이동 시 서서 움직이는 것은 위험합니다. 안전벨트는 꼭 매 주세요. • 버스, 호텔, 기타 지역에서 귀중품을 분실하지 않도록 귀중품은 본인 책임하에 잘 관리해 주세요. • 내리고 타실 때는 안전상 위험하오니 버스가 완전히 정차된 이후에 내려주세요.
식당에서	• 한국에서는 식사 후 발생되는 문제(식중독, 배탈 등)의 책임 소재 관계로 외부 음식, 반입, 반출을 금합니다. 양해바랍니다. 물론 사용하신 물통으로 식당에서 물을 받는 것도 위생 상 나쁩니다. • 개별적으로 가져오신 주류는 식당 반입을 금합니다. 방에서 드시는게 좋습니다.
호텔에서	• 호텔시설 이용 시(목욕탕, 수영장 등) 미끄러지지 않도록 조심하세요. • 금연방에서 흡연 시 벌금이 발생될 수 있으며, 타인에게 피해를 줄 수 있으니 유의해 주세요.
호텔에서 외출 시	• 일정 이후에 발생된 사고는 본인 책임입니다. 항상 주의해 주세요. • 외출 시 호텔 브로쉬어, 호텔안내 카드, 가이드 및 인솔자 연락처는 꼭 소지해 주세요. • 한국의 차량통행 방향이 고객의 국가와 반대일 수 있으니, 횡단보도 건널 때에는 반드시 좌우측을 확인하고 건너세요. 또한 무단횡단은 절대로 하지 말아야 합니다. • 외출 시 자전거 및 오토바이와 부딪치는 사고가 종종 발생합니다. 항상 주의바랍니다.

목욕탕 및 온천여행 시	• 목욕탕 바닥이 미끄럽습니다. 가끔 목욕 중 넘어지는 사고가 발생됩니다. 항상 조심해 주세요. • 몸에 문신이 있으신 분은 대중목욕탕에 가시는 것을 삼가주세요. • 혈압이 높으시거나 심장이 약하신 분, 그리고 술을 드신 분은 가능한 온천 및 대중목욕탕 이용을 자제해 주세요. • 온천 탕에서는 5분 정도 담그시고, 5분씩 3회 정도 즐겨주세요(너무 오래 탕에서 몸을 담그시면 건강에 좋지 않을 수도 있습니다). • 온탕을 즐기신 후(젖은 머리, 얇은 옷)은 감기 걸릴 수 있으니 항상 철저히 관리하시기 바랍니다.
기타 사항 및 고객관계 시	• 일부 고객의 이기적인 행동으로 고객 간의 말다툼이 가끔 발생되고 있습니다. 함께 여행시 언어 문제 및 기타 행동에서 배려하는 자세로 임하여 주시고, 눈살을 찌프릴 수 있는 개인적인 행동들은 스스로 자제해 주세요. 항상 즐겁고 가치 있으며 의미 있는 여행길이 될 수 있도록 고객 간의 상호 배려와 양보는 대단히 필요합니다.

Table 1-2 좋은 가이드가 되기 위한 논의

■항상 긍정적으로 행해야 할 자세

- 고객에게 감성을 담은 따뜻한 미소
- 시간과 장소에 적합한 복장
- 고객만족을 실현 할 수 있는 인내심
- 불평행동에 대한 지혜로운 자세와 처리
- 친절, 긍정, 공손, 편안한 가이드 안내
- 조사와 연구를 통한 정확한 안내 멘트
- 여행에 대한 흥미와 관심을 갖게 하는 지속적인 노력과 연구
- 버스 운전사 및 현지 안내가이드에 대한 배려
- 여행참가 고객들의 이름 기억하기
- 여행법규 및 관계 기관의 약관 이행하기(모든 여행지에서)

■기억하고 잊지 말아야 할 자세

- 항상 여행고객의 즐겁고 유익한 여행을 위하여 일하고 있음을 잊지 마라! -모든 고객들에게 공평한 자세로 임하고 특별인에게 호의적 태도는 삼가 주십시오!
- 항상 평정심을 유지하고 오버하지 하지 않도록 하라!
- 위선적이고 경망스러운 행동은 삼가 주십시오!

- 객관적인 정보만 말하며 주관적인 말과 행위는 주의하라!
- 지정된 쇼핑센터와 식당에 대해서만 안내를 하도록 하라!
- 문제가 될 수 있는 사전정보 또는 구설수에 오를 수 있는 정보는 가능한 주지마라!
- 알지 못하는 정보를 절대로 거짓으로 말하고 전해주려 하지마라!
- 정확하게 시간을 준수하고 무슨일을 행하든 늦어서는 안 된다!
- 음주는 절대로 삼가 주십시오!

Unit 2

Korea Overview

Domestic Tour Guide English

Unit 2

Korea Overview

♣ 한국관광 시작하기 ; Origins tourism in KOREA

대한민국은 3면이 바다이며, 일본/중국과 접하고 있어 국제무역의 허브인 반도국가이다. 지리적으로 중위도 북반구에 위치하고 아름다운 자연을 갖고 있으며 4계절을 지닌 면적 10만 33평방km의 나라이다. 네덜란드 면적의 2배, 독일면적의 1/3의 면적을 지닌 한국은 약 5천1백만명의 인구를 갖고 있다. 문화와 무역교류측면에서 관광을 중요시하고 있으며 약1,700만명의 외국관광객을 유치하고 있다.

Korea is situated between China and Japan, and as a peninsula, is surrounded on three sides by ocean waters.

Due to its geographical location, Korea has served as a bridge between its neighboring countries, rising in importance as a hub for international trade.

Its location in the mid-latitudes in the Northern hemisphere gives it four distinct seasons and a beautiful natural landscape. Its total surface area is 100,033 square kilometers, which is a third of the size of Germany and twice the size of the Netherlands. the total population of Korea was approximately 51 million.

Tourism has long been a source of economic development for our country. The Republic of Korea is a country visited by more than seventeen million international travelers every year. With its long history in culture and tradition, the country has a lot to offer to travelers.

Photo 2-1 historical culture and tradition place in korea

한국관광공사는 외국인의 국내여행안내와 편의를 위하여 국번없이 1330서비스를 운영하고 있으며 연중 24시간 무휴, 무료서비스로써, 외국인의 국내안내 및 통역, 여행불편 신고, 베니키아 호텔예약, 관광경찰 연결서비스 등을 하고 있다.

The KTO's 1330 Korea Travel Hotline provides information and services for most regions of Korea as well as interpretation services. 1330 Korea Travel Hotline, operated by Korea Tourism Organization (KTO), is a one-stop helpline available as a public service for local and international travelers. For any inquiries or complaints relating to Korean tourism, either beforehand or during your stay in Korea, you can seek assistance here as well.

서울은 한국의 수도로써, 언제 어느 시기에 방문해도 대단한 매력을 줄 수 있는 관광

도시이다. 매일 매일 새로움을 느낄 수 있는 서울의 강남은 전 세계에 전파를 탄 '가수 사이'의 '강남스타일'과 같이 최첨단 유행 패션 및 트렌드 변화를 이끌고 있는 곳이다.

Seoul, Korea's capital city is filled with many things to see and enjoy. It is a fascinating city to visit in any season of the year but you can make your trip even more fulfilling by visiting certain attractions at certain times of the day. The constant change keeps Seoul exciting so that even a long stay here will feel new every day. For tourists who don't have time to spare, it can be difficult to choose where to go.

Photo 2-2 Gangnam Station, credit, seoul city

Gangnam sprang to the forefront of Korean tourism after Psy's song "Gangnam Style" hit the international airwaves Known as the most prosperous area in all of Seoul, Gangnam is almost synonymous with words like fashion, trendy and cutting edge.

Visit Gangnam to feel the excitement of youth at the base of impossible-to-count skyscrapers. Experience Gangnam, an area so completely trendy and modern, it will be hard to find a trace of traditional culture! Set aside one day of your travels to discover the hidden charms and delights of Gangnam.

♣ 관광버스 이용하기 : The Ride on the Bus

인천공항에서 관광버스 이용은 1층 정보센터를 이용하면 상세히 알 수 있으며, 터미널 밖 티켓 부스에서 표를 구할 수 있다. 공항버스는 2타입으로 목적지까지 직행하는 디럭스와 중간경유지를 거쳐 운행하는 스탠더드 버스가 있다.

Airport buses run from Incheon International Airport to most parts of Seoul. Tickets may be purchased at the ticket booths just outside the passenger terminal (arrival area) on the first floor. Detailed inquiries on bus routes and bus stops can be made at the Airport Information Desk, conveniently located on the 1st floor.

Check your bus route and purchase tickets at the Airport Bus Ticket Booth inside the arrivals hall (1F) by gates 4 and 9 or outside by gates 4, 6, 7, 8, 11, 13, and 9C. Find the bus stop location written on your ticket.

Go to the bus stop and check the bus route and departure time. When on the bus, make sure to listen to the English recording so you don't miss your stop.

There are two types of airport buses: deluxe and standard. Deluxe buses operate on non-stop or shortened routes to major hotels and destinations. These buses make fewer stops (shorter travel time) and have comfortable seats with more space.

Standard buses tend be more crowded with smaller space and make more stops. Please note that the fare for the two bus types is different, even if they are going to the same destination.

Photo 2-3 Passenger Terminal 1F at Incheon International Airport

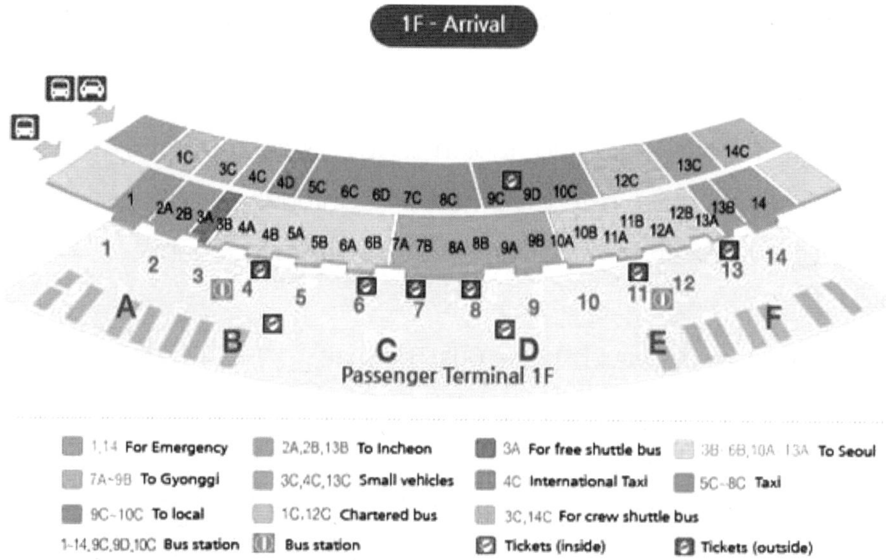

한국에는 다양한 종류의 택시가 있는데, 일반, 디럭스, 점보, 그리고 국제형이며, 인천공항1층출구 12,13번사이에는 공항 콜밴 카운터를 이용 할 수 있다.

In Korea, there are a variety of taxi types: regular, deluxe, jumbo, and international. The base fare for a regular taxi is 3,000 won (for the first 2km) while the base fare for deluxe and jumbo taxis are 5,000 won (based on taxi fare in Seoul).

Please also note that regular taxis charge an extra 20% of the base fare after midnight (24:00–4:00), while no such additional fare is applied for deluxe and jumbo taxis.

Passengers who would like to use Call Van Service, please visit the Airport Call Van Counter located in between Exit No. 12 and 13. it may cause you overcharge fare due to the unapproved business in the airport facility.

한국에서 관광지를 다니고자 할 때 여러 방법이 있으나, 가격대비 티켓비용측면에서 버스가 가장 합리적이며, 시내 중심에 있는 터미널 서비스도 잘 유지하고 있다.

They are many ways to travel around Korea, but the most popular way to get from region to region is by buses. Both express and intercity buses have extensive networks throughout the country and prices of the tickets are considered to be very reasonable.

Photo 2-4 Exterior of Seoul Express Bus Terminal

The buses are maintained clean and have very accommodating atmosphere that offers an enjoyable ride for passengers, in addition to timely departures and arrivals. In most cases, both the express and intercity bus terminals are located closely at the cities' center.

그러나 서울 종합터미널에서 각 지역으로 운행되고 있는 버스는 버스 탑승 위치가 다르므로 출발 전 꼭 확인해야 하며 직행과 일반으로 구분되어 운영되고 있다.

However, in some cities such as Seoul, the terminals are found at different locations in the city. Therefore, you are advised to double-check the boarding place of your bus before your departure. The last thing to check before booking the ticket will be looking out for bus terminals with the word jonghap, which serves both types of bus services.

Here, visitors can check the times and choose which of the two is more convenient, depending on your travel itinerary. These buses are operating either on ilban (일반, regular) or jikaeng (직행, straight) routes.

The difference between the two buses is a number of stop-over made, while the jikaeng bus goes straight to its destination.

Non-stop buses like jikhaengs can have different sign written as mujeongcha (무정차, non-stop) on the front of the bus.

한국에서의 시내버스 운영은 색깔별로 구분되어져 있으며, 대중교통으로써, 그 기능과 역할을 하고 있으며, 서울의 버스는 Blue, Green, Yellow, Red색으로 구분하여 운영되고 있다.

In Korea, city buses are one of the most convenient and readily available forms of transportation. Throughout the country, city buses provide an easy way to reach any destination, with special colors or numbers to designate each route.

Buses in Seoul are classified by color to designate the type of bus: blue buses travel on major roads and run for relatively long distances through Seoul; green buses travel shorter distances and carry travelers between transfer points such as subway stations and longer bus routes; red buses are express buses that travel from Seoul to suburban areas; yellow buses operate on a closed circuit within a district of Seoul.

Promoting this efficient management system, many other regions in Korea have also introduced similar designated bus systems to ensure the punctuality of public transportation.

Photo 2-5 Bus in downtown Seoul, credit, Seoul city

버스요금은 다른 버스라인 및 지하철과 연계하여 사용할 수 있는 할인적용 채로 카드나 현금으로 지불된다.

Bus fare can be paid either by cash or transportation card when boarding. If using a transportation card, passengers can get a transfer discount when changing to the subway system or another bus line.

To receive the discount, be sure to tap your card on the card reader by the exit doors before getting off the bus. Riders paying with cash cannot get the transfer discount so we highly recommend using a transportation card.

한국을 방문하는 국제업무자들이나 관광객들은 서울 이외의 지역으로 5코스 2일일정으로 운영되고 있는 K-Travel Bus를 이용하는 것이 언어의 문제점이나 편리성측면에서 합리적일 수 있으며, 강원, 2018년 평창올림픽코스, 전라남도, 경북, 인천/강화도코스, 대구지역의 주요 문화와 관광지를 둘러볼 수 있다. 각 코스별로 일주일에 1회 운영되고 있으며, phone, email, 그리고 online website로 예약이 가능하다.

Tourists visiting Korea and international workers alike can take advantage of a special foreigner-exclusive tour bus, operating to select regions in order to promote tourism throughout the country.

Travelers using K-Travel Bus can easily visit areas outside of Seoul, which may have been hard to reach before due to the language barrier. Now, travelers can rest assured that their trip will be a success, with guides they can understand and accommodations they can trust.

Each two-day course visits representative tourist attractions of Korea and includes cultural experiences international visitors are sure to love.

The five courses are full of things to see and do. In Daegu, travelers will enjoy a foot bath at Yangnyeongsi Museum of Oriental Medicine and picking fruits at Guam Farm Stay Village.

Incheon's Ganghwado Island features a traditional tea ceremony at the birth home of Kim Koo, a famous Korean politician. A visit to the ski jump deck to be used in the 2018 PyeongChang Olympics is in store for tourists on the Gangwon course. Tourists more interested in history will enjoy either the Jeollanam-do Course, with a hanbok experience and gayageum performance at Naganeupseong Folk Village, and a Hahoe mask-making experience on the Gyeongbuk course.

Each course operates once a week, with reservations accepted via phone, email, and online website. For more detailed information, please visit the official website.

♣ 지하철 공항선 : Airport Subways

공항지하철 로선은 지하1층 여객터미널을 거쳐 공항철도역을 통하여 이용 할 수 있으며, 버스,택시,지하철은 잘 발달된 지불시스템과 함께 대중교통으로의 역할을 다하고 있다. 특히 지하철 운용서비스는 한국인이나 해외방문자들에게 호평을 받고 있다. 지하철은 현재 서울 수도권 지역을 비롯하여 부산, 대구, 광주,대전지역에서 운영되고 있다.

AREX(Airport Express) station is located in B1 floor of Transport Center(1st floor of Passenger Terminal → B1 floor of Passenger Terminal → Transport Center → Airport Railroad Station).

Korea has not only a great public transportation system but also a well-developed payment service that is widely accepted for payment on buses, subways and taxis operating throughout the country.

Subways serve as a convenient means, probably the most favored public transportation by both Koreans and visitors from aboard. It connects you from one point to another with less hassle than often seen on the open roads and thus, making it easy for tourists to get around as well.

Subways are currently being operated around five major cities including, Seoul Metropolitan Areas, Busan, Daegu, Gwangju and Daejeon.

Photo 2-6 Seoul Metropolitan Subway Map

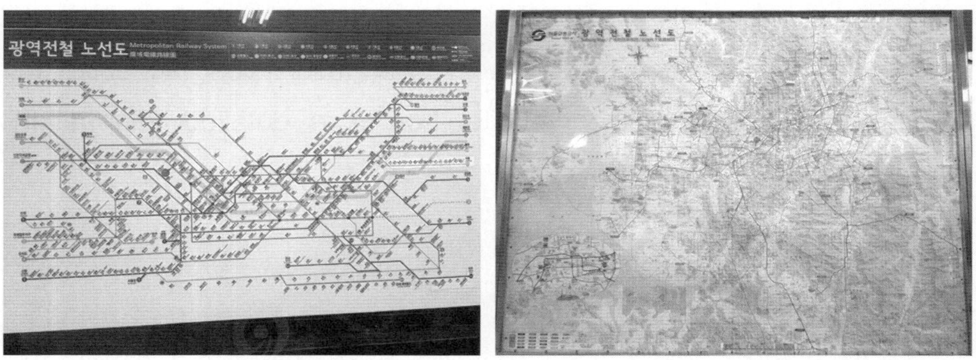

서울의 지하철 로선은 1호선에서 9호선으로 색깔별로 구분 운영되고 있으며 각 지하철의 이름이 명명되어 있다. 지하철 운임 지불카드와 함께 T-money, Cashbee or

M-Pass로 지불할 수 있으며, 서울의 지하철역에는 라커시스템도 갖추어져 있어 외국인도 편안하게 사용할 수 있다.

Seoul Metropolitan Areas rank the top in terms of its size and number where it centers the city from Line 1 to 9 and additional lines branching out into the metropolitan area.

Also, each subway station has a name, number, and a color representing the subway line, and with just a little guidance, anyone can use the metropolitan subway systems with ease.

These transportation cards can be purchased from subway stations and convenience stores. The best part of this service is that it is available to all citizens and international visitors' use, saving 100 won on each trip over the fare when paying with cash, as well as providing a discount when transferring.

In order to use subways, the first step to take is purchasing a right card depending on your needs. Passengers can either buy a Single Journey Ticket or get rechargeable cards like T-money, Cashbee or M-Pass for multiple uses. You may receive a 500-won refund for the Single Journey Ticket deposit by returning the ticket to a deposit refund device at your final destination.

Simply insert the ticket into the device, and collect your refund. Many of the subway stations in Seoul are equipped with paid lockers.

In addition, the user's guide of these lockers are offered in multiple languages. The fees for using the locker may vary depending on the term of use and operator of each convenient facility.

Photo 2-7 Ticket vending, refund and card recharge machine

Table 2-1 Subway Lockers

Term of use: Basic storage time 2-4 hours
Fees: Based on basic storage time, Small lockers 1,000-2,000 won / Medium lockers 1,500-3,000 won / Large lockers 2,000-4,000 won (additional fees applicable when basic storage time is exceeded)
Payment: Though it vary by lockers, there are many lockers that do not accept cash for payment. Therefore, payment can be made via transportation card (T-Money or Cashbee) or a credit card.

T-money and Cashbee are transportation cards that can be used on public buses and subways in several different metropolitan cities and locations throughout the nation.

With this transportation card, travelers can save the hassle of purchasing single journey subway tickets for every ride and enjoy discounts on rides during transfers from one bus to another, one subway line to another, or from bus to subway or vice versa (within a transfer time limit).

Photo2-8 T-money cards / Cashbee cards

♣ 철도정보 : Railroad information

여행객을 위한 한국의 철도는 고속열차(KTX)와 일반열차(ITX-새마을, 새마을호, 무궁화호, 누리로, 통근열차)를 통칭하는 간선여객열차 운행을 통해 운송 서비스를 제공하고 있으며, 2004년 개통한 KTX는 개통 초기 1일 평균 72천 명으로 출발하여 2015년 9월에 누적 승객 5억명을 돌파하였다(2015년 일평균 16.6만 명 이용).

현재 300km 이상의 장거리 여행 교통수단 중 약 57%의 점유율을 차지하는 등 국내 대중교통 중 가장 높은 성장률을 기록하고 있으며, 고객의 니즈와 여행 트렌드를 적극 반영하여 다양한 관광열차상품을 개발하고 매년 서비스를 개선해나가고 있다.

특히 2013년 4월 12일, 천혜의 자연경관 백대두간이 자리 잡고 있는 중부내륙권관광벨트를 달리는 관광전용열차를 개발하였으며, 철도관광의 패러다임이 한 단계 더 업그레이드시켜 현재는 협곡열차 O · V-train 운행, S-train, DMZ-train, A-train과 G-train이 개통하여 전국 5대 관광벨트를 구성하여 운영 중이며, 인천공항과의 연계는 서울을 경유하여 대전, 대구, 부산, 목포, 여수시 등과 연계하여 다른 관광지와 연계시키고 있다.

KTX (Korea Train express) is a high speed rail express train that connects Incheon Airport to Seoul, Daejeon, Daegu, Busan, Mokpo, Yeosu, and other cities.

There is a train pass sold by Korea Railroad Corporation (KORAIL) for foreign visitors or foreign residents of Korea.

These special tickets will allow unlimited travel on KORAIL-managed trains for a certain time period.

There are no limits on the number of times you can travel or where you can travel during the duration of your pass. The pass may also give you additional discounts on accommodations and tourist attractions, helping you enjoy more of Korea.

The KORAIL Pass (also known as KR Pass) is exclusively for the foreign travelers' use. Each pass may only be used within the designated period of time, as specified by each ticket type which will be introduced below.

photo2-9 Normal korail pass ticket

The KORAIL Pass holders can make use of all railroad service offered by KORAIL (including the high speed KTX trains), following the usage period.

One can choose to have the days from a single day to maximum of seven days in total, though, frequency of travel or the travel areas are not restricted.

Please however, do note that terms and conditions of use may be limited depending on traveling period, such as during national holidays and/or summer vacation seasons, and may also require additional charge when boarding.

There are two types of KR passes available – consecutive day(s) pass and flexible pass. In particular, the flexible pass is available in 2-day and 4-day pass, and you can randomly choose your desired travel date within 10 days upon redeeming the KR Pass.

However, you should activate the pass on your actual travel date at the ticket counter of any KORAIL stations before traveling.

Table 2-2 Rail Pass information

※ Consecutive Day(s) Pass

- Normal Pass : Passengers over age 26
- Youth Pass : Passengers between ages 13-25
- Saver Pass : Group passengers of 2-5 people

※ Flexible Pass

- Normal Pass : Passengers over age 26
- Youth Pass : Passengers between ages 13-25
- Saver Pass : Group passengers of 2-5 people

Ticket prices for KORAIL Pass will vary depending on the age group and terms of use applies. Travelers may purchase a KORAIL Pass voucher (e-ticket) from overseas distributors or from the KORAIL's official website.

Travelers booking the pass online will receive an e-ticket, which must be exchanged for the pass upon arrival in Korea. In case of no reservation before arriving in Korea, you can still purchase a voucher for the pass at appointed travel agencies available in Korea.

To know more about KORAIL Pass, go to www.letskorail.com.(English, Japanese, Chinese).

Applicable for regular trains (KTX, KTX-Sancheon, ITX-Saemaeul, Saemaeul, Mugunghwa, Nuriro, commuting trains, ITX-Cheongchun) and 5 tourist trains (O-Train (Central Inland Region Tour Train), A-Train (Jeongseon Arirang Train), S-Train (Namdo Sea Sightseeing Train), G-Train (West Gold Train), DMZ-Train). The pass is not eligible for use on first class seats, subways or other touring trains not aforementioned.

Table 2-3 exchanging ticket sales information

- Incheon Airport Railroad Information Center: 07:00-21:30 (open all year round)
- Seoul Station: 05:00-24:00 (open all year round)
- Busan Station: 05:00-24:00 (open all year round)

※ Exchange of train tickets is available at all train stations nationwide. However, operating hours for every train station may vary from abovementioned hours.

[Note]

- At the time of exchange of voucher for the pass ticket, present the passport that was used when making the reservation, e-ticket, and the credit card used for the payment.

- E-tickets must be paid for and exchanged for KR Passes within 180 days of making your reservation, or your reservation will be automatically cancelled. (There are no cancellation fees for e-tickets while a cancellation fee may follow if booked from overseas).
- The KR Pass cannot be reissued if lost.

※ Inquiries: KORAIL Customer Service Center +82-1599-7777 (English Service Center).

♣ 관광 촉진 : Tourism Promotion

한국관광공사를 비롯해 지자체 및 기관들은 지속 증가하고 있는 해외여행 수요를 국내로 전환하기 위해 '근로자 휴가확산+국내로 여행촉진' 캠페인을 실시하고 인바운드 시장 다변화를 위해 몽골, 카자흐스탄 등 잠재시장 개척에 주력하고 있다.

이를 위하여 한국관광공사(Korea Tourism Organization)는 한국관광품질인증제 확대 및 고품질 콘텐츠 발굴 방안 등을 통해 한국관광산업의 체질을 근본적으로 개선하는 한편 숙박제도 정비 및 규제완화, 근로자 국내여행비용 제도적 지원, 동남아 관광객 대상 비자조건 완화, 지역 대중교통 문제개선 등 다양한 정책을 추진하고 있다.

특히 최근에는 관광공사, 유럽과 미주지역에 SNS로 한국관광 매력 전파로 관광촉진 홍보방안을 마련하여 펼치고 있으며, 구 · 유학생으로 구성된 SNS 기자단 '헬로 코리아 (Hello Korea)' 출범시켜, 구 · 미주 지역의 방한 관광객 유치확대를 위하여 노력하고 있다.

이들은 한국의 문화, 관광, 여행 등 콘텐츠 제작에 필요한 전문교육을 비롯, 한류관련 이벤트나 문화활동 홍보, 주요관광지 취재활동 지원, 기자단 증명서 발급 등 다양한 지원과 혜택을 부여해 SNS를 활용한 한국관광 홍보를 촉진할 계획이다.

국내 관광지 구석구석을 찾아다니며 한국의 관광과 문화를 구 · 미주에 전파 활동을 시작했으며,국내의 문화관광 콘텐츠를 직접 체험한 후 구미주 지역에 페이스북, 유튜브, 트위터, 인스타그램 등 개인 SNS 채널과 공사의 공식 채널인 '헬로 코리아

(www.facebook.com/Hellokorea)' 페이스북을 활용하여 체험 후기와 관광지 홍보 등을 하고 있다..

한편, KTO는 적극적인 SNS 마케팅을 통한 해외시장 개척을 위해 '주한일본인네트워크' (일본), '와우코리아 서포터즈(Wow Korea Suppoters)' (동남아시아 · 중동), '한유기' (중국), '코리아 버디스(Korea Buddies)' (홍콩 · 대만 · 몽골) 등 지역별로 SNS 기자단을 운영 중이며, 전 세계를 대상으로 한국의 관광매력을 널리 홍보하고 있으며 한국 관광 촉진 정책을 최 일선에서 담당하고 있다.

The Korea Tourism Organization to manage Visitkorea.or.kr, its foreign language web page promoting tourism in Korea ("VisitKorea").

Members of VisitKorea are classified as individual or group members, and are sub-classified as Korean or foreign individual members or Korean or foreign group members.

Any individuals and groups that wish to become members of VisitKorea may obtain membership by filling in and submitting membership forms online.

Korea Tourism Organization (KTO) has released a new promotional advertisement 'Korea, KTO advertisement was devised to boost Korea's brand image as a tourist destination in relation to the Seoul, Hangang River, Digital Media City (DMC), and Gangnam-daero Boulevard etc.

The new advertisement offers a look into the unique lives and culture of Korea such as the 24/7 food delivery service, nightlife of Seoul, traditional food and art, and the haenyeo (women divers) of Jeju Island.

KTO have been to introduce heroes who represent Korea's culture and tradition. These heroes are neither K-pop superstars nor famous actors. They are actually far from the spotlight. They are real masters who are superbly skilled at diverse cultural assets of Korea. We are living in an era in which technology has amazingly progressed to the stage where almost everything you need can be searched for and found within a few moves of the fingertips, through portable devices.

Thus, this has led to the emergence of mobile application services. Such developments are also seen in the fields of business travel, with fewer people depending on tour guides and more relying on their smart devices instead.

The majority of independent travelers prefer this trend of self-motivated travel, also known as a "smart tour," choosing to use mobile applications to guide them than joining a tour package program.

To fulfill the increasing need for travel mobile applications as well as to promote tourism in Korea, Korea Tourism Organization (KTO) offers an easy and convenient mobile service known as 'VisitKorea' for both international and domestic visitors alike.

By using the KTO's travel app, going around the country is no longer a frightening experience, but an informative one as you will be well-versed with the latest travel news, popular sightseeing destinations, eateries and more. Above all, the information provided on this app is of top quality, allowing travelers to plan a more accurate itinerary.

Foreign nationals entering Korea are generally required to have a valid passport and a Korean visa assigned by overseas branch of Korean embassy or consular offices.

However, many are now permitted visa-free for a limited period under certain conditions following the "Citizens of the Countries under the Visa Exemption Agreement".

In order to check whether you're allowed to enter Korea without visa issuance and for other requirements, please contact the Korean immigration offices or visit the following websites to confirm.

A Korean embassy or consulate can issue two types of visa: a short-term visa for the visitor who wants to stay up to 90 days or a special long-term visa for periods longer than 90 days. A visitor with a special long-term visa is required to apply for alien registration at a local immigration office within 90 days of arrival.

한국을 방문하는 모든 국내 · 외국인은 세관에 신고를 하게 되어있으며, 내국인의 관세면제 한도는 $600로 제한되어 있으며, 그 품목과 항목도 국내산업의 보호를 효과적으로 수행하기 위하여 원재료 · 반제품에는 낮은 세율을, 가공도가 많음에 따라 높은 세율을 적용하는 관세를 원칙으로 하고 있다.

한편 국내조달이 불가능한 자본재에 대하여는 설비투자에 따른 자금부담을 완화시켜주기 위하여 관세감면제도 및 관세분할 납부제도 등과 같은 관세상의 지원을 마련고 있으며, 동 · 식물 검역을 강화하여 국내농산물 보호 정책은 물론 환경오염에 대한 폐해를 철저히 하고 있다.

All visitors who enter Korea must submit a written baggage declaration to a customs officer upon entry. If a passenger declares non-duty free articles voluntarily, the declared amount will be accepted and the clearance procedure will be expedited, unless the declared price of articles is questionable. More information about customs allowances and currency regulation can be found at the website.

For items that are taxable, US $600 per capita from the total dutiable value shall be exempted from imposition of duty tax. Additional duty free exemptions are: 1 bottle of liquor (less than 1 liter, not over US $400), 1 carton of cigarettes (200 cigarettes, 50 cigars or 250 grams of tobacco) and 2 ounces of perfume (about 60㎖). For amounts that exceed the duty exemption, duty on the amount over will be charged per capita. Also, the liquor and cigarette exemptions are only permitted for those over 19 years of age.

Passengers who carry any plants or soil including fruits (mango, orange, papaya, etc.), vegetables, seeds, orchids, nursery stock or cut flowers, etc., must describe the items and immediately declare them upon arrival. If you have any question about plant quarantine, please contact the National Plant Quarantine Service.

♣ 국내항공사(National Airlines)

국내항공사는 국제선취항과 국내선 취항, 일반항공사와 저비용항공사(LCC)로 구분해 볼 수 있으며, KE와 OZ는 국제선 장거리 노선이 많고, 저비용항공사인 진에어, 제주항공, 티웨이, 이스타, 부산에어, 에어서울은 단거리 노선이 비중이 높다.

한국의 항공사는 대체적으로 지연율이 낮은 편이며, 최근 국제선 취항율 증가에 의한 저비용항공사는 최근 지연이 잦았던 중국 노선의 비율이 줄면서 국제선 지연율이 감소추세를 보이고 있으며 서비스도 향상되고 있다. 국제선 항공사는 외국 타항공사와 여객/운임/화물등의 운송업무에 상호 협력체제를 구축하고 있는데 KE의 Sky Team, OZ의 Star Allance가 그것이다.

Provide convenient and safe air transport service Aim to become an aviation powerhouse leading the Pan Pacific region. Expand the serviced cities and international routes to make a leap forward to the largest air transport hub in Asia.

Hold strategic air negotiations with countries in the Central and Latin America as well as Africa and actively pursue the Open Skies Agreement with EU and ASEAN, thus expanding the international aviation network.

Promote Open Skies Agreement with North East and North South Asian countries or increasing the supply power with the advent of the prevalence of Low Cost Carrier (LCC) service.

Our national airline, Korean Air, was formed in 1969 as Korean Air

Lines. In many ways, Korean Air was a world leader in passenger aviation, introducing the world's first computerized reservations system.

Korean Air established itself as a respectable company and carrier by opening its transpacific route in 1971 and its first Seoul-Paris freight route in 1973.

Always looking ahead, the company laid the groundwork for the future when it ordered American Boeing Company's B747 Jumbo in 1972, plus 6 additional Airbus A300 models in its early years.

Korean Air introduced its 100th aircraft in 1995 and displayed consistent growth until the mid 1990s. It was then that new challenges arose, including oversaturation of the aviation industry and increasingly intense competition.

Korean Air is a founding member airline of SkyTeam, the global airline alliance formed in 2000. The alliance currently consists of 20 member airlines flying to 1,062 destinations in over 177 countries worldwide with 17,343 flights every day. **SkyTeam** is committed to offering passengers quality service and high-end comforts. The 20 SkyTeam member airlines make it possible for you to travel the world in a better way.

Photo 2-10 The 20 Sky Team member airlines

Today, Korean Air is an innovative leader in the global aviation industry known for its dedicated service that surpasses client expectations. It is not only adored by domestic passengers, but also loved by customers all over the world, and it is soaring to higher levels.

Moving forward, our goal is always 'Excellence in Flight' and to be recognized as an industry leader by promoting sustainable growth through strengthened competitiveness and by being able to quickly and flexibly respond to market changes and customer needs.

At the end of May 2017, Korean Air owned 162 aircrafts and operated scheduled flights to 129 cities in 46 countries worldwide, including 13 cities in Korea.

Asiana Airlines Established in 1988 with the management ideology, 'maximum safety and customer satisfaction through service', Asiana Airlines had developed into a truly global airline.

Asiana Airlines envisions that 'customers are transported safely, promptly and comfortably to their desired destinations at their preferred time' as the core belief and fulfills 'customer satisfaction through superior safety and service' as the corporate philosophy.

Asiana Airlines promises our members that It will provide more benefits as a member of the Star Alliance.

Star Alliance network is a premium international airline network with one of the highest number of daily flights, destinations, destination countries, and member companies. Formed in 1997, Star Alliance is the first ever airline alliance and boasts a world-class scale, service quality, and safety. At the end of December 2017, Asiana Airlines owned 83 aircrafts and operated scheduled flights to 65cities, 79routes in 23 countries worldwide, including 10 cities, 11routes in Korea.

They have pursued safety as highest priority and the world's greatest airline, making intensive efforts for sustainable growth. We hope you enjoy a fun, comfortable journey with Asiana Airlines.

Jeju Air is one of the representative domestic airlines in South Korea that is very popular among the locals.

It operates not only the busiest route, Gimpo Airport–Jeju Airport, but also more than 20 major routes in Asia including Japan, China, Taiwan, Philippines, Vietnam, Thailand and Guam as well as other domestic routes.

한국의 인기 있는 국내항공사중의 하나인 Jin Air는 24대의 항공기로 국제선과 국내선 취항을 하고 있으며 방콕을 비롯한 아시아 주요도시에 15곳의 국제선을 운영하고 있다. 진에어는 2008년 7월17일 김포-제주노선에 취항하여 첫 운항을 시작하였으며 2015년 2월 1천만명, 2017년 7월 취항9주년을 맞아 1,900만명을 돌파하였다.

한국 공항공사의 통계자료에 따르면, 2016년도 김포-제주노선 탑승객 약 1,690만명 중, 국내 LCC이용객수는 약 1,000만명으로 59.7%의 점유율을 기록했으며, 진에어는 약300만명의 여객을 수송하여 국내LCC가운데 점유율 29%로 1위를 차지하고 있다.

One of the popular domestic airline in Korea is **Jin Air**, which also offers both domestic and international flights by the number of aircraft in fleet to 24. It operates more than 15 routes international routes to major Asian cities, including Bangkok, Cebu, Hong Kong, Guam and etc. Jin Air's first flight took place on July 17, 2008 on the Gimpo–jeju route. After accumulating 10million passenger trips by February 2015, They reached 19 million passenger trips on 9th anniversary by July 2017.

According to statistics from the Korea Airports Corporation, among the 16,900,000 passengers who flew between Gimpo and Jeju in 2016, an estimated 10million, or 59.7%, traveled on domestic low cost carriers, and Jin Air transported 3million passengers. Jin Air comes in first place among the low cost carriers, boasting 29% share of the domestic low cost carrier market.

Air Busan first launched its flight departing Busan, the second largest city in South Korea, and eventually expanded routes and now operates fourteen domestic and international routes today. Speaking of its logo, it is designed as an image of a seagull and its wings that look like a sea wave and a sky, all of which represent the image of Busan very well. To add, Air Busan provides the largest space between the seats.

The fourth domestic airline in South Korea is **Eastar Jet**, which is currently operating services to regional destinations such as Gimpo, Gunsan, and Cheongju. Like the color of its logo, the uniforms feature a red-violet color that you'll find very pretty. Lastly, it's T'way. This airline operates 6 international routes from Gimpo and Incheon to Bangkok, Fukuoka, Sapporo, Saga, Taipei and Jinan in China.

Air Seoul is a Korean LCC based at Seoul Incheon International Airport. A subsidiary of Asiana Airlines, the carrier commenced service operations on 11-Jul-2016, with a four times daily Seoul Gimpo-Jeju service. During the initial stages, Air Seoul operates with three A321s from Asiana, with plans to take delivery of two more aircraft in 2017.

♣ 환경 · 문화 보호정책과 국립공원 관리(Cultural assets, Parks and Protected Areas)

한국 정부는 지속가능한 대한민국이라는 가치아래 환경보호를 위하여 다양한 분야에서 민, 세계, 미래를 향해 진취적인 자세를 견지하고 있다. 특히 2009년 국가 온실가스 감축목표(2020년, BAU 대비 30%)를 설정한 이후, 산업계, 일반시민 등과 함께 목표달성을 위한 다양한 정책을 전개해 왔다.

한편, 한국의 국립공원 관리는 공단을 중심으로 나라의 자연풍광을 대표하는 경승지이자 생태계의 보고이며, 국민의 쉼터 역할을 해내고 있는 자연 그대로의 모습과 경제적, 생태학적, 역사 · 문화적 가치를 안고 있는 소중한 국가자산인 국립공원을 미래세대에게 물려줘야 할 책임을 갖고 보존하고 있다.

현재 국립공원관리공단은 대한민국 21개의 국립공원을 지키고, 가꾸고, 관리하는 일에 열정을 다하며 '건강한 국립공원', '행복한 국민'을 만드는데 노력하고 있다.

이를 위하여 국립공원 생태계의 엄정한 보전과 기후변화에 적극 대응하며 국민에게 휴식과 치유가 있는 행복한 국립공원을 만들고자, 자연공원법 제44조 및 제80조의 규정에 따라 국립공원관리청인 환경부장관의 권한을 위탁받아 국립공원의 보호 및 보전과 공원시설의 설치?유지?관리를 효율적으로 수행하고 있다.

국립공원의 주요 기능과 역할은 다음과 같다. ① 자연생태계와 자연 · 문화경관 조사 · 연구 및 보전, ② 생물종 다양성 증진을 위한 야생 동 · 식물 복원 및 증식, ③ 자연자원 생태변화 관찰, ④ 탐방프로그램 개발 · 운영 등 건전한 탐방문화 정립, ⑤ 탐방객 안전관리 및 공원시설의 설치 · 유지관리, ⑥ 공원자원 훼손예방 및 불법행위 단속, ⑦ 공원사업시행, 행위허가 및 협의 업무, ⑧ 공원시설사용료 징수, ⑨ 공원이용에 관한 계도 · 홍보 기능 등을 수행하고 있다.

Korea has established the modern protected area system in 1960.

A look at the evolution of tourism in Korea would be incomplete without a quick study of our national parks and protected areas. The systemic conservation and celebration of korea's parks over the next century would help shape korea's identity, both at home and abroad.

The National Park System Plan divided South Korea into 8 regions, with the goal of preserving each distinct ecosystem for future generations. In 1967, the country's first national park was established in Jiri mountain, and in the 50 years that followed, 21 national parks and marine conservation areas were created.

Photo 2-11 Korea's first national park

It have designated and managed various types of 1,300 protected areas including national parks, ecosystem & landscape conservation areas, wetland protected areas, nature reserves, forest genetic resources reserves, Baekdudaegan protected areas, marine environment conservation areas and marine protected areas.

The ecosystem and its biodiversity in protected areas are protected by the relevant laws and national plans. As a result, RAMSAR COP10 was successfully held in 2008 in Korea. Based on the agreement at World Summit Sustainable Development, Korea established and implemented the first national strategy for sustainable development 2006-2010.

Korea also set up a green growth as a national policy and made strenuous efforts for a natural environment protection and sustainable development. The modern protected area system, build the relevant information and improve the capacity building of the staff for the better management of protected areas.

Covering 39 sites including national parks under Ministry of Environment (MOE) jurisdiction, this project was initiated with a number of preparatory works for many years since the first discussion in 2005 and the participation of the domestic & international experts.

Through the systematic implementation of the possible responses after the close review, it is expected that Korea protected areas system can become the world best class and the management can be effectively improved.

Korea has undergone a major expansion in its protected area system, driven by a strong vision from the government, with a promise to complete a comprehensive ecologically–representative system by 2015, increasing cover from around 10 percent to 15 percent of the country s land surface.

Natural resource management has until now received less attention in Korean protected areas than management issues such as visitor services; nonetheless, overall condition of natural resources seems to be fairly good, although data are incomplete.

Statistics for the number of threatened species that remain in danger gives cause for concern and needs to be monitored carefully in the future. Of the threats analysed, poaching and invasive species seem to be of the most immediate concern to the Koreans, although the former is reported to be declining in protected areas.

The fragmented nature of the protected areas system and climate change will both potentially be even more important in the future.

Restoration and landscape connectivity efforts are heartening and appear to be working, although it is still too early to judge final success for most efforts.

Korea has world class visitor services in protected areas, particularly in terms of facilities and interpretation.

The commitment of time and resources is impressive. Very high visitation, with the accompanying exercise and relaxation, must have positive health impacts and thus reduce national health and social costs.

High visitor numbers inevitably put some protected areas under pressure, but impacts are often concentrated and it is preferable to manage visitors rather than stem demand and therefore support for the park system.

It might be possible to provide more alternatives, for example developing alternative walks to mountain peak trails: more guided walks; broadening the range of visitor opportunities; and providing specialist cultural heritage or wildlife experiences.

♣ 문화재 보호(Cultural Heritage Protection)

한국의 문화재청(The Cultural Heritage Administration,CHA)은 소중한 과거의 문화유산을 국민 소통 · 참여형 서비스로 국민들의 문화 적 긍지와 보존에 대한 열의를 이끌어 내어 미래를 열어주는 값진 자산이자 민족의 혼과 얼이 담긴 귀중한 유산을 보존하기 위하여 노력하고 있다.

21세기 문화의 시대를 맞게 우리의 소중한 문화유산에 대한 사회적 관심과 향유 형태도 크게 변화하고 있는바, 문화재청에서는 문화재 보존 · 관리와 더불어 문화재에 숨결을 불어 넣고 국민들의 생활 속에서 향유기회를 높이는 문화재 활용 분야도 균형 있게 나가고 있다.

The Cultural Heritage Administration (CHA) is responsible for much cultural management in protected areas, along with Buddhist authorities in the case of active temples. Korea has a beautiful nature and a wealth of priceless cultural heritage as befits its five thousand year history and traditional culture.

Korea's cultural heritage includes tangible and intangible cultural heritage, monuments and folklore cultural materials of historic, artistic, academic and scenic value as national, ethnic or world heritage formulated artificially or naturally.

Throughout the years, Korea has cultivated its own unique cultural heritage in which the emotions and culture of its people are ingrained. Its cultural heritage also has an array of attributes ranging from artistic sensibility to scientific sense.

Photo 2-12 korea's Cultural Heritage

The Cultural Heritage Administration (CHA) is continuing to provide people with more opportunities to appreciate the value of its cultural heritage and to make every effort to preserve its precious cultural heritage which is not only the quintessence of human culture and nature but also the source of life.

Much of the cultural management within protected areas is of a high standard, but deterioration is clearly occurring and that there is currently a separation between natural and cultural management.

The Korean protected area system has a strong legislative base, comprehensive policies, a relatively good and apparently secure budget, agreed control and enforcement measures and a strong planning system at national and local level. Policies appear to be implemented well and effectively.

Increasingly the Korean protected area system is being linked to the international system through cooperation with other protected area agencies.

However, governance is currently confused, with different legislation and policies resulting in duplication; current attempts to address are not wholly successful.

Lack of support for enforcement from police and local courts is a problem and there are differences between national and local government aspirations for protection that should be addressed.

There are currently efforts by MOE(Ministry Of Environment) to examine a number of ways of clarifying the situation. Korea has over the last few years made enormous efforts to increase its international role in protected areas and has to a very large extent succeeded, both regionally and internationally.

The current assessment is a significant part of this process and shows an important commitment not only to make Korean expertise more widely available to others but also to learn from experiences in other countries.

♣ 국제적인 영향과 산업경향(Global Shock and Industry Decline)

한국의 가장 중요한 수출산업은 조선, 섬유, 자동차, 철강, 전자산업이며, 수출은 한국경제 성장 의존도가 크며 수출업종이 경제성장을 견인하고 있다. 최근 자유화시장 경제체제이지만 쌀은 국제시장과 국내시장 간의 심각한 가격차이로 인하여 보호받고 있으며, 모바일 시장은 개발자들이 기술적 제약 없는 혜택에 힘입어 성숙된 시장으로 알려져 있다.

South Korea relies largely upon exports to fuel the growth of its economy, with finished products such as electronics, textiles, ships, automobiles, and steel being some of its most important exports.

Although the import market has liberalized in recent years, the agricultural market has remained largely protectionist due to serious disparities in the price of domestic agricultural products such as rice with the international market. South Korea today is known as a Launchpad of a mature mobile market, where developers can reap benefits of a market where very few technology constraints exist.

글로벌 산업측면에서 한국의 관광산업은 세계전쟁과 큰 경제적 침체에 영향을 받아왔다. 최근에는 9/11테러, 사스 창궐, 이라크 전쟁 등이 관광수입에 창출에 영향을 가져왔다.

As with the global industry, Korea's tourism industry was impacted by world events such as the Great Depression and the World Wars. More recently, global events such as 9/11, the SARS outbreak, and the war in Iraq took their toll on tourism receipts.

자연적인 재해, 건강 유해성, 정치적 불확실성, 테러공격으로부터의 예측 불가능한 상황에서도 관광은 지속적으로 성장성을 유지해왔으며, 6년 연속 세계 경제성장률보다 앞서왔다.

관광과 레저산업 분야의 전망은 좋다고 볼 수 있으며, 정부의 관광 인프라에 대한 투자가 계속되는 한 여행과 관광분야의 성장은 오랫동안 지속될 것이다.

Despite the increasing and unpredictable shocks from terrorist attacks, political instability, health pandemics, and natural disasters, Travel & Tourism continued to show resilience.

For the sixth successive year, growth in the sector outpaced that of the global economy. The outlook for business and leisure travel remains robust. Over the longer term, growth of the Travel & Tourism sector will continue to be strong, as long as governments continue to invest in the necessary infrastructure.

여행과 관광산업은 세계에 일자리를 창출하고, 수출 촉진과 지속적인 번영을 가져다 줄 것이며, 한국 국민들에게 문화유산의 가치와 환경, 문화, 사회 경제적 측면에서 보다 더 큰 기회를 줄 것이다.

Travel & Tourism creates jobs, drives exports, and generates prosperity across the world. It provides an enormous opportunity to further showcase the tremendous economic, social, cultural, environmental, and heritage value that the sector brings to people in Korea.

한국은 세계에서 2010년을 기준으로 20번째로 큰 외래 관광객 방문국가로 850만 명이 방문했으며, 최근에는 한류 영향으로 동남아국가, 홍콩, 타이완, 중국으로부터 많은 관광객이 찾고 있다.

South Korea, making it the 20th most visited country in the world, up from 8.5 million in 2010. Recently, the number of tourists, especially from China, Taiwan, Hong Kong, and Southeast Asia, has grown dramatically due to the increased popularity of the Korean Wave (Hallyu).

한국의 중국관광객은 미국의 미사일 방어시스템의 서울의 배치에 따른 그룹투어의 금지에 후에 공식적 통계로 볼 때 4월 중국 객은 2/3로 줄었다.

중국의 3월15일부터 미국의 고고도 미사일의 한국 배치에 대응하여 중국 단체관광객의 방문 거부를 단행했다.

남한의 북에 대한 핵위협에 대한 방어개념이었지만 중국은 자기들의 핵 억제력의 일환이라고 보고 경제적 측면의 분노 행위를 표출하고 있는 것이다.

South Korea – Chinese tourist numbers to South Korea plunged by two-thirds in April after Beijing banned tour groups over Seoul's deployment of a US missile defence system, official statistics showed.

Beijing imposed a boycott from March 15 on Chinese tour groups visiting the South in a spat over the US Terminal High Altitude Area Defense (THAAD) system.

It is purely to defend against threats from nuclear-armed North Korea, but Beijing fears it could undermine its own nuclear deterrent and has reacted with fury, imposing a series of measures seen as economic retaliation.

한국관광공사(KTO)에 따르면 금지령 후 년초대비 4월 한달 66.6%줄었으며, 작년동기대비 27.2%가 감소된 결과를 보이고 있다. 이런 현상은 한국의 면세점 운영 등에 큰 타격을 주고 있다.

April was the first full month of the ban, and saw a total of 227,811 Chinese tourists visiting South Korea, down 66.6 percent on the 682,318 a year earlier, according to the state-run Korea Tourism Organization (KTO).

Total visitor numbers were down 27.2 percent from last year to 1.07 million, KTO said, blaming a "huge decline in Chinese visitors due to China's ban on tours to South Korea". The tumbling figures have taken a heavy toll on duty-free shops in South Korea.

The popular Myeongdong shopping area of Seoul. Beijing has banned Chinese tour groups from going to the South, hammering its tourist market and the duty-free shops of retail giant Lotte, which has been targeted for providing land for the controversial defense system.

중국관광객-유커는 한국 관광산업의 핵심이었으며, 방문 외래관광 객의 47%를 점유하고 있었다. 그러나 제주도는 사라진 중국관광객 대신 국내관광객의 방문이 쇄도하여 증가를 보이고 있다.

한편, 정부와 문화체육관광부는 방한 외래 관광객 유치에 대한 시장 다변화를 위하여 일본 및 동남아등의 광고예산을 증가시키고, 베트남어, 인도네시아어 등의 표지판을 세우며 관광촉진 전략을 펴고 있다.

Chinese visitors are key to the tourism industry in Korea ? the Chinese make up 47 percent of all tourist entries there. The prevalence of Chinese tourists has increased to the point where Korean media has even created a specific word for them ? 유커 (yoo-kuh). The term, which was adapted from the Chinese word for tourists, does not have an inherently negative meaning.

The announcement shook South Korea's tourism and retail industries, which rely heavily on customers from China. Jeju Island, one of South Korea's most iconic and popular tourist destinations, has actually seen an increase in tourism since the ban took effect.

Korea's tourism and duty-free sectors could see up to an 80 percent decrease in sales, a loss of up to $11.7 billion, if China maintains its crackdown. According to preliminary numbers from the Jeju Tourism Association, the number of Chinese tourists has indeed dropped following the ban announcement.

One of the most vulnerable areas is the duty-free industry, which relies heavily on the Chinese – around 70 percent of duty free sales in Korea come from Chinese visitors. While the early numbers suggest that Jeju may be able to survive the drop in Chinese tourists thanks to domestic travelers, other industries may not be so lucky.

However, the total number of tourists to Jeju actually increased over that period, thanks to a rush of domestic tourists taking advantage of the empty island.

Meanwhile, the Korean government is eagerly reaching out to new markets to make up for these possible losses. An official from the Ministry of Culture, Sports and Tourism told that they are diverting their advertising budget from China and focusing on Southeast Asia and Japan.

South Korea has been struggling to fill the gap with promotional campaigns to attract more visitors from other countries, mainly from Japan and those in Southeast Asia.

♣ 한국관광 현상(Tourism in Korea Today)

현재 한국관광산업은 대부분 국내관광에 의존하고 있으며, 버스와 기차의 광범위한 네트워크의 덕택으로 어떠한 주요도시든 당일관광으로 이루어질 수 있다. 총 국제관광객의 점유율 수는 일본, 대만, 홍콩 등 동남아관광객이 75%를 점유하고 있다.

The majority of the South Korean tourist industry is supported by domestic tourism. Thanks to the country's extensive network of trains and buses, most of the country lies within a day's round trip of any major city.

International tourists come primarily from nearby countries in Asia. Japan, China, Hong Kong and Taiwan together account for roughly 75% of the total number of international tourists.

In addition, the Korean Wave has brought increasing numbers of tourists from Southeast Asia and India.

In the past, during the 1980s, the liberalization of international travel has begun to take place in catering to the globalization of the South Korea society.

Since then, South Koreans have been able to travel freely abroad. The busy lifestyle of modern South Koreans, leading to difficulties in mediating vacations with family or friends, and the increase in one-person households, have contributed to the growing number of South Koreans traveling alone.

According to the results of a plane ticket analysis in 2016, the top foreign destination for South Koreans is Osaka, followed by Bangkok and Tokyo. Moreover, Osaka, Tokyo, and Shanghai have high re-visit rates for South Koreans.

However European destinations such as London, Paris, and Rome have fallen in re-visit rating, due to geographical distances, expensive air fares and high costs. The Japanese public's image of South Korea deteriorated significantly. Japanese tourists to South Korea declined by half from 3.5 million in 2012 to 2.3million in 2016, while South Korean tourists to Japan doubled from 2 million in 2012 to 4.5 million in 2016.

2010년 이후로 국내관광객은 꾸준히 증가하여 연간 총 2억 3천8백30만 명에 이르고 있고, 지출은 2014년에 약 14조 원에 이르고 있다. 외래방문객은 2016년 1,720만 명이었으며(2015년 대비 30.3%증가), 관광수입은 171억 달러였다. 또한 내국인의 해외관광은 2010년 이후 급격히 증가하고 있으며 2012년부터 2017년까지 연간 평균 8.2%의 증가율을 보여 2016년 2천2백40만 명의 해외 관광자이고 그들의 총 지출은 231억 달러였다.

The number of Korean domestic tourists has increased since 2010. The number of people who participated in domestic travel (which includes one day trips) was about 238.3 million. It increased by 4.9% compared to 2014 (227.1 million). In 2014, Korean's domestic tourism expenditure was ₩14.4 trillion. In 2016, Korean's visitor arrivals 17.2million increased by 30.3% compared to 2015 and tourism Receipts was $17.1billion.

Also, Korean oversea tourists are keep increasing since 2010. From 2012 to 2017, the number of people travelling overseas has risen by about 8.2% on average. In 2016, number of Korean oversea tourists was about 22.4million. And Korean oversea tourism expenditure was $23.1billion.

한국의 역사문화관광은 옛 수도인 서울, 경주, 부여를 포함하고 있으며, 자연적인 관광명소는 백두대간을 포함하여 지리산, 설악산, 단양 고수동굴, 환선굴, 해운대와 만리포 등을 들 수 있다.

제주도 뿐만 이니라 남서해안의 많은 작은 섬들과 동해안의 울릉도까지 왕복여객선으로 다녀올 수 있으며, 최근 들어와 독도방문 국내관광객들이 방어에 대한 정치적인 결과로 많이 증가하고 있다.

South Korea's historical tourist attractions include the ancient capitals of Seoul, Gyeongju and Buyeo. Some natural landmarks include the peaks of the Baekdudaegan, particularly Seorak-san and Jiri-san, the caves of Danyang and Hwanseongul, and beaches such as Haeundae and Mallipo.

Apart from Jeju island, there are many smaller islands. Excursion ferries are quite common along the south and west coasts and also to Ulleung-do Island, off the east coast. Limited tourism mainly by South Koreans to the Liancourt Rocks (Dokdo) has grown in recent years as a result of the political status of the rocks.

보령 머드축제와 청도 소싸움축제와 같이 여러 지자체에서 연간 축제를 개최하고 있으며, 한국의 수도 서울은 9백9십8만 1천673명의 인구에 많은 관광매력 물과 쇼핑장소, 축제와 공연장 등 문화적인 공간을 지니고 있어 사람들이 모여드는 곳이다.

문화체육관광부에 따르면 서울은 한국의 문화예술 화랑, 도서관, 박물관 36.4%가 집중되어 있는 곳이기도 하다.

Many local districts hold annual festivals, such as the Boryeong Mud Festival and the Cheongdo Bullfighting Festival.

The population of Seoul is 9,981,673 and it's the largest city in South Korea. As many people gather, there are many cultural spaces such as festivals, performances, shopping places, and tourist attractions in Seoul.

To foreigners, Seoul is an attractive place because traditional Korean culture and modern culture co-exists. People in South Korea come to Seoul to enjoy various cultural activities. Due to the metropolitan area centralization of cultural infrastructure, there is a cultural gap between Seoul and other regions.

According to the Ministry of Culture, Sports and Tourism, 36.4 percent of the total cultural infrastructure such as public library, museum, and art galleries are concentrated in Seoul.

문화체육관광부와 한국관광공사는 국내에서 꼭 가보아야 할 25곳의 웰니스 매력지를 발표했다. 웰니스 관광은 세계적인 현상이며 건강을 유지하고자 스파, 레저 리조트와 같은 건강과 힐링에 초점을 맞춘 것과 관계가 깊다.

그 매력물은 네 가지로 구분될 수 있는데, 한방, 미용, 명상 치유, 숲 치유 등이다. 지정된 매력지와 보다 많은 정보는 개별 매력지 웹 또는 Visit Medical Korea website에서 찾아 볼 수 있다.

The Ministry of Culture, Sports & Tourism and the Korea Tourism Organization have released a list of the 25 Must-go Wellness Attractions in the nation.

Wellness tourism is currently booming around the world and relates to sites where the focus is on health and healing, such as spas, leisure resorts, and health maintenance.

The attractions have been divided into four categories of Hanbang (oriental medicine), Beauty Spa, Healing Meditation, and Forest Healing.

The hanbang category includes Herb Lab Bomdong and four other sites. Visitors interested in healing meditation can visit one of the three designated spots such as Healience Zen Village in Gangwon-do.

The largest category is beauty spa, with a total of 13 attractions with the Herb Healing Center at Herb Island in Gyeonggi-do topping the list.

The remaining four locations are forest healing areas which include Cypress Forest Woodland in Jeongnamjin.

The full list of designated attractions and more information can be found on the official Visit Medical Korea website, as well as on the individual websites of the attractions.

Tourism Guide Quiz

1. What is '1330 service'?
2. What is the Han Style?
3. Introduce Korean's visitor arrivals.
4. Jiri Mountain is known for its National Park in korea. What is it?
5. What do you think is the most important tourism place or value in Korea?

수행 Tips : The ability to raise 4차 산업혁명과 여행 · 관광산업의 미래변화에 대한 사례

한국관광 브랜드-Imagine Your Korea!

- 브랜드란 살아 숨 쉬는 생명체이며, 좋은 브랜드는 우리 가슴 속에 각인된다. 브랜드가 의미 있는 존재로 남으려면 변화하는 고객들의 욕구와 필요에 의하여 끊임없는 변화와 혁신에 대한 창의적인 노력이 요구된다.
  한국을 관광목적지로서 전 세계 관광객들에게 인상적이며 차별화된 모습으로 기억되게 하려면 이를 위해 한국관광의 매력을 효과적으로 표현할 수 있는 브랜드가 필요하다.
- 한국의 인물과 문화, 역사와 환경, 상품과 서비스, 국가 방향성, 고객의 니즈와 트렌드를 살펴본 결과 Diverse(조화롭고 다양한 즐길거리가 가득한 한국), Vibrant(지

치지 않는 생기와 활력이 느껴지는 한국), Creative(새로운 가치를 창출하는 한국), Intriguing(흥미를 자극하고 유발하는 한국)이라는 네 가지의 핵심가치를 도출하였으며, 이를 통해서 한국관광 브랜드 아이텐티티를 Creative Motivation으로 설정하였다.

• CREATIVE MOTIVATION
 – 나의 감각과 안목을 높여주는 창의적 자극
 – 브랜드 슬로건 : 슬로건 'Imagine your Korea'는 활기찬 쇼핑거리, 매력적이고 창의적인 문화컨텐츠 등 한국의 다양한 관광자원을 여행자들의 관점에서 표현

• Imagine : 한국의 관광자원에 기초하여 영화, 드라마 속 장면들이 현실이 되는 한국, 평범한 일상도 특별하게 만들어주는 매력 있는 한국, 수많은 문화유산에, 명동의 활기찬 쇼핑거리까지 무한한 즐길 거리로 가득한 한국

• Your : 여행자 관점에 기초하여 FIT 관광객의 증대에 발맞춰 그들의 관점에서 매력적인 관광지로 변화하는 한국 고객들이 직접 참여하고 체험할 수 있는 문화컨텐츠가 가득한 관광선진국 한국 다변화하는 관광객들의 요구를 충족시켜주는 한국

• 슬로건 디자인 컨셉 : 한국관광 브랜드 슬로건에 대한 이해도와 기억용이성을 돕기 위해 브랜드 슬로건의 디자인이 입혀졌으며, 새롭게 개발된 디자인은 한국관광 브랜드의 창의적이고 매력적인 모습, 활기차고 다양한 모습과 한국을 찾는 모든 관광객들을 환영한다는 의미이다.

• 브랜드 플랫폼 : 한국의 무한매력을 K-Food, K-Wave, K-Spirit, K-Place, K-Style를 통해 소개하며, 새로운 한국관광 브랜드를 통해 전세계인들이 한국관광에 대하여 끊임없이 상상할 수 있도록 지속적인 커뮤니케이션 활동을 추진한다.

• 커뮤니케이션 메시지 : 발길이 머무는 곳마다, 눈길이 닿는 곳마다 색다르고 독특한 체험으로 방문자 모두에게 기대 이상의 경험을 선사할 것이다.

• 관광객들이 한국을 사랑하는 이유, Reasons To Believe; K-Food(사계절 다양한 식재료와 색다른 요리법으로 즐기는 독특한 먹거리), K-Wave(K-POP, K-DRAMA,K-MOVIE 등 독창적인 한국만의 콘텐츠), K-Spirit(한국과 한국인을 규정짓는 무한한 창의성과 열정), K-Place(현대적인 감각과 전통이 조화를 이루는 한국만의 신선한 명소), K-Style(트렌드 헌터의 마음을 설레이게 하는 세련되고 특별한 라이프 스타일)

자료출처 : 한국관광공사

Unit 3

Korean Peninsula

Domestic Tour Guide English

Unit 3

Korean Peninsula

한국은 한반도의 남쪽지역 북동아시에 위치하고 있는 나라이다. 한국의 국경은 북쪽으로 북한, 동쪽으로 남동해안과 접하고 있는 일본, 서쪽으로 황해와 접하고 있으며, 남서 앞바다의 가장 큰 섬 제주(1,845스퀘어 킬로미터)를 포함한 총 면적은 9만 9천 268스퀘어 킬로미터이다.

내륙의 길이는 1,030km, 가장 좁은 폭은 175km이다. 북쪽 국경선을 접하고 있는 북한은 동쪽으로 일본, 서쪽으로 중국과 접하고 있으며, 총면적 10만 33 스퀘어 킬로미터이다.

South Korea is a country in north-eastern Asia that occupies the southern portion of the Korean Peninsula.

South Korea is bordered on the north by North Korea, on the east by the East Sea (Sea of Japan), on the southeast and south by the Korea Strait, which separates it from Japan, and on the west by the Yellow Sea.

It has a total area of 99,268 sq km (38,328 sq mi), including numerous offshore islands in the south and west, the largest of which is Cheju (area, 1845 sq km/713 sq mi).

It is surrounded by the ocean on three sides, making it a unique geographical location. With Seoul as its capital city, the landsite is roughly 1,030 km (612 miles) long and 175 km (105 miles) wide at its narrowest point. Korea's total land area is 100,033 square km, neighboring Japan to the east, China to the west, and sharing a northern border with Democratic People's Republic of Korea (North Korea).

대부분 서울 수도권지역에 거주하고 있는 한국의 총 인구는 5천1백63만 4천618명이며(2016년7월 기준), 서울 이외의 경제발전을 이루고 있는 높은 인구밀집 지역의 도시로 부산, 인천, 대구, 대전, 광주, 울산 등이 있다.

The total population of south Korea is approximately 51,634,618 (July 2016 data) with most of them residing in the Seoul metropolitan area. Outside of Seoul, other large and economically advanced cities such as Busan, Incheon, Daegu, Daejeon, Gwangju and Ulsan also have higher population densities than other cities in Korea.

한국은 2차 세계 대전 후 1948년 북한은 러시아, 남한은 미국의 영향 권 하에 정부가 수립되었다. 서울은 남한에서 가장 큰 도시이며 수도이다.

South Korea was established in 1948 following the post-World War II partitioning of the peninsula between the occupying forces of the United States in the south and the Union of Soviet Socialist Republics (USSR) in the north. The capital and largest city of South Korea is Seoul.

한국은 세계 경제 2위, 3위 국가인 대단히 부유한 일본, 빠르게 성장하고 있는 중국과 지리적으로 큰 위협으로 느낌을 받고 있어, 러시아 일본, 중국의 침략과 지배에 대한 두려움의 이유가 되기도 하였다.

유럽의 이탈리아가 프랑스, 스페인, 오스트리아와 이웃하여 몇 세기 동안 위협을 받아온 것과 같이 동등한 위치이다.

이탈리아는 북쪽의 기술협조와 산업 원천 및 시장에 대한 영향력을 잘 이끌어 지역발전을 가져왔다. 같은 의미에서 한국도 두려움으로부터 희망의 원천과 큰 기회가 될 수 있다.

이미 경제적 측면에서 지리적인 행운이 따르고 있는바, 중국은 한국의 가장 큰 무역 파트너였던 미국을 넘어서고 있으며, 한국의 기업들과 약 50만 명 이상의 학생들과 업무 자들이 중국에서 잘 하고 있다.

Korea is, to the world's second-and third-largest economies. Japan is hugely rich, while China is developing rapidly. Korea's greatest fear has been geographic. Squeezed between China, Japan, and Russia, it has had reason to fear invasion or domination.

The closest European equivalent is Italy, which was threatened for several centuries by neighboring Austria, France, and Spain. It has turned to Italy's advantage, providing at least its northern half with booming markets, sources of industrial and technological cooperation, and wider scope for Italian influence.

South Korea's great opportunity is to do the same, turning geography from a fear into a source of hope. The economic basis to exploit this good geographical luck already exists: China has overtaken the United States as South Korea's top trading partner. South Korean firms have done well in China, and more than half a million South Korean citizens work or study in China already.

한국의 위치는 아시아 중심에 있으며, 정치 및 경제적으로 범 아시아 발전을 이끌고 있고, 정치 및 산업과 경제에 강한 영향력을 갖고 있다.

South Korea's position as a mid-sized power in the heart of Asia can become a strength-above all in political terms, but also in economic and industrial terms. South Korea should be taking the initiative in promoting the development and deepening of pan-Asian economic and political institutions.

♣ 헌법과 정부(Constitution and Government)

한국의 헌법은 1948년 7월17일 공포되었으며 정부는 국경일로 정하였다. 헌법의 첫 번째 개정은 1952년 7월이었으며 1987년 10월27일 국민투표까지 9번 개정을 하였다.

대한민국 헌법은 정부의 기본적인 원칙은 자유민주주의를 채택하였고, 다양한 법률 하에 국민의 자유와 권리를 주창하고 있다.

복지국가 설립의 필요성을 인식하고, 사회, 문화, 정치, 경제를 포함하여 모든 분야에 동등한 권리를 보장하고 있다.

또한 대한민국의 헌법은 국민은 근로, 납세, 교육, 국방의 의무를 지니며, 국제 평화를 위하여 노력해야 한다고 제정하고 있다.

The country's Constitution was promulgated on July 17, 1948 after a month and half of work for its enactment.

The government observes it as a national holiday. The first amendment to the Constitution was made in July 1952, while the 9th and last amendment was passed by referendum on October 27, 1987.

The country's Constitution adopts liberal democracy as the basic principle of governance. The Constitution guarantees the people's freedom and rights under various laws.

It also guarantees equal opportunities in all sectors, including politics, economy, society and culture, and recognizes the necessity of establishing a welfare state.

The Constitution also stipulates that all people have the obligation to pay taxes, engage in national defense, educate their children, and work.

The Constitution states that the country should endeavor to maintain international peace.

It stipulates that international treaties signed by the country and generally accepted international laws have the same effects as domestic laws.

Under the Constitution, the status of aliens is guaranteed in accordance with international laws and treaties.

국회는 국민의 대표기구로써, 국가의 모든 법은 국회에 의하여 만들어지며, 현재 4년 임기로 선출되는 국회의원 수는 300명으로 고정되어 246명은 지역에서 선출되고, 54명은 비례비율로 정당별로 선출된다. 1948년 5월에 선출되어 시작된 국회는 현재 20대 국회로써, 2020년 5월까지가 임기이며 국회의사당은 서울을 관통하고 있는 한강 변 여의도에 위치해 있다.

The National Assembly is an institution that represents the people's opinions. All the laws of the country are made by the National Assembly.

At present, the National Assembly has 300 fixed members, each of whom is elected for a term of four years.

The National Assembly is composed of 246 members elected in local constituencies and 54 members elected by political parties for the purpose of proportional representation.

The first National Assembly was launched in May 1948. The members of the current 20th National Assembly (May 2016 – May 2020) were elected in the election held in April 2016. The National Assembly building is located in Yeouido near the Hangang River that flows through Seoul.

헌법재판소는 특별법에 의하여 탄핵소추권과 정당해산권을 갖고 있으며, 3명의 재판관은 대통령이 지명하고 3명은 국회에서 지명되며 3명은 대법원장이 지명한다. 헌법재판소장은 국회의 동의하에 대통령이 지명한다.

중앙선거관리위원회는 국민투표 및 정당과 정치자금을 공정하게 관리하며 중앙선거관리위원은 정치행위와 정당 활동이 금지되어 있다. 임기는 6년이며 위원장은 위원들이 선출한다.

The Constitutional Court has the right to review whether a specific law is unconstitutional, to judge an appeal for the impeachment of a high-ranking official, and decide on the disbandment of a political party under the Constitution.

The Constitutional Court is composed of three judges appointed by the President, three judges appointed by the National Assembly, and three judges appointed by the Supreme Court Chief Justice.

The President of the Constitutional Court is appointed by the President with the consent of the National Assembly.

The National Election Commission handles matters associated with elections, fair management of referendums, political parties, and political funds. A member of the commission is not allowed to join a specific political party or engage in political activities. Their term is six years. The chairman is elected from among the members.

국가인권위회는 국민들의 기본적인 권리를 증진하고 보호를 통하여 주권이라 할 수 인간의 존엄과 가치를 실현시키고 존경받을 수 있는 역할과 업무를 수행한다.

The National Human Rights Commission of Korea (NHRCK) performs the role of respecting and realizing the dignity and values of human beings as sovereign individuals by protecting and promoting their basic rights.

The commission was launched in November 2001 in light of the people's earnest desire for improvement of the country's human rights conditions expressed during the democratization process.

The commission also handles cases concerning human rights infringement or discrimination involving a foreigner residing or working in the country.

한국은 1995년 6월에 지방자치 제도를 채택했다. 지방자치 헌장은 1949년에 제정되었으나 한국전쟁, 1960년 4월 학생혁명, 1961년 쿠테타 등 정치적인 격변 동안 시행되지 못했다.

The country adopted the local autonomous system in June 1995. The Local Autonomy Act was enacted in 1949, but local autonomy was not implemented during the period of political upheaval, including the Korean War, the April 1960 Student Revolution, the May 1961 Coup d'état.

Local governments are divided into high-level and low-level local governments. With the inclusion of Sejong Special Autonomous City in July 2012, the number of high-level local governments was increased to seventeen (i.e. Seoul Special City, six metropolises, eight provinces, and Jeju Special Self-Governing Province).

The number of low-level local governments stands at 226 (i.e. si/gun/gu). The heads of local governments and councilors are elected through direct election. The term for local government heads is four years, and they can be reelected for up to three terms.

한국은 다른 나라와 협조와 친선관계 증진을 위하여 노력하고 있으며, 2012년까지 189개 나라와 외교관계를 맺었고, 수립하였고, 112나라와 대사관계를 42곳에 영사업무, 4개 대표부를 운영하고 있다.

South Korea strives to promote friendly and cooperative relations with other countries. By July 2012, the country had established diplomatic relations with 189 countries, operating permanent embassies in 112 countries, in addition to 42 consular offices and 4 representative offices.

한국은 UNESCO, IMF, APEC, IAEA, ILO, WHO 등 다양한 국제조직의 일원으로 적극적인 역할을 수행하고 있으며 1991년 UN의 회원이 되었고, 1996년 OECD회원으로 1947년 이후 IOC회원으로서 활동하고 하고 있다.

The country is committed to carrying out positive activities as a member of diverse international organizations such as UNESCO, IMF, APEC, IAEA, ILO, WHO. South Korea became a member of the UN in 1991, and joined the OECD in 1996. The country has also carried out activities as a member of the IOC since 1947.

South Korea does its best in the sector of international cooperation in keeping with its enhanced economic strength. The country takes part in programs designed to provide support for impoverished countries through the World Bank, the IMF, and the OECD. Recently, the country has also joined worldwide efforts for peacekeeping, global economic stabilization, environmental conservation, etc.

한국의 해외 원조 프로그램은 한국 국제협력 단에 의하여 협조체제를 구축하고 있다. 이 체제는 1961년 설립하였으며 발전경험을 공유하기 위하여 지원되는 나라를 돕기 위하여 조직 프로그램이 이루어진다.

South Korea's foreign aid programs are coordinated by the Korea International Cooperation Agency (KOICA). This body was established in 1991, and organizes programs designed to provide support for developing countries and to share South Korea's own development experience.

KOICA provides ODA (Official Development Assistance) of US$400–500 million annually to developing countries in Asia and Africa; these funds contribute to numerous areas, including education, health, agriculture/forestry/fisheries, public administration, and industrial energy, among others.

한국은 또한 UN평화유지 예산지원 등으로 다양하게 세계 평화와 안전에 공헌하기 위하여 노력하고 있다.

South Korea is also pleased to be making a contribution to world peace and security through taking part in a wide variety of UN peacekeeping operations and by supporting the UN peacekeeping budget.

Currently, South Korean troops are stationed in eight countries including Lebanon, South Sudan, India, Pakistan, and West Sahara, where they are tasked with the maintenance of order, rehabilitation, medical services, and other activities.

♣ 국기(National Flag) : 태극기(Taegeukgi)

고결한 태극기, 한국에 대한 영광, 자유, 정의에 진지한 충절 서약을 의미한다.

The noble Taegeukgi, solemnly pledge allegiance to the Republic of Korea, to its glory, liberty and justice.

Photo 3-1 Construction of the Flag of Korea

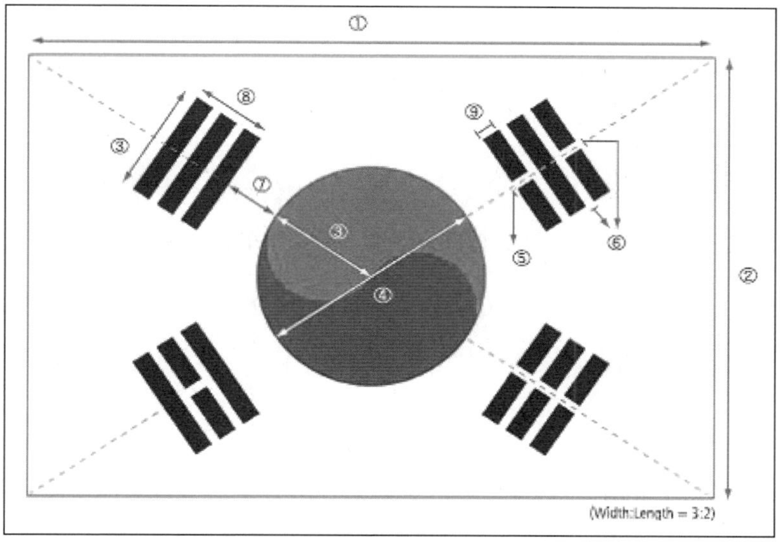

① Diameter of circle×3	② Diameter of circle×2	③ Diameter of circle×1/2
④ Length of flag×1/2	⑤ Right angle(90 degrees)	⑥ Diameter of Circle×1/24
⑦ Diameter of circle×1/4	⑧ Diameter of circle×1/3	⑨ Diameter of circle×1/12

The Taegeukgi consists of a white background, a red and blue taegeuk circle in the center, and four black trigrams (collectively called geongongamri), one in each corner of the flag. The white background represents brightness, purity, and peace, qualities that are highly valued by the people.

The taegeuk, which has long been a commonly used motif, denotes the harmony between the negative cosmic forces (yin : blue portion) and the positive cosmic forces (yang : red portion), depicting the truth of nature that all things are created and evolve through the interaction of yin and yang.

The four black trigrams are specific representations of the movement and harmony of these forces. In detail, the geon symbolizes the sky, the gon the earth, the gam water, and the ri fire. Together, they create harmony around the taegeuk mark. In short, the Taegeukgi flag embodies the vision of the Korean people who, like the universe, seek continuous creation and enrichment.

By upholding the spirit and significance of the Taegeukgi, the people seek to realize unity and unification and contribute to the happiness and peace of humanity.

♣ 국가찬양 : 애국가(The National Anthem – Aegukga)

화려하고 멋진 강과 산으로 덮여 있는 삼천리, 위대한 국민, 진실로 위대한 길에 머물러야 한다.

Three thousand ri of splendid rivers and mountains covered with mugunghwa blossoms. Great Korean people, stay true to the Great Korean way.

Photo 3-2 aegukga of the Song of Korea

1. Until that day when the waters of the East Sea run dry and Mount Baekdusan is worn away, God protect and preserve our nation; Hurray to Korea.
2. As the pine atop the near mountain stands firm, unchanged through wind and frost, as if wrapped in armor, so shall our resilient spirit.
3. The autumn sky is void and vast, high and cloudless; the bright moon is our heart, undivided and true.
4. With this spirit and this mind, give all loyalty, in suffering or in joy, to the love of country.

Generically, aegukga refers to any song that expresses love for one's country. However, the term has become synonymous with Korea's national anthem.

Following adaptation by several composers, the lyrics gradually took the form we know today. Korean composer Ahn Eak-tai felt that this foreign melody was unfit for Korea's national anthem.

In 1935, he composed the Symphonic Fantasy Korea, the finale of which became the current melody for the national anthem. Even though the Provisional Government of the Republic of Korea adopted this tune as their national anthem,

it was only known abroad. In Korea, the lyrics continued to be sung to the Scottish folk song until the Korean government was established in 1948 following the nation's independence from Japan.

At that time, the current version of Aegukga was sung during official government functions, and gradually, with its inclusion in all student textbooks, it gained popular acceptance.

Afterwards, the song was widely disseminated abroad and finally became established as the national anthem of Korea.

Whenever people sing Aegugka, which, for almost a century, has been part of the people's destiny both in good times and bad, they are reminded of the love that their forefathers held for the nation.

♣ 국화(National Flower) : 무궁화(Mugunghwa)

한국인들은 성공뿐만 아니라 경험해왔던 시련의 국가 상징 차원에서 국화를 소중히 여긴다.

Koreans cherish the national flower because it honors the country's noble spirit and symbolizes the many successes as well as tribulations that the nation has experienced.

Mugunghwa varieties are grouped based on the colors of their blossoms. The groups are dansim, baedal, and asadal. The flower is a symbol in the flags of government and national organizations, decorations, and badges.

Photo 3-3 Mugunghwa Image

① White dansim ② Red dansim ③ Purple dansim

④ Blue dansim ⑤ Baedal ⑥ Asadal

Dansim : White, red, purple, or blue flower with intense red or purple center
Baedal : Pure white flower
Asadal : White flower with intense red center that fades to pale pink at the petal edges

The mugunghwa, or the rose of Sharon, is an object of deep affection. Meaning "eternal blossom that never fades," it has been an important symbol of Korean culture for centuries.

Ancient records show that even before the Gojoseon era (ancient Korean kingdom), the mugungwha was treasured as a "blossom from heaven".

As further testimony of its cultural value, the Silla Kingdom (57 BC ~ AD 935) called itself Geunhwahyang, meaning Country of the Mugunghwa.

The ancient Chinese, too, referred to Korea as the "land of wise men where the mugunghwa blooms."

Over time, the public affection grew stronger when a phrase extolling the flower's beauty was included in the national anthem in the late 19th century.

Those words are "Mugunghwa samcheonli hwaryeogangsan (Three thousand ri (equivalent to 1,200 kilometers, the length of the Korean Peninsula) of splendid rivers and mountains covered with mugunghwa blossoms)".

Even during the dark days of Japanese colonial rule, the people's devotion to the flower never faded.

Hence, it was only natural for the government to adopt it as the national flower after Korea regained its independence from Japan.

Tourism Guide Quiz

1. Can you explain the National Flag of Korea, the Taegeukgi?
2. Explain Korean Peninsula briefly.
3. How can you improve your English skill as a tour guide?
   Based on your experience, share your ideas.
4. Explain what the National Flower of Korea, Mugunghwa, symbolize.
5. Introduce "the National Anthem ? Aegukga" briefly.

수행 Tips : The ability to raise 통역안내사 영어 면접시험 예상문제

전문지식과 응용능력이 중요시되고 있으며, 국가관, 사명감 등 정신자세는 필요충분조건입니다. 의사발표의 정확성과 논리성, 창의성 등에 좋은 평가를 받을 수 있습니다.

1. Han Style란?
2. 관광통역안내사로서 갖추어야 할 자세와 덕목은?
3. 한국의 주요산업과 수출품목에 대하여 설명하시오?

4. 추석이란?

5. 외국인 관광객의 여권분실시 조치사항은?

6. 한글의 우수성에 대하여 설명하시오?

7. 석굴암에 대하여 설명하시오?

8. 한국의 관광브랜드에 대하여 설명하시오?

9. 조선왕릉에 대하여 설명하시오?

10. 경복궁의 의미에 대하여 설명하시오?

11. 6차산업이란?

12. 창덕궁에 대하여 설명하시오?

13. 덕수궁에 대하여 설명하시오?

14. 외국인이 김치냄새를 싫어 할 경우 어떻게 소개 할 것인가?

15. 저가항공의 장점과 단점은?

16. 다도해 해상공원에 대하여 설명하시오?

17. 남대문의 역사적 의의에 대하여 설명하시오?

18. 팸투어란?

19. 해양관광에 대하여 설명하시오?

20. 달러/엔화 상승이 관광객 유치에 미치는 영향은?

21. 한국의 관광기념품에 대하여 설명하시오?

22. PCO란 무엇인가?

23. 프리미엄 가이드란?

24. 유네스코 지정 문화/자연/기록 유산에 대하여 설명하시오?

25. DMZ에 대하여 설명하시오?

26. 관광통역안내사의 직업 사명감은 무엇이라고 생각합니까?

27. 한국을 대표하는 관광기념품에 대하여 설명하시오?

28. 지난해에 우리나라를 방문한 총 외래 관광객 수와 10대 방문국가는?

29. 해외여행중에 가장 인상 깊었던 장소를 소개해보세요?

30. 관광통역안내사를 하려는 동기는?

31. 의료관광산업이란?

33. 세계지질공원(Geo Park)이란?

33. 한지에 대하여 소개해 보시오.

34. Opitional Tour란?

35. 외국인 중 가장 인상깊었던 사람은?

36. 1일 여행에 대하여 소개할 곳은?

37. 서울의 night tour에 대하여 소개해 보시오.

38. city tour bus에 대하여 설명하시오.

39. 산업적 관광자원이란?

40. 관광안내사의 자질에 대하여 설명하시오.

41. 팔만대장경에 대하여 설명하시오.

42. Temple Stay에 대하여 설명하시오.

43. 유형문화재란?

44. 무형문화재란?

45. 좋아하는 책 또는 인상깊게 보았던 영화에 대하여 설명하시오.

46. 남산골 한옥마을에 대하여 설명하시오.

47. 사물놀이란?

48. 왜 전 직장을 그만두었는지 그 이유에 대하여 말씀해 보세요.

49. 실사구시란?

50. 동의보감에 대하여 설명하시오.

51. 태극기의 그 의미에 대하여 설명하시오.

52. 한국의 종교에 대하여 설명하시오.

53. 서울의 유명관광 목적지에 대하여 설명한다면?

54. 한강에 대하여 설명하시오.

55. 반나절 관광지역을 간단히 설명하시오.

56. 한국 최고의 테마파크는?

57. 왜래방문객을 위한 한국의 쇼핑시장과 백화점에 대하여 설명하시오.

58. 태권도의 역사에 대하여 설명하시오.

59. 사찰음식에 대하여 설명하시오.

60. 한방에 대하여 설명하시오.

61. 한국의 유명 전통 음식에 대하여 설명하시오.

62. 거북선에 대하여 설명하시오.

63. 한국의 전통음악에 대하여 설명하시오.

64. 한국의 전통음식인 비빔밥에 대하여 설명하시오.

65. 투어 중 교통사고로 발생된 사건에 대한 긴급대처 방안은?

66. 서울의 4대 소문에 대하여 설명하시오.

67. 탈춤에 대하여 설명하시오.

68. 인바운드 투어와 아웃바운드 투어에 대하여 설명하시오.

69. 관광개발을 저해하는 요인은 무엇이라고 생각합니까?

70. 단체행사 중 호텔체크아웃 시 관광객에게 사전에 전달해야 할 사항 및 업무요령에 대하여 설명하시오.

－A journey of a thousand miles begins with a single step.－

Unit **4**

Seoul Overview

Domestic Tour Guide English

Unit **4**

Seoul Overview

♣ **서울관광의 기원**(Origins of Tourism in SEOUL)

서울은 한반도 중심에 위치하고 있으며, 수세기에 걸쳐 한 왕조에서 다음 왕조까지 경제와 국방 측면에서 항상 중요한 전략적 요충지였다. 백제, 고구려, 신라가 모두 이 지역을 차지하기 위하여 싸웠으며 현재 한국의 수도이다. 조선시대(1392-1910)에 공표된 수도이며 현재까지 서울의 역할을 하고 있다.

Located at the heart of the Korean Peninsula, Seoul has always been an important strategic point throughout the centuries in terms of defense and the economy, from one kingdom to the next.

The three kingdoms of Baekje, Goguryeo, and Silla (BCE 57 - AD 688) all fought over the area that is now Korea's capital. The Joseon Dynasty (1392-1910) declared Seoul its capital, a role that Seoul still plays to this day.

In the early period of Seoul's history the Three Kingdoms were fighting for hegemony in Korea and the Seoul area was often contested due to its strategic location in the Han River valley. The Joseon Period ran from 1392 up to the Japanese invasion in 1910 and Seoul was its capital. It was the longest ruling Confucian dynasty in history and during its reign the Joseon monarchy consolidated absolute rule over Korea.

서울은 같은 시대에 전자, 전화, 물, 손수레 차, 전기 차가 존재해 온 동아시아 최초의 도시이다. 이 모든 것들이 미국과의 주요무역에 기인하였으며 전후 서울은 거대한 재건축과 현대화에 초점을 맞추었다. 현재 서울의 인구는 한국인구의 24%를 구성하고 있으며, 주요 산업기반측면에서 세계 7번째 도시에 위치해 있다.

Seoul became the first city in East Asia to have electricity, trolley cars, water, telephone, and telegraph systems all at the same time. Much of this was due to major trade with the United States. In the post-war years Seoul was the focus of an immense reconstruction and modernization effort. Today the population of the Seoul area comprises 24% of the total population of South Korea and Seoul ranks seventh in the world in terms of the number of major companies based there.

Seoul hosted the 1988 Summer Olympics and was one of the venues of the Football World Cup in 2002. In 2004 the South Korean Government came up with a highly controversial plan to relocate the capital to the Gongju area in order to ease the population pressure on Seoul and set up the seat of government at a safer distance from North Korea.

서울의 무역중심지는 옛 조선시대의 다운타운 지역이라 할 수 있는데, 대부분 왕궁, 정부사무실, 기업들의 본사, 호텔, 전통시장이 위치해 있다. 중심지 북쪽에는 북한산이 남쪽에는 작은 산 남산이 위치하고 있다. 한강건너 강남은 다른 주변 이웃보다 새롭고 부유한 곳이라 할 수 있으며 여의도는 국회의사당이 위치하고 있는 한강 중심에 있는 큰섬이다.

The traditional heart of Seoul is the old Joseon Dynasty city, which is now the downtown area, where most palaces, government offices, corporate headquarters, hotels and traditional markets are located. To the north of downtown is Bukhan Mountain, and to the south is the smaller Namsan. Across the Han River are the newer and wealthier areas of Gangnam-gu and surrounding neighbourhoods. Yeouido is a large island in the middle of the Han River and is home to the National Assembly.

♣ 서울로 여행가기(Getting Travel SEOUL)

한국은 미국으로 KE, UA항공사 등이 취항하고 있으며 서울로는 CX, CA, 등의 항공사가 취항하고 있다. 미국 서해안으로부터 13시간보다 적게 걸리고 런던으로부터 11시간, 동경은 2시간 30분, 홍콩은 3시간 30분, 북경은 1시간 30분이면 도착할 수 있다. 인천국제공항은 서울 서쪽 52km(31마일), 김포공항은 서울 서쪽 19km(12마일)에 위치해 있다.

South Korea is connected with the United States by Korean Air, Japan Airlines, United Airlines, and Northwest Airlines among others. Carriers routed through Seoul include Cathay Pacific, China Airlines, Malaysian Airlines, and Singapore Airlines.

It is less than 13 hours from the US West Coast, 11 hours from London, $2\frac{1}{2}$ hours from Tokyo, $3\frac{1}{2}$ hours from Hong Kong, and $1\frac{1}{2}$ hours from Beijing. Incheon International Airport (IIA) is 52km (31 miles) west of Seoul, Gimpo Airport, 19km (12 miles) west of Seoul.

Several airlines, including Jeju-Air, Korean Air, and Asiana, conduct air travel within Korea. Daily flights from Gimpo Airport to Jeju-do, Busan, Gwangju, Daegu, Yeosu, Pohang, Jinju, and Ulsan are available on domestic carriers with flight times of 40?65 minutes.

The best way out of Incheon International is currently by bus, with routes to Gimpo (the main airport for domestic flights), numerous points in downtown Seoul, Incheon City, and Gyeonggi Province.

Departures coincide with the first and last flights and run regularly in between. Buses take about 50 minutes to travel between the airport and downtown Seoul.

대한항공은 공항에서 훌륭한 서울 및 강남의 호텔에 편안한 리무진 버스를 운행하고 있으나 러시아워 같은 피크타임에는 공항철도나 지하철을 이용하는 것이 좋다.

Korean Air (KAL) runs a convenient Limousine shuttle from the airport to many of the nicer Seoul and Gangnam hotels, as well as to/from Gimpo Airport. The Incheon airport train linking Gimpo and Incheon airports runs only hourly, on the hour and it is inconvenient for people to take the subway to Gimpo and then continue on to Incheon.

At peak times, such as rush hour, this train/subway option makes sense. At other times of day it is easy to take the bus. Service between Incheon Airport and Seoul Station is expected to begin in 2010, a connection that will be warmly welcomed.

The fare for the commuter train is up to W3,400 (depending on the station you exit) between Incheon and Gimpo. See www.arex.or.kr for further details. The Limousine Bus service covers Gimpo and Seoul, with tickets priced for standard and deluxe buses at W9,000 and W14,000 respectively.

Subways are a transportation facility of the urban railroad system that is operating in Seoul. Since the opening of Line 1 on August 15, 1974, 9 lines now are currently operating.

Trains run from 5am to midnight at three-minute intervals during rush hours, and at six-minute intervals at other times. Smoking is prohibited on platforms as well as in the cars. From Seoul Railway Station, it goes to six major destinations: Cheongnyangni Railway

Station and Songbuk district to the north, and to Incheon (39km/24 miles west), Suwon (41km/25 miles south), Jamsil, and Guro.

At the entrance of subway stations, there are a subway sign and the station name. Station names are indicated in Chinese and English for foreigners. Station numbers are also indicated in different colors, so passengers can easily recognize which subway line it is.

택시는 목적지까지 도착하는데 편리한 방법이며, 서울시에서는 외국인을 위한 통역 서비스가 있는 택시서비스 운영을 하고 있으며, 예약은 국제택시 홈페이지를 이용하여 예약할 수 있다.

Taxis are a convenient way to get to your destination. To help with communication,Seoul Metropolitan Government operates foreigner-dedicated

taxis and provides interpretation services. A direct reservation is possible via the homepage for International Taxis Immediate use of the taxi is available even without a prior reservation if there is a taxi that is standing by.

International Taxi services basically require a prior reservation via telephone (+82-2-1644-2255) and homepage. Call +82-2-1644-2255 for English/Japanese consultations, which are available all year round 24 hours a day 365 days a year. A direct reservation is possible via the homepage for International Taxis Immediate use of the taxi is available even without a prior reservation if there is a taxi that is standing by.

The hiring and educating of taxi drivers and call center operations are supervised by the Seoul Metropolitan Government. Taxi drivers have certifications in foreign language proficiency. The information desk and boarding area that are exclusively for International Taxi users are located at the Incheon International Airport and Gimpo International Airport. Payment is possible with credit cards or T-money.

Medium taxis can accommodate up to five passengers. The "International Taxi" sign is on the roof of each taxi. Cabs with "Japanese" signs mean that the driver can speak Japanese.

Large taxi vans can accommodate up to nine passengers. The body of the vehicle is black and "International Taxi" signs are displayed on the sides.

Luxury taxis can accommodate up to 5 passengers. The color is black. The sides of the vehicle and the roof lamp will have the "International TAXI" sign.

While you can differentiate between a privately and company owned taxi by their roof lamp, you can also easily spot company owned cabs by the company name and numbers on their side doors. The basic fare for these taxis is 3,000won for the first 2 km with an increase of 100 won per 142m.

공항버스 운영시스템을 도입하고 있는 서울시의 버스 운영은 - blue, green, red, or yellow - 색으로 구분하여 그 기능을 달리하고 있다.

Airport buses operate in Seoul. Seoul's transit system has buses in one of four colors - blue, green, red, or yellow - depending on their function. Blue buses (main line) provide services on major trunk roads between downtown Seoul and satellite cities.

Green buses (branch line) service routes between subway stations and nearby residential areas and main bus lines. (These routes are often also serviced by village buses.) Red buses (wide area line) service routes between major areas (downtown, Gangnam,

Yeongdeungpo, etc.) and metropolitan satellite cities (Ilsan, Bundang, Uijeongbu, etc.). Yellow buses (circular line) serve circular belt roads in the downtown and major metropolitan area.

Yellow Bus : First Number (Areas where buses are operating) /Second Number(serial number (1~), Airport Bus : First Number (6; 0~7)) / Third Number (serial number; 00~).

요금지불은 교통카드와 현금으로 지불할 수 있으며, 한번 탑승 지불금은 정액 요금제이고 T-money 등 다양한 교통카드 지불시스템이 있다.

Fares can be paid by cash or transportation card. One-time boarding charges a flat-rate fare where you can pay by cash or transportation card.

Fares for Seoul city buses and Maeul (village) buses can be paid by T-money, U-Pass, EB Card, Cashbee, and Korail Membership Card. Deferred payment transportation cards, which are compatible with T-Money and U-Pass, can be used as well.

서울, 경기도, 인천버스와 수도권 지하철은 통합 지불시스템으로 10km마다 요금이 올라간다. 서울 광역버스, 경기도 일반버스, 직행 디럭스 버스, 인천버스, 레드버스는 인천버스 운영 요금시스템은 기본적으로 30km이며, 각각 5km마다 추가요금 100원을 지불해야 한다(성인요금 기준).

Seoul, Gyeonggi-do, Incheon buses and metropolitan subways are under the Metropolitan Integrated Fare System, so they charge a basic fare up to 10km. Using Seoul metropolitan buses, Gyeonggi-do general buses, non-stop deluxe buses, Incheon buses, and red buses for more than one transfer will cost a basic rate up to 30km, and you will be charged an extra 100 won for each additional 5 km (based on the adult fare).

Multiple-passenger boarding and a transfer discount are applicable only to city buses, and this offer can be approved only if the same passengers travel to the same destination.

♣ 건축물의 문화적 수용력에 대한 인식(Recognizing the Culture-Shaping Capacity of Architecture)

서울시는 또한 '안전하며, 부유하고, 꿈꾸며, 숨쉬는' 도시 행정개혁 추진에 대한 강한 인식을 갖고 25개 핵심 프로젝트를 진행해 왔다.

The city government is also strongly committed to pushing ahead with administrative reform. with the goal of turning Seoul into a "Safe, Warm, Dreaming, and Breathing City". Of these projects, 25 have been designated as key projects. The city government plans to narrow 12 lane roads by one or two lanes, a total of 15.2km, within the historical downtown "four gates" area of Seoul, in areas such as Cheonggyecheon, Daehak-ro, and Sejong-daero, where subway stations are extremely crowded.

서울 4대문 안에 자동차의 위협이 없이 보행자와 자전거를 탈 수 있도록 창조적인 공간으로 기획했다. 서울의 상징 랜드 마크 중의 하나로 경복궁, N-서울타워, DDP를 포함하여 서울 경관지를 지정했다.

This is part of the plan to create spaces where pedestrians and bikers feel comfortable moving around the city without being threatened by speeding cars, at least within the historical "four gates" area of Seoul.

A number of iconic landmarks, including Gyeongbokgung Palace, N-Seoul Tower, and the Dongdaemun Design Plaza (DDP), define Seoul's landscape.

건축물의 문화 창조 수용 활동에 대한 인식하에 시정부(SMG)는 연간 기본 계획에 SAF(서울 건축제)를 조직화했다.

In recognition of the capacity of architecture to shape and create culture and in the hope of fostering such culturally creative architectural activities, the Seoul Metropolitan Government (SMG) has been organizing the Seoul Architecture Festival (SAF) on an annual basis.

부가적인 전시회 중의 하나가 서울의 건축물에 대한 자연과 우월성을 증진시키는 것이었다. UIA(국제 건축가연합) 2017은 건축물과 관련된 주요 국제 이벤트가 될 수 있을 것이며, 시정부와 한국 건축물 연합회는 2011년 국제건축연합회를 주관하였다.

A number of additional exhibitions were held to promote the innovative nature and superiority of architecture in Seoul. UIA 2017 will be a major international event related to architecture, for which the SMG and the Union of Korean Architectural Associations won the bid to host at the Union Internationale des Architects (UIA) in 2011.

UIA전시회는 3년마다 다른 장소에서 개최되는데, 서울은 1948년 이후 북경과 동경에 이어 아시아에서 3번째 개최되는 곳이다. 영혼이 있는 도시라는 주요 테마 하에 개최되는 UIA 2017은 호스트시티답게 전통과 현대를 완벽하게 조화를 이루어진 특징 전시와 프로그램이 될 것이다.

The UIA exhibition is held in a different city every three years. Seoul is the third city in Asia to host the event since 1948, after Beijing and Tokyo.

Under the overarching theme of "Soul of City," Seoul UIA 2017 will feature programs and exhibitions that strike a perfect balance between tradition and modernity, much like the host city has.

The great diversity of the participatory and interactive programs attests to the sincerity of the "Humane City," which was the overarching theme of this year's festival.

Every weekend during the festival period, famous architects and cultural figures were invited to take citizens on tours of various architectural works in the city.

서울 전람회의 대부분 참여프로그램은 도시와 주제라는 다양한 전시로 특징될 것이며, 전시회는 10가지 주요 주제가 될 것인데, 세계 주요도시에서 진행되고 있는 일반적인 것과 공공주도와 관계된 것이 될 것이다.

For the most part, the biennale will feature diverse exhibitions by topic and city, along with participatory programs at the Seoul Lab. The exhibitions will address 10 major topics related to the commons as well as major public initiatives underway in cities worldwide.

The biennale will address a wide range of important urban issues facing Seoul today, including urban spacing and organization, development and renewal, architecture and technology, urban environment, and urban management and solidarity.

♣ 금메달 따기(Going for Gold)

1988년 국제 올림픽 위원회는 1988년 올림픽과 장애인올림픽 개최지로 'SEOUL 1988'로 지정하였다. 인프라 개발이 이어졌는데, 한강 남동쪽 송파지역에 건설된 잠실 올림픽 스타디움과 도심에서 공항까지 빠르게 다다를 수 있는 교통망 구축에 관한 것 등이다.

In 1988, the International Olympic Committee named 'SEOUL1988' as the host city for the 1988 Olympic and Paralympic Summer Games.

Infrastructure development followed, Including the expansion of the Jamsil Olympic Stadium and the construction in the Songpa District in the southeast of the city south of the Han River, a rapid transport line connecting the airport with the city's downtown.

서울의 상징 표현은 삼태극인데, 삼태극은 한국을 대표하는 전통적인 한국인 표현과 심상 이미지를 나타내는 것이다.

The Seoul emblem features a samtaeguk pattern. A samtaeguk is a traditional Korean pattern and visual image which represents Korea.

This pattern is widely used as decoration on fans, gates of Korean-style homes, artefacts, and folk crafts.

두 가지 형태의 올림픽 상징 특징은 구심력과 원심력인데, 한국으로 향하는 세계인의 대표화된 중심개념과 인간의 번영과 행복을 지속시킨다는 원심력 행동의 세계적 조화를 상징한다.

The Olympic emblem features patterns in two forms, centripetal and centrifugal; the centripetal motion represented the people of the world coming together in Korea, thus symbolising worldwide harmony, while the centrifugal motion represented a march onward in search of man's lasting happiness and prosperity.

공식포스터는 컴퓨터그래픽 기술로 행해졌으며, 한국을 상징하는 조용한 아침의 나라를 상징하는 푸른빛과 밝은 오랜지색을 혼합했다.

The official posters were done with computer graphic techniques, and light blue and bright orange colours were blended to symbolise Korea as the Land of Morning Calm. In addition to the official poster the Organising Committee for the Seoul Games decided to produce 27 types of sports posters to introduce sports of the Seoul Olympic Games and to establish a familiar image of the Games.

한국 올림픽 게임의 상징이 민주주의 채택국가의 추진력을 의미한다는 측면에서 북한은 참가하지 않았으나, 쿠바, 이디오피아와 니카라구아가 함께하여 159개 국가가 참여하였고, 52개 국가가 메달을 획득하였으며 31개국이 금메달을 받았다.

Awarding the Summer Games to South Korea provided the impetus for the country to embrace democracy. The Democratic People's Republic of Korea (North Korea) boycotted, and was joined by Cuba, Ethiopia and Nicaragua. Still, records were set with 159 nations participating, 52 winning medals and 31 taking home gold medals.

Photo 4-1 The Seoul 88' Olympic Games Emblem and The official poster

1988년 서울 올림픽 위원회는 노래를 통하여 전 세계인의 우정과 화합을 강화하고 축제참여를 고무시키는 차원에서 모든 IOC멤버 국가에게 올림픽 게임 광고와 서울올림픽 공식 노래를 공급해주기로 결정했다.

In 1988, the Seoul Olympic Organizing Committee (SLOOC) decided to produce and distribute an official song of the Seoul Games to publicize the Games to all the IOC member nations, encouraging their participation in the festival and consolidating the harmony and friendship of the entire world citizens through the song.

미국 작사가 'Whitlock'과 이탈리아 작곡가 'Moroder'에 의하여 만들어진 공식 올림픽 노래 "손에 손잡고"는 그룹 코리아나에 의하여 불렸다.

The song "Hand in Hand" was written by Italian composer Giorgio Moroder and American songwriter Tom Whitlock, and performed by singing group Koreana. "Hand in Hand" topped popular songs in 17 countries including Sweden, West Germany, the Philippines, Spain, Switzerland, Austria, Japan and Hong Kong and was listed among the top 10s of the popular songs in more than 30 countries.

Photo 4-2 The 2002 Seoul World Cup Stadium(Credit: seoul city)

2002년 FIFA월드컵 17회 월드컵 경기였으며, 한국과 일본에서 2002년 5월31일에서 6월30일 사이에 개최되었다.

The 2002 FIFA World Cup was the 17th staging of the FIFA World Cup which took place from 31 May to 30 June 2002 in South Korea and Japan.

It was the first World Cup to be held in Asia, the first to be held on a continent other than Europe or the Americas, the last World Cup during which the golden goal rule was in force and the only World Cup to be jointly hosted by more than one nation as FIFA amended its statutes in 2004 to officially forbid co-hosting bids.

서울 월드컵 경기장은 5개의 소공원으로 만들어졌다. 즉 평화(peace), 하늘(sky), 노을(sunset), Nanjicheon and Naji Hangang 공원이다.

The Seoul World Cup Stadium and is made up of five smaller parks: Pyeonghwa (Peace) Park, Haneul (Sky) Park, Noeul (Sunset) Park, Nanjicheon and Naji Hangang Park. Pyeonghwa Park, a symbol of the peace and harmony of the world, is the flagship park of the five and was built in memory of the first World Cup Soccer Finals of the new millennium.

Haneul Park is the highest in location of the five, while the sunset viewed from Noeul Park is especially beautiful. Nanjicheon Park features a natural creek where diverse plants grow. Nanji Hangang Park, located on the banks of the Hangang, features various sports and leisure facilities.

홍대 자유시장은 한일월드컵 동안 문화이벤트로 2002년 개설되었으며, 끝난 후에도 지속적으로 유지되고 있다. 문화와 젊음의 장소로 서울의 인기지역 중의 한 곳이다.

Hongdae Free Market was established in 2002 as a cultural event during the Korea-Japan World Cup and has been held continuously there after.

One of Seoul's popular area for the young, hip, artistic and cultural hubs, Hongdae (Hongik University) offers more than a vibrant nightlife, nice restaurants and cozy coffee shops.

Every Saturday, Hongdae's 'Playground' (the recreation ground in front of the main entrance to Hongik University) becomes a marketplace where young artists display their creative artwork and a performance venue for Korean indie bands. Looking for a unique souvenir or gift, the 'Hongdae Free Market' is definitely one of the best places to visit.

Items displayed at the free market are all handmade original creations. Thus, most of them are very unique items that are not readily available in other places. Some of the creations on display at the market include hand-painted shoes, bags, hats and t-shirts; silver jewelry and ceramic accessories, postcards and many more.

♣ 관광서울(Tourism in SEOUL)

한국의 수도 서울은 현대적인 문화와 오랜 전통이 잘 어울러져 성장하고 있는 도시다. 서울은 흥미 있는 매력물로 충만하며 고궁, 사원, 역사적인 장소를 탐방할 수 있고 과학센터, 수족관, 현대 박물관 공원을 함께 접해 볼 수 있는 지역이다.

The capital of South Korea, Seoul is a thriving city that skillfully blends old traditions and style with modern culture. Seoul is simply bursting with interesting attractions and visitors will be able to explore ancient palaces, temples and historical sites, which are situated alongside modern amusement parks, aquariums and science centers.

서울은 한국의 옛것은 찾아보고자 하는 관광 자에게 좋은 장소로 만들고자 전통과 관습에 대한 많은 것을 유지하기 위하여 관리해 왔다.

Seoul has managed to maintain many of its customs and traditions, making this a good place for visitors to gain an insight into ancient South Korea. Originally named Hansung when it was founded during the Koryo Dynasty, Seoul has long been a city rich is culture and history as well as the most densely populated city in the entire world.

However, rather than feeling crowded, Seoul has an intimate air and the large population means that there is plenty to do in the city after the sun sets such as dancing, dining and karaoke and visitors can be sure that there is always something to see and do in this vibrant city.

서울은 역사적인 덕수궁을 포함하여 볼 것이 많은데, 다양한 불교사원, 전통시장, 명동과 같이 번화한 현대적인 곳, 홍대와 이태원과 같이 활기찬 밤거리 등이 그것이다.

There is much to see, including the historic Deoksugung Palace, a variety of Buddhist temples, traditional markets, the bustling modern center of Myeongdong, and the buzzing nightlife of Itaewon and Hongdae. For those seeking peace and quiet, Citizen's Park is perfect for picnics, watersports, and the national pastime of kite flying.

■ visit an old palaces Gyeongbokgung

빛나는 행복의 궁 경복궁은 태조에 의하여 창건되었으며 힘의 상징이었다. 왕과 왕비가 1592년 일본과의 전쟁에 의하여 불타기까지 사용했다.

Gyeongbokgung, the Palace of Shining Happiness, was Taejo's residence and seat of power. He and his successors used it until 1592 when it was burned during warfare with Japan. If you inquire more closely, you will discover that Gyeongbok's throne hall, the Geunjeongjeon (Hall of Government by Restraint), rebuilt in 1867, was the very centre of Taejo's governmental heart. Here the king sat to receive ministers ranged in orderly ranks before him, made judgments, and issued proclamations.

1926년 일본식민통치하에서 옥좌 복도와 정문사이에 거대한 식민빌딩(조선총독부청사)를 지었다.

In 1926, Japanese colonial rulers built a mammoth colonial Capitol Building between the front gate and the throne hall. This was an obvious symbolic severance of the link between the Korean people (the gate) and the royal family (the throne hall). In 1998, finally fed up with this affront, the city tore down the building in celebration of Korea's 50th year of independence from Japan.

국립고궁박물관은 경복궁 안에 2005년에 오픈하였는데, 왕조의 유물과 경복궁과 창덕궁, 덕수궁의 조선왕조 보물을 4만점을 수집해 놓았다. 또한 국립민속박물관은 매일 사용되어지는 공예품과 사용방법 입체모형을 경복궁 안에 세웠다.

The National Palace Museum of Korea opened in 2005 inside the Gyeongbok Palace area, with a collection of over 40,000 pieces of Joseon-dynasty royal treasures taken from the Royal Museum in Deoksu Palace, and from Changdeok and Gyeongbok palaces and the Royal Ancestral Shrine. Also inside the palace grounds stands the National Folk Museum of Korea, which houses artifacts of everyday use and dioramas showing how they were used.

■ Changdeok Palace

창덕궁은 한국의 가장 많은 전통한옥이 잔존하고 있는 지역에 위치하고 있다. 북찬동과 삼청동 근처에는 오래된 나무집들이 줄지어 있는데, 조그만 찻집과 카페들이 들어와 있다. 이들 개성화된 거리 동쪽에 뛰어난 덕행의 궁 창덕궁이 있다.

Changdeok palaces is one of the city's largest surviving areas of traditional Korean housing (hanok). The neighborhoods of Bukchan-dong and Samcheong-dong are full of small winding streets lined with old wooden houses and a plentiful supply of teahouses and cafés. Abutting these characterful streets to the east is Changdeokgung, the Palace of Illustrious Virtue.

창덕 후편에는 비밀정원이라고 알려진 비원이 넓게 놓여있다. 원래 거주 왕가의 사적 공간이었기 때문이다.

Behind Changdeok lies the extensive acreage of Biwon, known as the Secret Garden, so-called because it was formerly a private park for the resident royal family. In wooded and hilly terrain, footpaths meander past ponds and pavilions and over small bridges. The most picturesque of these sites is Bandoji (Peninsula Pond), shaped like the outline of the Korean Peninsula. From its shore extending out over the water stands a small, exquisite, fan-shaped pavilion from which Injo, the 16th king, could cast a line for a bit of quiet fishing. Entrance is through Changdeok Palace.

■ Deoksu Palace

높은 덕행이 오래 지속되는 궁, 덕수궁은 시청광장 앞에 위치하고 있으며 잔존하고 있는 궁중에 가장 오래되지 않았다. 15세기말에 별궁으로 건축되었으며 조선왕조 말 불행의 시기의 역할로서 중요한 곳이다.

Deoksugung, the Palace of Virtuous Longevity, whose gate faces City Hall Plaza. Deoksu is not the oldest of the surviving palaces – it was built as a villa toward the end of the 15th century – but it is important for its role at the unhappy end of the Joseon dynasty.

King Gojong, who was forced to abdicate in favor of his son Sunjong in 1907, lived in retirement and died here in 1919 after having seen his country annexed by the Japanese in 1910 and his family's dynasty snuffed out after 500 years.

There's also a royal audience hall and two startlingly European-style stone buildings, with Ionic and Corinthian columns, designed in 1909. The palace grounds offer a welcome relief from the city's hustle and bustle, especially in the autumn when its aisle of ginkgo trees is aflame in gold.

■ Changgyeonggung Palace

창경궁은 1418년 선왕 태종을 존경하는 마음에 세종시대에 지어졌다. 창경궁은 창덕궁과 접하고 있는 유일한 궁이며 창덕궁이 정궁의 역할을 하게 되면서 인접해 있는 창경궁은 왕실의 생활공간으로 그 활용빈도가 높아졌다.

Changgyeonggung Palace was built by King Sejong in 1484 to honor the former King Taejong.

It is the only palace among Joseon's palaces that faces the east. It was used as a auxiliary residential area in Changdeokgung Palace.

Honghwamun, the main gate of Changgyeonggung palace, faces east as is Myeongjeongjeon hall, the main building of the palace. This gate is believed to have been first built in the 15th year of the reign of King Seongjong(1484) and then burnt down during the Japanese invasion of 1592 and rebuilt in the eighth year of the reign of King Gwanghaegun(1616).

This is typical of the early Joseon architecture, featuring a two-story pavilion 3kan wide and 2kan deep(a kan is a traditional word of length between two columns showing different dimension according to the period), and multi-brackets atop the columns.

There are three wood plank doors in the front and crimson arrow-like ornaments above the doors There is a flight of stairs in the northern part of the structure leading to the second story. The second story is wood floored and the ceiling structure is visible from the floor. Walls extend from the gate.(Treasure No. 384)

Okcheongyo is such a bridge for Changgyeonggung palace. This 9.9m long and 6.6m wide bridge was built in 1483. The middle of the bridge is raised for kings to walk on. All main halls of the Joseon palaces are approached across a stone bridge over a stream.

The bridge is supported by twin arches. There is a carving of a monster mask between the arches to expel evil spirits. Four pillars divide the railing into five panels on either side of the bridge, and each panel has two openings.(Treasure No. 386)

■ Traditional markets

서울에는 여러 가지 작고 큰 전통시장이 있는데, 풍물시장과 의학시장과 같은 볼거리가 많은 것을 제공해주며 100여 년의 오랜 역사 동안 시장 기능을 하고 있다.

Seoul has several small and large traditional markets, ranging from markets with a long history of 100 years to markets that offer many things to see such as a medicine market and pungmul markets.

백여 개의 시장과 이웃하고 있는 남대문시장의 쇼핑센터와 좌판은 10시부터 해가 질 때까지 오픈하며, 진정한 할인은 주말 자정시간 이후에 구매하는 것이다.

The hundreds of neighborhood markets, and you have Namdaemun Sijang, the shops and stalls are open from 10am until sunset, though it's said that the real bargains are bought after midnight on weekends.

Remember to barter for any purchase. The stalls selling watches, jewellery, kitchenware, and bric-a-brac are everywhere, with clothing outlets occupying most of the shop space. There are also numerous street food stalls, serving a tempting array of seafood snacks.

남대문시장의 3배 규모인 동대문 시장은 종로5가와 6가 남쪽에 길게 늘어진 큰 규모이다. 실크시장의 눈요기의 향연-미적인 양단과 화려한 색깔의 실크좌판들은 진실로 눈부신 전시이다. 이시장의 역사는 조선시대의 근원인 14기라 할 수 있다.

Triple the size of Namdaemun and you have Dongdaemun Sijang (Great East Gate Market), a large area that stretches south of Jongno 5-ga and 6-ga. Feast your eyes on the silk market here (which operates similar hours to Namdaemun) – stall after stall of brilliantly colored silk and synthetic brocades, a truly dazzling display. The history of this market goes back to the 14th century and the roots of the Joseon dynasty.

At either market you can find almost anything you want, and, perhaps, many things you'd rather not find. On weekends the crowds are so intense, you have simply got to move with the flow to survive.

Hawkers shout out bargains, and the louder the better. This is also a good place to sit down to a sundae, stuffed intestine, or that most pungent of Korean delicacies, beondegi (silkworm larvae). Really, you haven't experienced Seoul until you have spent some time at Namdaemun or Dongdaemun markets.

광장시장은 100년 이상 동안 서울의 중심에 위치해 왔다. 1905년 일본의 침략으로 잃어버린 국가의 주권을 되찾기 위하여 광장회사의 창립으로 출발해왔다.

Gwangjang Market has been situated in the center of Seoul for more than 100 years. The market was started with the establishment of Gwangjang Co. in order to restore Korea's national sovereignty, which was lost due to the Japanese invasion of Korea in 1905. Silks and satin, linen and cotton, women's clothing, bedding, and handcraft items are sold here. Import stores are frequented by young people who want vintage fashions.

2008년에는 서울 민속 벼룩시장이 청계천가에 오픈되었다. 이 시장은 민속품, 생활필수품, 선물용품, 전통상품, 음식 등을 관광객들이 한곳에서 쇼핑과 먹거리를 즐길 수 있도록 판매한다.

In 2008, the Seoul Folk Flea Market was opened near Cheong-gyecheon Stream. The market sells folk items, daily essentials, souvenirs, traditional goods, and food, which allows visitors to enjoy shopping and eating all under one roof.

The market is divided into seven zones that are marked with the colors of the rainbow, such as red, orange, yellow, green, blue, indigo, and purple. The red zone is a food court. The orange zone sells local specialty produce, crafts, and decorative stones.

The yellow zone sells vintage goods such as typewriters and telephones. The green zone sells antiques such as traditional antique furniture and art. The blue zone sells fashion accessories, paintings, calligraphic works, and hanji (Korean traditional paper). The purple zone sells miscellaneous goods, electronics, and tools.

노량진 해산물 도매시장은 서울 중심에서 가장 신선한 해산물을 살 수 있는 가장 좋은 장소이다. 지하철 노량진역 1번 출구에 위치하고 있으며 바다로부터 온 모든 종류의 활어를 다량으로 풍부하게 구할 수 있다.

The Noryangjin Fisheries Wholesale Market is the best place in downtown Seoul to get fresh seafood. It is located near Noryangjin Station of Subway Line No. 1. All kinds of live seafood, which are fresh from the sea, area available in abundance. During lunchtime, dinnertime, and late at night, the market is bustling with customers who try to get fresh seafood at good prices. There is a wholesale market where fish and other marine life from oceans far away as well as those caught or raised in the seas around Korea are sold. The concrete floor is covered with seawater and the place is crowded with plastic containers from all over the country.

약령시장은 특별한 약초산업지역으로 지정되어 있다. 이 시장은 1960년 말에 일상적인 시장으로 하나둘씩 약초 상점이 생겨나면서 출발하였다. 경제발전과 함께 이 시장은 양적 · 질적으로 큰 성장을 가져왔다.

Yangnyeong Market has been designated as a specialized medicinal herb industry zone. The market was formed in the late 1960s as herbal shops started to flock to the current market place one by one. Along with economic development, the market has qualitatively and quantitatively grown bigger.

Consumers can get hard-to-find medicinal materials such as frogs, terrapins, and freshwater shrimp, which are used as folk remedies, from this market.

The market sells cactus fruits, cockscomb seeds, corn silk, and mulberry roots at affordable prices as well. Customers can get herbal tea packaged in convenient plastic pouches by simply paying 10,000 won as a fee to an herbal processing shop. It takes about 3 hours to make these tea pouches. At the ginseng market, customers can buy fresh ginseng, red ginseng, fine ginseng roots, and a variety of honey, as well as Korean yeongji mushroom.

TV, 세탁기, 냉장고와 같은 한국의 전자기기는 세계 여러 나라에 한국 홍보 촉진에 가장 좋은 업무 중의 하나이다. 용산 전자시장은 전기나 전자와 관련된 어떤 것이든 살 수 있는 곳이다.

Korea's electronic appliances like washing machines, refrigerators, and TVs have done the best job of promoting Korea around the world.

You could go as far as to say that anything related to electricity or electronics can be obtained at Yongsan Electronics Market. Electro Land is at the entrance to Yongsan Electronics Market from the Gangbukgangbyeon Road and is an arcade complex that sells electronic appliances and computers as well as video and audio equipment.

There are many lighting stores and places that sell parts for electronic appliances around the Yongsan Electronics Market intersection. Parts related to electricity are mostly at Wonhyo Electronics Mall across the street from Electro Land. The various malls of Yongsan Electronics Market are always crowded with all kinds of people who come to look for what they need.

■ Myeong-dong and Insa-dong

명동은 모든 사인보드 불빛 때문에 "밝은 지역"을 의미한다. 명동은 쇼핑의 천국이며 항상 활기가 넘치고 거리에는 많은 인파가 모이는 곳이다.

Myeong-Dong means "Bright Town" Because of its all lighting sign boards. Myeong-Dong its just a shoppers heaven. Myeongdong' streets are always crowded and full of vitality. If you look at the history of Myeong-dong, you find that it grew as the Chungmuro area developed into a commercial district during the Japanese occupation.

It was the place for writers to gather in the sixties, a place of romance along with the guitars and jeans culture in the seventies, a place where the smell of teargas was always in the air in the eighties, and then a place for teenagers in the nineties.

명동은 서울의 중앙에 자리하고 있는데, 이 지역에 많은 사람들이 모여들고 있는 이유는 모든 골목길에 다양한 문화를 접하고 즐길 수 있는 먹거리, 쇼핑장소 등이 가득차 있기 때문이다.

Myeong-dong is in the middle of Seoul. The reason so many people flock to this area is that every alleyway is filled with places to shop, eat, and enjoy a diverse range of cultural aspects. It is also the most popular tourist spot for foreign visitors. Myeongdong is part of Jung-gu and is situated between Chungmuro, Euljiro, and Namdaemun. Except for the Chinese Embassy and Myeongdong catholic church, most of the area is malls or arcades. It is also the center of Korea's finance and a street of the latest trends.

명동에서는 당신을 도와 줄 영어로 말할 수 있는 많은 쇼핑점들이 있어 어떠한 언어 장벽에 대해서도 걱정 할 필요가 없다.

There is no need to worry about any language barriers as there are many shop have English speaking persons to help you out. In a shopping block radius of few streets will feel as if going round & round at the same place because there are at least 5 of each big Korean names cosmetic's brand shops in proximity close to each other. This are just shops but there are huge shopping mall's such as Lotte fit-in, Shinsegae department store, Migliore, H&M,Zara, Noon Square & M Plaza.

인사동은 서울에서 관광객의 뜨거운 장소중의 하나이다. 골동품 판매자들에게 유서깊은 곳인데, 질 좋은 고려청자 등을 판매하는 작고 특별한 상점들이 많이 있는 곳이다.

Insadong is one of the city's tourist hotspots. A time-honored location for antiques dealers, there are a huge number of small specialist shops selling fine Goryeo celadon, Silla pottery, and Joseon-era furniture, along with numerous art galleries, art supply stores, teahouses, restaurants, and a few bookshops.

Although some of the antiques stores face the street, others lurk in back alleys snuggled between tiny restaurants, teahouses, junk dealers, and music stores. Some vendors spread their wares on blankets on the ground. It's a real bargain hunter's wonderland, but be cautious (as anywhere) with prices for items – especially antiques – that seem too inexpensive to be true. Hanji paper items, from cards to wrapping paper to dolls, are high-quality.

주말에 인사동 거리에는 축제분위기인데, 한국인들과 외국인들이 거리와 상점에 몰려온다.

At weekends, the streets of Insadong take on a festive atmosphere, as Koreans and foreigners (the area is a favourite with the expat community) crowd the streets and shops. With its network of tiny side alleys and its main flowing avenue filled with shoppers, Insadong is something of a flashback to an older, smaller city. Insadong is also well known for its traditional (jeontong chatjip) and not-so-traditional (dabang) teahouses, where bell jars of dried herbs line the shelves. Ginseng is the most popular, but various other home-made brews are also served.

Tourism Guide Quiz

1. Introduce dongdaemun market.
2. Recommend one of the best attractions in Seoul.
3. Tell me the characteristics of Myeong-dong and Insa-dong.
4. Explain one of the traditional markets in Seoul.
5. Introduce The Seoul World Cup Stadium.

수행 Tips : The ability to raise 통역안내사 우리말 면접시험 예상문제

전문지식과 응용능력이 중요시되고 있으며, 국가관, 사명감 등 정신자세는 필요충분조건입니다. 의사발표의 정확성과 논리성, 창의성 등에 좋은 평가를 받을 수 있습니다.

1. 한류문화에 대하여 설명하시오.

2. 창덕궁의 특성은?

3. 사물놀이에 대하여 설명하시오.

4. 관광안내 중 긴급상황(테러 및 자연재해)이 발생하였을 때 대처 방안은?

5. 3면이 바다인 우리나라 해안별 특징을 설명하시오.

6. 여행업의 종류와 등록기준은?

7. 관광상품의 특성에 대하여 설명하시오.

8. 저비용 항공(LCC)란?

9. I.SEOUL.YOU의 브랜드가 의미하는 바는?

10. 융 · 복합관광이란?

11. 공항도착시 가이드의 준비사항은?

12. 4차산업시대에 관광산업의 변화에 대하여 설명하시오.

13. 쇼핑안내 시 주의사항에 대하여 설명하시오.

14. 세계유산-문화유산이란?

15. 수하물 도난 및 분실시 대처방안은?

16. 근정전에 있는 품계석은?

17. 신라와 백제문화의 특징에 대하여 설명하시오.

18. 법보/승보/불보사찰이란?

19. 승탑과 부도가 의미하는 바는?

20. 항공기의 출발지연이 발생하였을 경우 대처방안에 대하여 설명하시오.

21. 항공사 마일리지 제도의 장점은?

22. 한국의 의료관광에 대하여 설명하시오.

23. 서울에서 중요지역외 외국인에게 소개할 만한 곳은?

24. 우리나라 해상국립공원 4곳은 어디인가?

25. 5대 적멸보궁은 무엇이며, 어디에 위치하고 있는가?

26. Slow City란?

27. 유네스코의 세계 유산의 유형과 종류에 대하여 설명하시오.

28. Concierge란?

29. 우리 문화의 우수성에 대하여 설명하시오.

30. 삼보사찰이란?

31. SIT란?

32. 남사당이란?

33. 국제회의의 개최효과에 대하여 설명하시오.

34. 조선시대 왕실의 도자기 관리관청은?

35. 중국 전담여행사의 역할은?

36. 계절에 따른 금강산의 명칭을 설명하시오.

37. 조선시대 객사(客舍)란 무엇인가?

38. 조선시대 대한팔경은?

39. 계절성이란?

40. 관광통역가이드의 직무에 대하여 말씀해 보세요.

41. 문화재 보호법이 정하고 있는 4대 문화재는?

42. 창덕궁의 세계 유산적 가치는?

43. 신기전이란?

44. 바루공양이란?

45. 대한민국 국보지정 기준은?

46. 수원화성의 문화적 우수성에 대하여 설명하시오.

47. 조선시대 5대궁궐의 정전과 정문을 설명하시오.

48. 실학의 발생배경에 대하여 설명하시오.

49. 5대 궁궐은?

50. 크루즈 여행의 특성에 대하여 설명하시오.

51. 대표적인 실학자에 대하여 설명하시오.

52. 우리나라 국립공원 중 최초의 국립공원과 가장 최근의 국립공원은?

53. stop over란?

54. 역사왜곡을 믿고 있는 외래관광객에게 어떻게 설명할 것인가?

55. 위안부 문제와 관련한 아베신조 정권이 주장에 대한 본인의 견해는?

56. 애국가에 대하여 설명하시오.

57. 1인당 면세한도와 면세한도액에 포함되지 않는 면세통관 품목은?

58. 독도의 위치와 일본측이 제기한 영토문제에 대한 본인의 의견은?

59. 국내의 대표적인 안보관광 상품-DMZ여행코스를 설명하시오.

60. 관광통역 안내사가 주의해야 할 사항에 대하여 말씀해 보세요.

61. 우리 고궁에 대한 대문의 역할과 기능에 대하여 설명하시오.

62. 백제역사 유적지구의 선정 의미와 등재된 8곳의 백제역사지구는?

63. 카지노산업의 긍정적 효과와 부정적 효과에 대하여 설명하시오.

64. 관광자원의 개념과 특성에 대하여 설명하시오.

65. 세시 절기 중 곡우의 의미는?

66. 관광산업의 중요성에 대하여 설명하시오.

67. 사적과 명승에 대해 설명하시오.

68. 2015년 세계기록유산으로 등재된 한국의 유교책판에 대해서 설명하시오.

69. 관광경찰의 역할은?

70. 관광이 경제에 미치는 영향은?

71. 무자격 통역안내사로 인해 발생되는 문제점에 대한 본인의 견해는?

72. 세계적인 건축가 안도타타오의 건축물이 국내에 설치되었는데, 이 분의 건축특징과 국내작품에 대하여 설명하시오.

73. 세계 문화유산 창덕궁의 비원을 소개해 보세요.

74. 여행사의 기능에 대하여 설명하시오.

75. 관광두레에 대하여 설명하시오.

76. 영화관광의 개념과 국내의 주요 명소에 대하여 설명하시오.

77. 당간지주란?

- Knock at the door and it will be opened -

Unit 5

Korean Lifestyle

Domestic Tour Guide English

Unit 5

Korean Lifestyle

♣ National Golidays(국경일)

한국은 정부에서 지정한 5개의 국경일이 있습니다.

In Korea there are five national holidays designated by the government: Independence Declaration Day (Samiljeol, March 1), which commemorates the March First Movement, one of the earliest public displays of Korean resistance against the Japanese occupation of Korea, and the promulgation of the Constitution of the Republic of Korea in 1948; Liberation Day (Gwangbokjeol, August 15), celebrating national liberation from Imperial Japan in 1945; National Foundation Day, which marks the foundation of Gojoseon, the first state of the Korean nation, on the 3rd day of 10th lunar month, 2333 BCE; and Hangeul Day (Hangeullal, October 9), which commemorates the invention and proclamation of the Korean writing system.

Table 5-1 National and public Holidays

Jan 1	New Year's Day Seollal	The first day of the year. The first day of the year by the lunar calendar. Three Day Celebration.
Mar 1	Independence Day	Commemorates the March First Movement, non-violent public resistance against the Japanese colonial rule, and the declaration of Korean Independence in 1919
Apr 8	Buddha's Birthday	Celebrates the birth of Shakyamuni Buddha. A variety of celebratory events are held in Buddhist temples across Korea,
May 5	Children's Day	A great variety of celebratory and fun events for children are held across the country.
Jun 6	Memorial Day	A national memorial service is held at the National Cemetery to honor and commemorate the achievements of war heroes and veterans
Aug 15	Liberation Day	Celebrates the 1945 liberation of Korea from Japanese colonial rule.
Aug 15	Chuseok	Known by different names such as Chuseok and Hangawi, this seasonal festival on the 15th day of the 8th lunar month brings families together for memorial services for their ancestors and celebratory events.
Oct 3	National Foundation Day	Commemorates the foundation of Gojoseon, the first Korean state, by Dangun in 2333 BCE.
Oct 9	Hangeul Day	Marks the invention and promulgation of Hunminjeongeum (Hangeul), the Korean writing system.
Dec 25	Christmas	Celebrates the birth of Jesus Christ with a great variety of religious and secular events.

자료출처 : korea.net

♣ Public Holidays(공휴일)

한국은 새해 첫날, 설날(음력 설, 3일간 지정)을 비롯하여 음력 8월15일, 추석 등과 같은 총 15일의 법정 공휴일을 정해놓고 있다.

The public holidays during which work is suspended by law in Korea include New Year's Day, Seollal (or Lunar New Year's Day, celebrated for 3 days). Chuseok (Mid-autumn Festival on the 15th day of the 8th lunar month, celebrated for 3 days), Buddha's Birthday (on the 8th day of the 4th lunar month), Children's Day (May 5), Memorial Day (June 6) and Christmas Day.

There are fifteen public holidays in total on which businesses are closed by law and employees have a day off, from which Constitution Day is excluded.

♣ Religion(종교)

한국은 세계의 모든 종교가 존재하는 나라이며 기독교, 불교, 유교, 이슬람교, 샤머니즈즘도 평화롭게 공존하고 있다.

Korea is a country where all the world's major religions, Christianity, Buddhism, Confucianism and Islam, peacefully coexist with shamanism. Given the great diversity of religious expression,the role of religion in South Korea's social development has been complex; and some traditions are best understood as important cultural properties rather than as rites of worship.

2005년 통계에 따르면, 한국인구의 53%가 종교를 갖고 있으며 2008년 통계는 510개의 종교 조직이 있다고 보여주고 있다.

According to the 2005 statistics, 53% of the Korean population has a religion, while the 2008 statistics show that there were over 510 religious organizations in Korea.

Among them Buddhism and Confucianism have been more influential than any others upon the life of the Korean people and over half of the country's listed cultural heritage are related with the two religions.

Since its arrival in Korea in 372, Buddhism has produced several tens of thousands temples across the country and currently has more adherents than any other religion.

Figure 5-1 size of religious group in korea

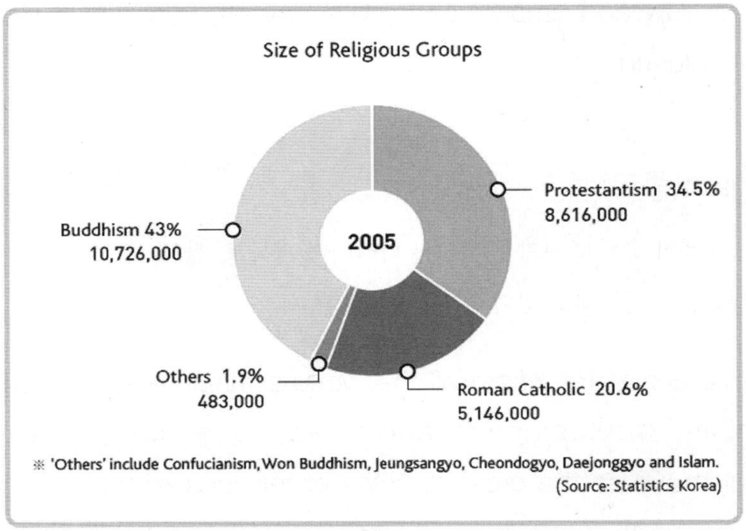

자료출처 : korea.net

종교생활의 다양성은 많은 인족과 문화를 빠르게 얻게 되는 방식인데, 한국은 법적으로 종교의 다양성을 보호하고 있다.

Diversity in Religious Life. Now rapidly on its way to becoming a multi-ethnic, multi-cultural, and multireligious society, Korea protects religious diversity by law.

People in Korea are free to lead a religious life according to their own choice and convictions, whether as followers of one of the major religions, namely, Christianity, Buddhism, Confucianism, and Islam, or as adherents of Korean native religions such Won Buddhism and Cheondogyo.

조선시대(1392~1910)는 유교를 이상 정책으로 채택했는데, 왕에 대한 효성과 덕을 강요하는 종교 이상의 보다 윤리적인 시스템이었다.

Adopted as the state ideology of the Joseon Dynasty (1392– 1910), Confucianism was more a system of ethics than religion and stressed the importance of loyalty, filial piety and other virtues.

Confucian followers also valued ancestral worship in the belief that the ancestral spirits can affect the life of their descendants, and tried to find auspicious sites for the graves of their ancestors.

Today, however, more and more people are turning from the practice of burial to cremation.

Photo 5-1 Chungdong First Methodist Church in Seoul. Korea' s first Protestant church founded in 1897

가톨릭은 조선시대 후기에 서구 성신부들과 북경을 방문하였던 사절단들에 의하여 중국을 통하여 전해졌다. 조선의 통치자들은 신자들을 박해하였으며 한국은 세계에서 4번째로 많은 가톨릭 성인들을 생기게 했다.

Catholicism was introduced to Korea from China through the envoys of late Joseon who visited Beijing and the Western priests who followed them.

The early Roman Catholics in Korea were subjected to severe persecution, but the religion continued to spread among the common people across the country. The persecution of Christian believers by Joseon's rulers led Korea to yield the world's fourth largest number of Christian saints.

개신교는 19세기 말경에 북미 지역에서 파견된 선교사들에 의하여 한국에 전해졌는데, 교육과 의료서비스를 통하여 국민들에게 빠르게 전도될 수 있었다.

Protestantism was brought to Korea during the late 19th century by North American missionaries, and quickly won people's hearts through school education and medical services.

Even today, Protestants in Korea operate a great number of educational institutions, middle and high schools, colleges and universities, and medical centers.

Photo 5-2 The interior of Myeongdong Cathedral in Seoul

한국에는 현대 한국역사의 다양한 격변기와 그들의 신자 수 증가노력에 의하여 원불교, 천도교, 대종교와 같은 성장하는 토착종교가 있다.

In Korea there is a rich array of native religions such as Cheondogyo, Won Buddhism and Daejonggyo which, although suffered various vicissitudes of modern Korean history, are still active in increasing the number of their adherents.

Cheondogyo, formed on the basis of the Eastern Learning (Donghak) of the 19th century, maintains the doctrine that "Man is Heaven," which exerted a strong influence upon the process of modernization in Korea.

Daejonggyo, established in the early 20th century to worship Dangun, the founder of the first Korean state, also affected the life of ordinary Korean people, boosting Korean nationalism.

1955년에 한국에 최초로 이슬람교가 출현하였으며, 1967년에 한국 무슬림연합이 창설되었다.

In 1955, there appeared the Islamic Society of Korea and the first Korean Imam, followed by the foundation of the Korean Muslim Federation in 1967.

Islam currently has about 60 places of worship across Korea and there are about 100,000 Korean Muslims. In addition to the major religions, shamanism has also played an important part in the daily life of the Korean people, trying to help them connect with the spiritual world and making predictions about their future.

Photo 5-3 The Seoul Central Mosque in Itaewon

♣ Clothing and Fashion

한반도에는 선사시대에 정주민이 존재한 이후 지속적으로 집에서의 삶과 먹거리, 입을거리와 관계된 독특한 전통문화를 부유하게 발전시켜왔다.

Since their settlement in prehistoric times on the land now known as the Korean Peninsula, the Korean people have developed a wealth of unique cultural traditions related to the way they dress, eat, and behave at home.

These traditions reflect the natural environment of their homeland, a terrain predominately covered by hills and mountains, bound by the sea on three sides and marked by four distinct seasons.

The Korean people learned to use various fabrics, such as sambe (hemp), mosi (ramie), cotton and silk to make a range of clothing that was not only attractive but also provided them with effective protection even during the harshest winters and the hottest summers. They made warm winter clothes using the technique of filling soft cotton between two layers of material, silk or cotton fabric, and sewing them together with fine stitching, and produced cool summer clothes with hemp and ramie. These clothes typically feature graceful lines and forms that create the serene aura characteristic of the traditional Korean clothes we know as hanbok.

과거에 역사적으로 한국인을 나타내는 것으로 단순함을 좋아하는 경향이었으며, 흰 옷은 다른 색깔과 디자인으로 꾸며졌다.

History reveals that Korean people in the past tended to prefer simple, white clothes to clothing decorated with different colors and designs. That is why they were often referred to as "the white-clad people" among their neighbors who admired them for being a peaceful people. Nonetheless, Korea has also had a long tradition of enjoying colorful clothes with complex designs depending on the period and the wearer's social status.

오늘날 한국에는 전통과 현대를 조화한 창조적이며 국제적으로 평판받고 있는 많은 재능을 지닌 패션디자이너들이 활동하고 있다.

Today, Korea is home to many talented fashion designers who have earned an international reputation with their creative designs which combine traditional Korean designs and patterns with a modern artistic sensibility. The beauty of traditional Korean clothes has been introduced to, and praised in, many parts of the world thanks to the remarkable success in recent years of many Korean films and TV dramas including Dae Jang Geum.

한국인들은 전통 옷보다 현대적인 서구스타일 영감을 받은 옷을 선호하는 것 같으며, 어떤 사람들은 결혼식이나 전통적인 휴일에 입기를 고수하고 있다.

Korean people today seem to prefer clothes inspired by modern Western styles to their traditional clothes, although some people still insist on wearing the latter on traditional holidays or for special family occasions such as weddings. Their love of tradition and yearning for the new sometimes led to the creation of attractive "modernized hanbok."

현재 서울 강남구에는 2012년 세계를 흔들었던 누구나 아는 노래 강남스타일 같은 부유한 거주 지역에 최고급 시설과 한국의 유행 패션거리가 있다.

Now a household name across the world thanks to "Gangnam Style," a K-Pop song that shook the world in 2012, Gangnam-gu in Seoul is a large district where wealthy residential areas sit alongside high-end art facilities and Korea's busiest fashion streets. The district now attracts numerous fashion-minded tourists from across East Asia and beyond with annual fashion festivals comprising international fashion shows and contests participated in by many rising designers.

국제 평판가들이 선호하는 또 다른 서울의 패션거리는 동대문구인데, 젊은이들과 젊은 마음을 리드하는 패션 품목을 창의적으로 공급하며 지역 패션의 허브로 성장하고 있는 곳이다.

Another fashion district in Seoul that enjoys an international reputation is Dongdaemun-gu, which has grown into a hub of the regional fashion industry, providing creative, affordable fashion items for youth and the young at heart. With its fully developed distribution and sales network, highly efficient production facilities, and throng of talented, aspiring designers, the district is now one of Seoul's most popular attractions among foreign tourists.

♣ Housing

한국인들은 집을 짓는데 독특한 건축기술을 발전시켜왔으며, 주거자들을 보호해주며 자연 환경을 알맞게 채택하는 것이다. 한옥(전통적인 한국인의 집)의 뛰어난 장점은 온돌이라 부르는 난방시스템을 밑에 장치하는 것이다.

Korean people have developed unique architectural techniques to build housing that is properly adapted to the surrounding natural environment, providing dwellers with better protection. A distinctive feature of the Hanok (traditional Korean house) is an underfloor heating system called ondol.

Literally meaning "warm stones" and developed during the prehistoric period, ondol refers to the system of channels running beneath the stone floor of a room through which heat is delivered from the fireplace in the kitchen.

It is also designed to effectively draw out the smoke through the under-the-floor passages connected to the chimney. Another important element of the traditional Korean house is the board-floored room (maru) located at the center and used for multiple purposes.

The room is usually larger than other rooms and is raised from the ground to allow air to freely circulate under it, creating a cool living environment during the warm summer season.

온돌과 마루의 혼합된 스마트한 시스템은 추운 겨울 뿐만아니라 무더운 여름에도 편안하게 거주할 수 있도록 하게해주는 전통적인 한국인들의 집이다.

The smart system combining ondol and maru makes the traditional Korean house a comfortable living space for its residents not only in the harsh winter but also in the scorching summer. The roof is typically covered with either ceramic tiles or thatching. While most of the roof tiles are dark gray, some exhibit more vibrant colors as demonstrated, for example, by the Official Residence of the Korean President Cheong Wa Dae, which literally means "Blue House" because, as the name shows, it is covered by blue roof tiles.

전통적인 한국인의 집은 일반적으로 목재로 건조하는데, 잘 관리하고 쓰면 다른 재질로 만든 건물보다 오래 거주할 수 있다. 예를 들면, 1363년 전에 지어진 경상북도 안동의 봉정사의 건낙전 홀은 한국의 가장 오래된 남아 있는 건축물인데 옛 모습 그대로 650년을 유지하고 있다.

While traditional Korean houses are generally wooden structures, they can survive as long as other buildings made with other materials if properly taken care of. Built before 1363, Geungnakjeon Hall of Bongjeongsa Temple in Andong, Gyeongsangbuk-do, for instance, is Korea's oldest remaining building, still maintaining its original structure intact after 650 years.

As an ideal location for their house, Korean people preferred a site protected by hills or mountains on three of its sides, with a stream or river passing in front, thus providing easy access to water. Houses built in such a place create a great harmony with the surrounding environment, attracting more and more admirers not just in Korea but outside it as well.

오늘날 서울의 60% 이상의 사람들은 현대적인 아파트에 살고 있지만, 이것은 재미있게도 크고 다양한 빌딩으로 오래된 온돌에 영감을 받은 히팅 시스템으로 새로움이 없는 것이다.

These days, over 60% of Seoul's population live in modern apartments but, interestingly, these tall, multistoried buildings are almost without exception furbished with a heating system inspired by the age-old ondol system. Similarly, newly built detached houses are also reliant on the legacy of the ondol system of heating the floor, although the traditional heat passages are now replaced by under-floor metal pipes with running water heated either by gas or electricity.

현재 이와 같은 온돌 히팅 시스템은 매일 온도의 변형 성을 가하여 다른 나라로 수출되기 시작했다. 한국에서 수년간 세련된 한옥을 간직하고 있는 지역은 서울 중심의 북촌과 다른 역사적인 지역 서촌까지 옮겨져 있다.

This heating system has now begun to be exported to other countries with wide variations in daily temperature. Korea was for a number of years an exquisite Hanok located in Bukchon, downtown Seoul, until he moved to Seochon, another historic district of the Korean capital.

♣ SPORTS

■ The 23rd Olympic Winter Games Pyeongchang 2018

세계인의 축제, 제23회 동계올림픽대회는 대한민국 강원도 평창에서 2018년 2월 9일부터 25일까지 17일간 개최된다. 대한민국 평창은 세 번의 도전 끝에 지난 2011년 7월 6일 열린 제 123차 IOC 총회에서 과반 표를 획득하며 2018년 동계올림픽 개최지로 선정됐다.

대한민국에서는 1988년 서울 올림픽 이후 30년 만에, 평창에서 개 · 폐회식과 대부분의 설상 경기가 개최되며, 강릉에서는 빙상 종목 전 경기가, 그리고 정선에서는 알파인 스키 활강 경기가 개최될 예정이다.

Pyeongchang, elected as the host city of the 2018 Olympic Winter Games after three bids, is well known for its beautiful natural scenery featuring lush forests and clean rivers.

Living up to its reputation for record snowfall, Pyeongchang established itself early on as the winter sports capital of Korea. Every year, swarms of winter sports enthusiasts visit Pyeongchang to enjoy the season to the fullest.

Despite having to prepare for a successful hosting of the Olympics, Pyeongchang also organizes a special event for young people around the world every year.

The "Dream Program" invites youths from snowless nations who have not experienced winter sports, and offers systematic training on skiing, ice skating, and other winter sports.

The program is considered a significant contributor to the global expansion of winter sports, 15events with 50,000 participants from 95 countries so far.

평창 겨울 올림픽이 다음해 2월에 열리는데, 30년 만에 개최되는 한국의 2번째 올림픽이 될 것이다. 1988년 서울의 여름 올림픽을 되돌아볼 면 큰 이벤트를 준비를 위하여 전 국가가 헌신적이었다.

The PyeongChang Winter Olympics, scheduled for February next year, will be Korea's second Olympic Games in close to 30 years.

Looking back on the Seoul 1988 Summer Olympics, that was a time when the entire country devoted itself to preparing for the big event.

A newly constructed highway was christened the Olympic Boulevard, and apartment complexes and city parks took on the Olympic moniker.

평창올림픽은 기억해야 할 중요한 행사이지만 약간 결정적인 전환점의 중심에 있다. 우선 첫째로 다양한 겨울 스포츠와 관련된 산업에 활기를 불어넣을 수 있을 것이며 강원지방 발전에 기여할 것이다.

It's important to remember, though, that the PyeongChang Winter Olympics are at the center of some crucial turning points. For starters, they will contribute to the development of Gangwon-do Province and invigorate various industries related to winter sports.

Moreover, they will be an opportunity to show the world our vision for the future by hosting a sporting event that offers 5G internet connection speeds.

Recently, there has also been talk of creating an inter-Korea sports team for the upcoming Olympics. Should this plan come to fruition, it would be a chance to stage an Olympics of Peace that would help ease tensions on the Korean Peninsula.

■ How South Korea Became a Sporting Powerhouse

한국은 2102년 런던 올림픽에서 메달 순위측면에서 5위로 세계를 놀라게 했다. 또한 축구팀이 동메달을 획득한 것에 주목할 필요가 있다.

South Korea's national team surprised the world by ranking 5th place in the medals table (gold, silver and bronze) at the 2012 London Summer Olympics. It is also worth noting that the team won the soccer bronze medal at those Games.

The potential of the country's soccer is explained by the presence of several South Korean players in European football (soccer) leagues.

Also, at the 2008 Beijing Olympics, the South Korean team won the gold medal for baseball with several South Korean players now enjoying great popularity among fans in the United States and Japan as members of local teams.

아시아 국가는 피겨스케이팅에 빈약한 지역이었으나 김연아는 훈련을 통하여 세계

기록을 깨뜨렸으며 변화시켰다. 펜싱은 기품 있는 서양선수들의 스포츠로 간주되었으나 한국선수들은 많은 메달을 획득했다.

Asians used to do poorly in figure skating, but Yuna Kim, a South Korean changed that by breaking world records in the discipline.

In fencing, which used to be regarded as a sport for westerners and the nobility, South Korean athletes have won many medals.

It is a well-known fact that many South Koreans have won both the PGA and LPGA championships.

It is also noteworthy that three or four Koreans continually rank in the top ten at each LPGA championship.

Formula 1 also visited Korea between 2010 and 2013 with the Korean Grand Prix held at Yeongam, Jeollanam-do, South Korea.

한국 스포츠 최우수 팀의 변화에 대한 중요한 요인으로는 스포츠를 사랑하는 많은 사람들과 효율적인 투자에 있다.

The most important factors behind South Korea's transformation into a sporting powerhouse are the country's large number of sports lovers and efficient investment.

The country strives to find promising young athletes, train them efficiently, and help them build their skills by accumulating a wealth of experience in domestic competitions.

There are also professional sporting facilities dedicated solely to the training of athletes selected for international events such as the Olympic Games or the Asian Games.

■ National Sports Infrastructure

한국의 많은 스포츠 동호인들은 스포츠를 즐기기 위하여 휴일 아침에 일찍이 모인다. 팀들은 흔히 이웃마을 팀과 게임과 시합에 참여하는데, 약 50만개의 동호인 팀들이 구성되어져 있다. 국가의 스포츠 인프라는 견고하며 광범위하다. 2013년의 경우 일상적으로 스포츠를 사랑하는 클럽 인들이 413만 명, 즉 전체 국가인구의 8.1%였다.

Many South Korean soccer lovers gather together early in the morning of a holiday to enjoy the sport. Teams from neighboring villages often take part in games and tournaments with the number of teams composed of neighbors currently standing at about 500,000.

The country's sports infrastructure is solid and wide-ranging. As of 2013, the number of ordinary sports lovers' clubs came to 4.13 million, i.e. 8.1% of the entire population.

The number of soccer lovers who have joined clubs (590,000) is at the top of the list, followed by the number of members of tennis, badminton, table tennis, gate ball, and daily calisthenics clubs.

The government strives to encourage people to engage in more positive physical activities by providing support for sports clubs. Most sports clubs hold events from time to time. Over the past few years, the number of marathon clubs has increased drastically.

In spring and fall, marathon competitions are held every weekend all over the country. An amateur marathon competition attracts thousands or even tens of thousands of participants.

A relevant organization estimates the number of people engaging in jogging, running, and marathon events at somewhere between 800,000 and 4 million.

Figure 5-2 한국 스포츠클럽과 숫자의 변화

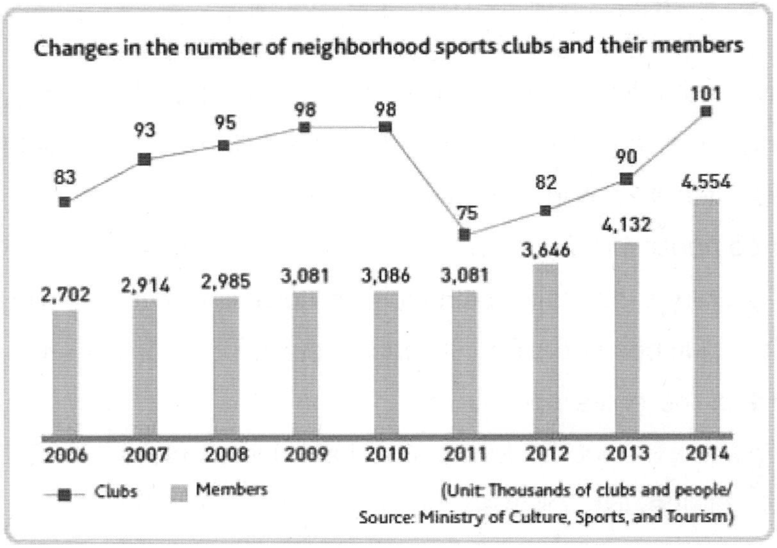

자료출처 : 문화체육관광부

Figure 5-3 주요 전문 스포츠 게임에 참여하는 관중 수

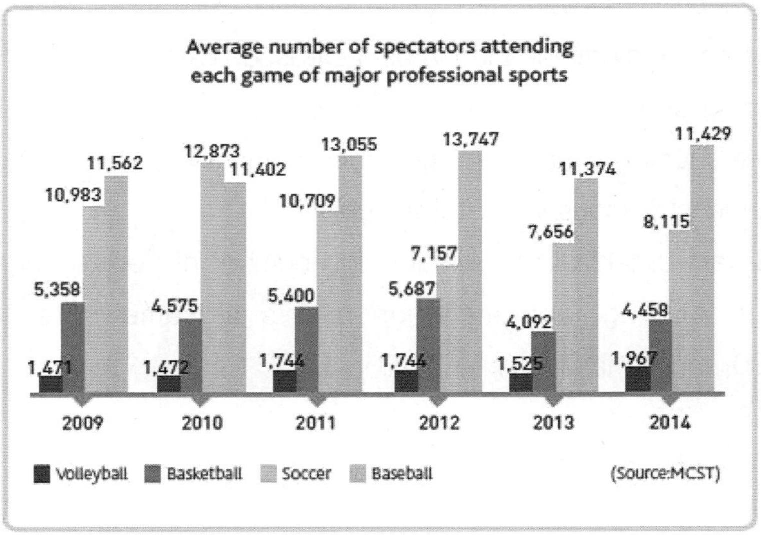

자료출처 : 문화체육관광부

A large number of people are attracted to professional baseball, soccer, and volleyball games. Rooting for one's favorite team is a fun pastime.

Professional baseball and soccer games are attended by 8 million and 3 million people, respectively, each year.

■ Collaboration of Sports and Science

2012년 런던 올림픽에서 금메달의 마지막 도약은 스포츠와 과학의 공동협력의 결과이다. 스포츠과학자들은 여러 기술들을 끌어 올릴 수 있는 최적의 조건들을 연구했다.

At the 2012 London Summer Olympics, a South Korean won the gold medal in the vault final. This achievement was the result of collaboration between science and sports. Sports scientists studied what the optimal conditions should be to pull through the hardest skills.

They reached the conclusion that the optimal time span for an athlete to touch the vaulting horse was 0.15 seconds and that the optimal angle between arm and body was 22 degrees in order to stay in the air longer and make more rapid turns.

한국 선수들은 신체조건에 적합한 최선의 조건에 기초한 훈련의 결과로 금메달을 획득할 수 있었다. 한국스포츠과학 연구소(KISS)는 스포츠동력, 생리학, 심리학 등 전문가들을 고용했다. 이 전문가들은 경재에서 가장 좋은 결과를 얻을 수 있도록 선수들을 도왔다.

The South Korean athlete was able to win the gold medal as a result of training based on optimal conditions suited to his body structure.

The Korea Institute of Sport Science (KISS) employs experts in sports dynamics, psychology, physiology, and so on. These specialists help athletes to achieve the best possible results in competitions.

Five experts accompanied the national team during the 2012 London Summer Olympics. There are sixteen sports-related societies in the country in total, all of which exchange information through an integrated computer system.

Korea has many practice and training facilities, including the Taereung Training Center in Seoul. The center in Taereung is equipped with training facilities, running tracks, indoor and outdoor courts, an indoor swimming pool that meet international standards, and a dormitory for 300 athletes.

진천에 있는 시설은 25개스포츠에 800명의 선수들에게 편의를 도모할 수 있도록 확장하였다. 다른 특별한 시설로는 선수들의 심폐기능을 향상시킬 수 있는 것으로 태백산 가까이 있는 함백산에 있다.

The facility in Jincheon have expanded to accommodate up to 800 athletes in 25 sports. Another facility specializing in the enhancement of athletes' cardiopulmonary functions is in Hambaeksan Mountain near Taebaek.

♣ Traditional Arts

■ Gugak

국악이라는 말은 문자 그대로 '국민의 음악'을 의미하며, 공식적인 행동과 춤, 노래를 포함하여 예술적 행위와 관계된 전통 한국인의 음악을 말한다. 한국 음악의 역사는 오랜 한국인의 역사와 함께한다고 할 수 있겠으나, 조선시대(1392-1910)의 왕 세종 통치, 15세기 초에 한국인의 음악은 깊은 연구의 주제였으며 가장 오래된 정률 표시법을 창의적으로 개발하였다. 이것이 아시의 정간보라 일컬어지고 있다. 세종대왕은 왕실 음악의 재구성하고자 노력하였는데, 2001년 인류의 무형문화유산을 대표하는 유네스코 지정 문화재, 종묘제례악이다.

The term gugak, which literally means "national music," refers to traditional Korean music and other related art forms including songs, dances and ceremonial movements. The history of music in Korea should be as long as Korean history itself, but it was only in the early 15th century, during the reign of King Sejong of the Joseon Dynasty (1392–1910), that Korean music became a subject of serious study and was developed into a system, resulting in the creation of the oldest mensural notation system, called jeongganbo, in Asia.

King Sejong's efforts to reform the court music led not only to the creation of Korea's own notation system but also to the composition of a special ritual music to be performed during the Royal Ancestral Rite at the Jongmyo Shrine–inscribed on UNESCO's Representative List of the Intangible Cultural Heritage of Humanity in 2001?and Yeomillak, or "Joy of the People."

전통적인 한국의 음악은 몇가지 형태로 구분되었다. 조선 귀족사회와 왕족들이 즐겼던 전통음악(장각 또는 정가로 불려짐); 판소리,산조,잡가를 포함한 민속음악; 축하이벤트에 왕을 위하여 연수되었던 정재(궁중연회 음악과 춤); 불교전통과 무속과 관계된 춤과음악과 같은 살풀이, 선무, 범패; 가곡과 시조와 같이 문학엘리트들이 사랑했던 시적인 노래 등이다. 수많은 민속 음악 중에 아리랑은 2012년 유네스코의 대표적인 인류무형문화재로 지정되었다.

Traditional Korean music is typically classified into several types: the "legitimate music" (called jeongak or jeongga) enjoyed by the royalty and aristocracy of Joseon; folk music including pansori, sanjo and japga; jeongjae (court music and dance) performed for the King at celebratory state events; music and dance connected with shamanic and Buddhist traditions such as salpuri, seungmu, and beompae; and poetic songs beloved of the literati elite such as gagok and sijo.

Of the numerous folk songs, Arirang-inscribed on UNESCO's Representative List of the Intangible Cultural Heritage of Humanity in 2012?is particularly cherished by the common people as there are many variations with special lyrics and melodies devised to touch their hearts.

The Korean people have also developed a wide range of musical instruments. These traditional musical instruments are generally divided into three categories: wind instruments such as the piri, daegeum, danso and taepyeongso; stringed instruments such as the gayageum, geomungo, haegeum, ajaeng and bipa; and percussion instruments such as the buk, janggu, pyeonjong, pyeongyeong, kkwaenggwari and jing.

■ Folk Dances

한국인들은 살풀이춤(정신을 정화시키는 춤), 굿춤(무속 의식 춤), 태평무(평화의 춤), 할양춤(게으름 뱅이들의 춤), 부채 춤(부채꼴의 춤), 검무(검춤),성무(수사의 춤)과 같이 다양한 민속춤들이 계승되어 왔다.

Korean people have inherited a great variety of folk dances such as salpurichum (spiritual purification dance), gutchum (shamanic ritual dance), taepyeongmu (dance of peace), hallyangchum (idler's dance), buchaechum (fan dance), geommu (sword dance), and seungmu (monk's dance).

Of these, talchum (mask dance) and pungmul nori (play with musical instruments) are known for their satirical targeting of the corrupt aristocracy of Joseon and their close connection with rural communities, which had long been the bedrock of Korean culture and tradition.

Most performances are presented in a marketplace or on the fields and involve drumming, dancing, and singing.

■ Painting and Calligraphy

그림은 고대부터 한국예술 양식의 항상 중요한 장르였다. 고대 한국의 예술은 고구려(기원전38-기원후668) 무덤의 벽화로 묘사되었는데, 일찍이 한국인의 인간성과 우주성 뿐만 아니라 예술적인 감수성과 기술에 대한 믿음의 소중한 단서가 되고 있다.

Painting has always been a major genre of Korean art since ancient times. The art of ancient Korea is represented by the tomb murals of Goguryeo (37 B.C. – 668 A.D.) which contain valuable clues to the beliefs of the early Korean people about humanity and the universe as well as to their artistic sensibilities and techniques.

The artists of Goryeo (918–1392) were interested in capturing Buddhist icons and bequeathed some great masterpieces, while the literati elite of Joseon was more attracted to the symbolism of plants and animals, such as the Four Noble Lords (Sagunja, namely, the orchid, chrysanthemum, bamboo, and plum tree) and the Ten Creatures of Longevity (Sipjangsaeng), as well as idealized landscapes.

18세기에 한국은 두사람의 위대한 미술인이 등장하는데, 김홍도와 신윤복은 그들의 작업에 일상적인 국민들의 생활상을 묘사에 열정적인 관심을 갖고 활동하였다.

Korea in the 18th century saw the arrival of two great artists, Kim Hong-do and Sin Yun-bok, both of whom developed a passionate interest in depicting the daily activities of ordinary people in their work.

Kim Hong-do preferred depicting a kaleidoscope of people in various situations and scenes of everyday life, whereas Sin Yun-bok, for his part, devoted his efforts to capturing erotic moments in works that were surprisingly voyeuristic for the period.

중국의 영향을 받아 한국에서 발전된 서예는 육필예술로써, 먹물의 미묘한 음영과 붓의 작동으로 힘과 개성 및 선의 미를 인식시키는 것이다.

Calligraphy, which developed in Korea under the influence of China, is the art of handwriting in which the beauty of the lines and forms of characters and the energy contained in brush strokes and subtle shades of ink are appreciated.

While calligraphy is an independent genre of art, it has been closely related with ink and wash painting since these forms use similar techniques and the tools commonly called the "four friends of the study" (i.e. paper, brush, ink stick and ink stone).

한국은 김정희(1786-1856)와 같은 대 서예가를 배출했는데, 그 자신의 스타일을 발전시킨 특별함으로 유명하며 추사체 또는 추사스타일(추사는 그의 펜이름)로 잘 알려져 있다.

Korea has produced an abundance of master calligraphers of whom Kim Jeong-hui (1786-1856) is particularly famous for developing his own style, which is known as Chusache or Chusa Style (Chusa was his pen name).

His calligraphic works fascinated even the Chinese masters of his time and are still widely admired for their remarkably modern artistic beauty.

■ Pottery

한국의 도자기는 오늘날 국제 수집가들에게 환호를 받는 매력물인데, 전통적으로 3 탑입으로 구분된다. 즉 청자(푸른색 청자), 분청(덧칠 도자기), 백자(흰 자기)이다.

Korean pottery, which nowadays attracts the highest praise from international collectors, is typically divided into three groups: Cheongja (blue-green celadon), Buncheong (slip-coated stoneware), and Baekja (white porcelain).

Celadon refers to Korean stoneware which underwent major development in the hands of Goryeo potters some 700 to 1,000 years ago. Celadon pottery is marked by an attractive jade blue surface and the unique Korean inlay technique used to decorate it. Gangjin of Jeollanam-do and Buan of Jeollabuk-do were its two main producers during the Goryeo Period (918-1392).

백자 도자기 제품은 조선시대를 대표하고 있는 자기예술이며, 이 제품은 거 표면에 유백색이 나타낸다. 페르시아로부터 중국을 통하여 수입된 귀중한 푸른 코발트 색소, 구리,산화철로 무늬로 그려져 다양하게 꾸며질 수 있다.

White porcelain ware represents the ceramic art of the Joseon Period (1392-1910). While some of these porcelain wares display a milky white surface, many are decorated with a great variety of designs painted in oxidized iron, copper, or the priceless cobalt blue pigment imported from Persia via China.

조선왕궁 도자기는 매우 높은 질의 상품을 얻기 위하여 경기도 광주의 자신만의 도예지에서 운영했다. 한발 앞선 기술이 백자상품 생산에 사용되었는데, 임진왜란(1592-1598)시기에 도예공이 납치되어 일본으로 소개되어졌다.

The Royal Court of Joseon ran its own kilns in Gwangju, Gyeonggi-do, producing products of the very highest quality. The advanced techniques used in the production of white porcelain wares were introduced to Japan by Joseon potters kidnapped during the Imjin Waeran (Japanese Invasion of Korea, 1592-1598).The third main group of Korean pottery, Buncheong, was made by Goryeo potters after the fall of their Kingdom in 1392. This type of pottery is characterized by its slip-coated surface and delightfully simple decorative designs created using several different techniques.

■ Handicrafts

과거 한국의 공예가과 여성들은 가정에서 필요한 품목 생산 기술의 범위를 발전시켰다. 등나무, 싸리나, 대나무로 아름다운 매트, 상자, 바구니를 짜냈고, 예리한 눈대중으로 조화와 균형을 이룬 옷장, 캐비넷, 테이블과같은 나무가구를 생산해냈다.

In the past Korean craftsmen and women developed a wide range of techniques to produce the items they needed at home. They made pieces of wooden furniture such as wardrobes, cabinets and tables marked by a keen eye for balance and symmetry, and wove beautiful baskets, boxes and mats with bamboo, wisteria or lespedeza.

They used Korean mulberry paper to make masks, dolls and ceremonial ornaments, and decorated diverse household objects with black and red lacquer harvested from nature.

Later they developed the art of using beautifully dyed oxhorn strips, and iridescent mother-of-pearl and abalone shell to decorate furniture.

Embroidery, decorative knot making (maedeup) and natural dyeing were also important elements of traditional Korean arts and crafts, which were widely exploited to make attractive garments, household objects and personal fashion ornaments.

■ Hallyu(Korean Wave)

한류라는 말은 아시아와 세계에 걸쳐 한국의 연예와 문화를 언급하면서 널리 사용되었다. 한류는 1990년대 중반에 처음 나타났는데, 1992년 중국과 외교관계를 맺으면서 한국 TV드라마와 팝 음악이 중국 언어사회에 큰 인기를 얻게 되었다.

1997년 CCTV방영된 '사랑이 무엇인지' 는 첫 성공의 하나인데 시청률 4.2%를 기록하였고, 150만 명의 시청자가 지켜보았다.

A term now widely used to refer to the popularity of Korean entertainment and culture across Asia and other parts of the world, Hallyu or the "Korean Wave" first appeared during the mid-1990s after Korea entered into diplomatic relations with China in 1992 and Korean TV dramas and pop music gained great popularity in Chinese-speaking communities.

When one of the first successful TV dramas, What Is Love, was aired by CCTV in 1997, it had an audience rating of 4.2%, meaning that over 150 million Chinese viewers watched it.

한국의 팝 음악은 특별히 댄스 음악이었는데, 중국 10대들에게 인기를 얻기 시작했고 라디오 프로그램으로 1997년 초에 소개된 이후 북경의 서울 음악방송국으로 불린다.

Korean pop music, especially dance music, began to gain popularity among Chinese teenagers after it was introduced in earnest in 1997 by a radio program called Seoul Music Room broadcast from Beijing.

The decisive moment in igniting Korean pop culture fever in China was the concert of Korean boy band H.O.T., held at the Beijing Workers' Gymnasium in February 2000. Korean news reports used the term Hallyu, or the Korean Wave, in describing this concert.

한류는 1999년 11월에 'Beijing Youth Daily' 에 기사로 알려졌으며 드디어 한국인을 인식하기 시작했다. 한류는 2003년에 일본에 상륙했는데 TV드라마 '겨울연가' 가 NHK를 통하여 방송되기 시작하면서부터이다.

The Korean Wave, acknowledged in an article published by Beijing Youth Daily as early as November 1999, began to finally be recognized by Koreans themselves from this point. The Korean Wave landed in Japan in 2003 when the KBS TV drama series Winter Sonata was aired via NHK.

The drama became an instant mega hit, making its male hero, Yon Sama, a household name, compelling his enthusiastic Japanese fans to visit various film locations, including Namiseom Island, in Korea.

한류의 열풍은 한국의 전통문화, 음식, 문학, 언어 등으로 확장되었으며 더욱 더 열광적인 지지자들이 창출하고 있다. 최근 현상으로 2013년 7월에 987개의 한류 조직이 형성되었으며 900만 명의 회원들이 활동하고 있다. 이 조직들의 대부분은 K-POP팬클럽인데, 요즈음은 관심있는 새로운 그룹들이 나타나면서 더욱더 다양화되고 있다.

The 'Korean Wave' craze has expanded to Korean traditional culture, food, literature and language, creating more and more enthusiasts. According to the latest figures, there were 987 hallyu-related organizations as of July 2013 with a combined membership of 9 million people.

A great majority of these organizations are K-Pop fan clubs, but lately new groups of people whose interests are more diverse have begun to emerge.

■ K-Pop

어떤 다른 분야보다도 더 빠르게 성장하고 있는 분야가 21세기 K-POP인데, K-pop 또는 한국 음악의 다양성이다. 즉 댄스 POP, POp발라드, 테크노 락, 힙합, R& B 등을 들 수 있다. 동아시에서 인기를 얻은 K-POP은 21세기 일본 음악시장에 뛰어들었으며, 동아시아와 동남아시아 성년들과 10대들 사이에 하위 음악문화로 성장했다.

One area that is growing more rapidly than any other is 21st century K-Pop, or Korean pop music, which spans dance-pop, pop ballads, techno, rock, hip-hop, R&B, and so on. First gaining popularity in East Asia, K-Pop entered the Japanese music market towards the turn of the 21st century, and grew from a musical genre into a subculture among teenagers and young adults of East and Southeast Asia.

Currently, the spread of K-Pop to other regions of the world, via the Korean Wave, is seen in parts of Latin America, Northeast India, North Africa, the Middle East, Eastern Europe and immigrant enclaves of the Western world.

The rise of K-Pop on the global stage is probably best represented by Psy's Gangnam Style, which swept the world as soon as it was released in late 2012.

The song was the first K-Pop title reach No. 1 on the British Official Singles Chart, took 2nd place on Billboard's Hot 100 in the US, and also topped the charts in more than 30 countries, including France, Germany, Italy, Spain, Russia, Canada, and Australia.

음악비디오 유투브는 다른 것보다도 더 많은 사람들이 시청하고 있는데, 약 20억 명을 넘겼으며, 세계적으로 강남스타일이 성공하며 K-POP 아이돌 그룹이 급상승하기 시작하였고 Big Bang, Beast ,Wonder Girls 등과 같은 아시아시장에 우위를 점하고 있는 그룹들이다.

The YouTube video of the song has been watched by more people than any other, with over 2 billion so far.

The worldwide success of "Gangnam Style" was preceded by a surge of K-Pop idol groups, such as TVXQ, Super Junior, Big Bang, 2NE1, Beast, Girls' Generation, 2PM and Wonder Girls, who dominated pop music markets across Asia.

TVXQ had a total of 65 tour concerts in Japan from 2006 to 2012, bringing together about 700,000 fans and selling over 6.3 million albums, while in late 2009 Wonder Girls became the first Korean group to enter the US Billboard Hot 100 chart with the song "Nobody".

The popularity of K-Pop singers is largely based on their excellent vocal abilities, dazzling stage presence and wellchoreographed, impeccable dance performances among other things.

While they may look comfortable and charismatic on stage, their performance is the result of many years of hard work rather than any inborn talent.

The year 2011 saw similar events held in several different cities around the world, starting with a K-Pop Festival that attracted over 45,000 fans to the Tokyo Dome in July. JYJ had concerts in Spain and Germany, and the artists of CUBE Entertainment performed in Britain and Brazil.

In October, Girls' Generation held a special concert at Madison Square Garden in New York whose success was covered on the front page of New York Daily News with a large photo of a concert scene and the rather sensational headline, "Attack of the K-Pop Stars."

In February the following year, another major K-Pop festival was held at the Palais Omnisports Bercy Stadium in Paris with over 10,000 fans coming from across Europe to fill the entire stadium.

■ Music

한국 클래식 음악사회는 보컬과 악기음악에 국제적으로 높은 수준의 예술가들을 지속적으로 배출시키고 있다. 예를 들면 2011년 세계 3대음악 경연대회 중의 하나인 국제 차이코프스키 음악 경연대회에서 바이올린과 솔로 보컬, 피아노부문에서 5개의 메달을 획득했다.

The Korean classical music community has continued to produce artists of the highest international standard in both vocal and instrumental music.

For instance, five young Korean artists won five prizes in the disciplines of piano, solo vocal and violin at the International Tchaikovsky Competition held in 2011, one of the top three international music competitions.

They were preceded by Korea's first generation of classical musicians, including two pianists, Han Tong-il and Kun-woo Paik, who fascinated international audiences between the 1950s and the 1970s and who still play to many enthusiastic fans.

Myungwhun Chung, the current maestro of the Seoul Philharmonic Orchestra, started his career in the world of classical music as a pianist, regularly playing as a member of the Chung Trio with his two sisters, Chung Kyung-wha, who won worldwide recognition as a violinist, and Chung Myung-wha, who plays cello.

Later he turned to conductorship and has conducted some of the world's most prestigious orchestras including the Berlin Philharmonic, London Philharmonic, and Paris Orchestra, before going on to serve as music director and resident conductor of the Op?ra de la Bastille in Paris.

■ Musical Theater

한국 뮤지컬 극장에 자주가는 사람들은 극장무대에 올려지는 희극뮤지컬에 더 많이 가고 있다. 좋은 질의 뮤지컬에 대한 수요의 증가는 원작자나 한국팀에 의한 캣츠, 시카고, 지킬과 하이드와 같은 세계 유명뮤지컬 공연의 결과이며, 한국배우들에 새로운 뮤지컬에 대한 연출과 작곡의 산물이다.

Korean theater goers have recently begun to pay more attention to musical comedies presented on theater stages.

The increased demand for good-quality musicals has resulted in the performance of world-famous musicals such as Jekyll & Hyde, Chicago and Cats either by the original or Korean teams, and the production of new musicals written and directed by Korean talents. Some of these Korean productions have been invited to perform in Japan and Southeast Asia.

Korea's thriving musical theater scene has resulted in the creation of a group of stars such as Choi Jung-won, Nam Kyung-joo and Jo Seung-woo, whose reputation has grown with stage musicals, and Yoon Bok-hee, Insooni and Ock Joo-hyun who have become great musical actresses based on their success on the K-Pop stage.

■ Modern Dance and Ballet

1962년 한국의 국립댄스회사의 시작은 현대 댄스관심에 큰 동기를 부여했다.

The launch of the National Dance Company of Korea in 1962 provided the momentum for a surge of interest in modern dance in Korea.

The changed environment eventually led to the birth of a great dancer, Sin Cha Hong (or Hong Sin-ja, born in 1943), who is now credited as Korea's first avant-garde dancer and premier performance artist.

She learned dance from Alwin Nikolais in the United States and worked there until 1990, and then returned to Korea to involve herself in various activities related with modern dance.

1980년대 한국은 2개의 발레회사를 창립하였는데, 유니버셜 발레(1984)단과 서울발레단(1986)은 한국과 해외에서 고전 발레공연을 하고 있다. 발레인기의 증가는 강수진을 비롯한 뛰어난 발레댄서의 출현에 기인한다. 강수진은 1986년 슈트트가르트 아시아 최초의 대선이며 현재는 수석댄서이다.

Korea in the 1980s saw the foundation of two ballet companies, Universal Ballet (1984) and Seoul Ballet (1986), which are still actively producing classical ballet performances in Korea and abroad.

The increased popularity of ballet resulted in the arrival of distinguished ballet dancers including Kang Sue-jin, who became the first Asian to be a member of the Stuttgart Ballet in 1986, where she is now a principal dancer. Other successful ballet dancers include Seo Hee who joined the ABT Studio Company in 2004 and became a principal dancer at the ABT in 2012, and Kim Ki-min who became the first Asian ballerina to join and become First Soloist at the Mariinsky Ballet in 2012.

■ Modern Art

비디오 아트의 창시자로 기억되고 있는 백남준으로 대표되고 있는 한국 현대예술의 1세대는 천경자, 백영수와 같은 탁월한 예술가의 세대로 이어지고 있다.

The first generation of Korean modern artists represented by Nam June Paik (1932-2006), who is considered to be the founder of video art, was followed by a new generation of distinguished artists such as Chang Ree-seok, Chang Doo-kun, Paek Young-su, Chun Kyung Ja, Tchang-Yeul Kim and Suh Se-ok.

Korea's rapid economic growth in the 1970s resulted in the establishment of numerous public and private art institutions of which about 60 are located in downtown Seoul, Insa-dong and Samcheong-dong in particular, such as Gana Art Space, Seoul Art Center Gongpyeong Gallery and Kyung-in Museum of Fine Art.

More recently, Cheongdam-dong in Gangnam-gu south of the Hangang River has emerged as a hub of Korean fine art. As for international art events, the Gwangju Biennale launched in 1995 has grown to be a major contemporary art exhibition in Asia.

Tourism Guide Quiz

1. Explain what Hallyu (Korean Wave) is.
2. Introduce Mr. Paik, a video artist, briefly.
3. List all the religions in Korea.
4. Introduce one of the traditional musicals in Korea.
5. Explain a national holidays in Korea.

수행 Tips : The ability to raise 여행안내 및 상품에 대한 신뢰성과 품질제고의 중요성 사례

신뢰성과 품질제고 노력으로 세계 8위의 관광대국으로 부상하고 있는 일본

국외로 해외로 여행을 떠나는 중국인 1억 명 시대로 접어들었다. 접근용이성이라는 지리적인 장점을 가진 아시아 각국은 부유해진 중국인 관광객 특수를 만끽하고 있다.

특히 일본은 그동안 중국인들에게 가장 인기 있는 여행지로 사랑받아온 한국과 홍콩을 제치고 지난해부터 인기 있는 해외여행지 1위로 부상했다.

일본을 찾는 중국인관광객은 전년의 거의 두 배에 육박하는 증가율을 기록하며 폭발적인 성장세를 이어간다. 일본을 방문하는 중국인 관광객의 여행목적은 순수하게 자연과 문화를 즐기기 위한 관광 목적과 일본제품을 구입하기 위한 쇼핑목적으로 나뉘는데, 특히 일본제품을 싹쓸이하는 중국 쇼핑객들은 지난 한 해 일본 사회에서 많은 화제를 낳으며 일종의 사회현상으로까지 떠올랐다.

긴자의 미츠코시(三越) 백화점에서는 중국 남성의 취향을 고려해서 디자인을 변경하여 특별 상품을 다양하게 시도하고 있다. 즉 양복과 함께 중국인을 겨냥해 만든 목 길이가 일본 표준보다 10㎝ 짧은 양말을 선보여 인기리에 판매하고 있다.

이와 같은 품질개선 서비스와 아울러 일본인 특유의 환대서비스를 접목하여 수요자의 입장에서 상품을 제작하여 고객 유치하고자 노력하고 있다.

또한 어디서 사든지 바가지를 쓰지 않고, 가짜 명품을 속아서 살 염려도 없어 안심할 수 있는 카메라 등의 전자제품에서부터 의약품, 가위, 문구용품 등의 일상용품에 이르기까지 하이엔드 기술을 자랑하는 세계적인 수준의 제품이 많기 때문이다.

특히 일본인의 섬세한 접객문화와 친절함, 정돈된 사회분위기도 중국인 관광객을 일본으로 불러 모으는 매력으로 작용한다. 일본을 찾은 많은 중국인 관광객들 중 재방문자의 비율은 25%가 넘고 있으며, 중국의 베이징, 상하이, 광저우에 거주하는 일본을 방문한 경험이 있는 중국인을 대상으로 실시한 조사에서는 재방문자 비율이 65%이상으로 나타나고 있다.

일본의 대표적인 관광입국(觀光立國)' 정책 ; ▷2020년 도쿄올림픽을 향한 관광 진흥 ▷인바운드 관광객의 비약적 확대를 위한 대처방안 ▷비자 요건의 완화 등 방일 여행의 용이화 ▷세계에 통용되는 매력 있는 관광지역 만들기 ▷외국인여행자 수용환경의 정비 ▷마이스(MICE: 국제회의, 전시회 등) 유치 · 개최 촉진과 외국인 비즈니스 손님의 대응에 대한 시책 등을 통한 4천만 명의 외국인 관광객 달성 목표 실현.

– Heaven helps those who help themselves –

Part 2

Korean Culture and Attractions

Unit **6**

UNESCO Treasures in Korea

Unit 6

UNESCO Treasures in Korea

1) World Heritage

세계유산은 1972년 유네스코(UNESCO, 국제연합교육과학문화기구) 세계 문화 및 자연유산의 보호에 관한 협약(Convention Concerning the Protection of the World Cultural and Natural Heritage)에 의거해 유네스코 세계유산위원회가 인류 전체를 위해 보호되어야 할 뛰어난 보편적 가치(Outstanding Universal Value)가 있다고 인정하여 세계유산목록에 등재한 유산으로 문화유산, 자연유산, 복합유산으로 분류한다.

문화유산 (Cultural Heritage)은 유적, 건축물, 문화재적 가치를 지닌 장소 등 (전체 세계유산의 77.5%), 자연유산 (Natural Heritage)은 생물학적 군락, 지질학적 생성물, 멸종위기에 처한 동식물 서식지 등, 복합유산 (Mixed Heritage)은 문화유산과 자연유산의 특징을 동시에 충족하는 가치를 담고 있는 유산이다.

Silla, on the other hand, was known for its artistic achievements and also for unifying the three kingdoms.

(1) Seokguram Grotto and Bulguksa Temple(1995)

located on the middle slopes of Tohamsan Mountain in Gyeongju, Gyeongsangbuk-do, is a Buddhist hermitage with an artificial stone cave built in 774 to serve as a dharma hall.

석굴암은 서기 751년 신라 경덕왕 때 당시 재상이었던 김대성이 창건하기 시작하여 서기 774년인 신라 혜공왕 때 완공하였으며, 건립 당시의 명칭은 석불사로 칭했다.

석굴암의 석굴은 백색의 화강암재를 사용하여 토함산 중턱에 인공으로 석굴을 축조, 이 석굴은 신라시대의 전성기에 이룩된 최고 걸작으로 평가되며, 그 조영계획에 있어 건축, 수리, 기하학, 종교, 예술이 총체적으로 실현된 것임. 현재 석굴암 석굴은 국보 제24호로 지정 관리되고 있으며 석굴암은 1995년 12월 불국사와 함께 유네스코 세계 문화유산으로 공동 등재되었다.

The hall houses an image of seated Buddha surrounded by his guardians and followers carved in relief, which is widely admired as a great masterpiece.

The cave faces east and is designed so that the principal Buddha receives the first rays of the sun rising from the East Sea on his head. The Seokguram Grotto of Silla Dynasty (National Treasure No. 24); served as the capital of Korea's Silla Dynasty (57 B.C.–A.D. 935) for about 1,000 years.

Completed the same year as Seokguram Grotto, Bulguksa Temple consists of exquisite prayer halls and various monuments, including two stone pagodas, Dabotap and Seokgatap, standing in the front courtyard of the temple's main prayer hall, Daeungjeon.

The two pagodas are widely regarded as the finest extant Silla pagodas: the first is admired for its elaborately carved details, the second for its delightfully simple structure.

(2) Gyeongju Historic Areas(2000)

It was the capital of Silla for about one millennium. The city still contains a wealth of archaeological remains from the Kingdom, and hence is often dubbed as "a museum without walls or roof." The photo shows a scene of the Silla mound tombs located in the city.

경주역사유적지구(Gyeongju Historic Areas)는 신라천년(B.C 57~A.D 935)의 고도(古都)인 경주의 역사와 문화를 고스란히 담고있는 불교유적, 왕경(王京)유적이 잘 보존되어 있으며, 이미 세계유산으로 등재된 일본의 교토, 나라의 역사유적과 비교하여 유적의 밀집도, 다양성이 더 뛰어난 유적으로 평가된다.

Among Korea's ancient dynasties, Silla is usually thought to be one of the most forward-thinking and aggressive eras in art, culture and science. Important treasures in the city include Cheomseongdae, a seventh-century astronomical observatory, as well as Seokguram Grotto, an eighth-century artificial stone cave that contains a Buddha statue and other rock art.

2000년 12월 세계유산으로 등재된 경주역사유적지구는 신라의 역사와 문화를 한눈에 파악할 수 있을 만큼 다양한 유산이 산재해 있는 종합역사지구로서 유적의 성격에 따라 모두 5개 지구로 나누어져 있는데 불교미술의 보고인 남산지구, 천년왕조의 궁궐터인 월성지구, 신라 왕을 비롯한 고분군 분포지역인 대능원지구, 신라불교의 정수인 황룡사지구, 왕경 방어시설의 핵심인 산성지구로 구분되어 있으며 52개의 지정문화재가 세계유산지역에 포함되어 있다.

In recognition of the city's value as a cultural asset worthy of humanity's common effort for preservation, the UNESCO World Heritage Committee inscribed "Gyeongju Historic Areas" on the World Heritage List in 2000.

경주 남산은 야외박물관이라고 할 만큼 신라의 숨결이 살아 숨쉬는 곳으로 신라 건국설화에 나타나는 나정(蘿井), 신라왕조의 종말을 맞게했던 포석정(鮑石亭)과 미륵곡 석불좌상, 배리 석불입상, 칠불암 마애석불 등 수많은 불교유적이 산재해 있다.

The areas are grouped in accordance with the nature of their historic remains – Mt. Nam, a renowned treasure trove of Buddhist art;

the Moon Fortress, a royal palace site; the Great Tumuli Park, a cluster of burial mounds; the ruins of Hwangnyongsa, a state temple; and the Mountain Fortress that served as the capital's defense structure. The listed cultural properties within the five locales amount to 52 items.

(3) Gochang, Hwasun, and Ganghwa Dolmen Sites(2000)

It is believed that humans began to inhabit the Korean peninsula around 700,000 years ago during the Paleolithic era. With an early agricultural society taking shape, the Bronze Age was in full swing around 1,000 B.C. The increased use of bronze tools, made from an alloy of copper and tin or zinc, characterized this period.

고인돌은 선사시대 돌무덤의 일종으로 영어로는 돌멘(Dolmen)이라고 함, 우리나라 청동기시대의 대표적인 무덤 중의 하나인 고인돌은 세계적인 분포를 보이고 있으며 지역에 따라 시기와 형태가 다르게 나타나고 있음.

As a result, tilling and livestock breeding developed into major means of livelihood. A widespread use of bronze implements yielded surplus farm products, which led to the emergence of power groups and social classes.

Bronze wares are most often excavated from megalithic barrows known as dolmens, or "goindol" in Korean, which literally means the "propped stone."

The dolmens are burial sites representative of the Bronze Age. While interment of the dead may have been the primary intention of early humans in creating the dolmens, the various burial offerings like earthenware, stone tools and bronze ware provide modern people with a vital glimpse into their society.

They are important archaeological remains from the early stage of civilization found in natural environments, not inside museums. Dolmens are found all over the world, but are notably concentrated in the Northeast Asian countries of Korea, China and Japan.

동북아시아 지역이 세계적인 분포권에서 가장 밀집된 곳으로 그 중 우리나라가 그 중심지역이라고 할 수 있으며, 우리나라에는 전국적으로 약 30,000여 기에 가까운 고인돌이 분포하고 있는 것으로 알려져 있는데, 그 중 세계유산으로 등재된 고창 · 화순 · 강화고인돌유적(Gochang, Hwasun and Ganghwa Dolmen Sites)은 밀집분포도, 형식의 다양성으로 고인돌의 형성과 발전과정을 규명하는 중요한 유적이며 유럽, 중국, 일본과도 비교할 수 없는 독특한 특색을 가지고 있음, 선사시대 연구의 중요한 자료가 되는 보존가치가 높은 유적으로 2000년 12월 세계문화유산으로 등재된다.

Among these countries, Korea is veritably the "kingdom of dolmens," with a far larger number of the stone cists distributed throughout North and South Korea. Some 30,000 dolmens have been found in South Korea and 10,000 to 15,000 in North Korea, which together account for over 40 percent of all dolmens identified around the world.

Gochang : The World's Densest Dolmen Cluster, Hundreds of dolmens in varying sizes are found along the foot of the mountain at Jungnim-ri, Sanggap-ri and Dosan-ri in Gochang County, North Jeolla Province. They are scattered over slopes stretching some 1.8 kilometers from east to west. As many as 447 dolmens have been identified so far here, demonstrating its reputation as the world's largest and densest cluster of dolmens.

고창고인돌유적은 전라북도 고창군 죽림리와 도산리일대에 매산마을을 중심으로 동서로 약 1,764m 범위에 447기가 분포하고, 우리나라에서 가장 큰 고인돌 군집을 이루고 있는 지역, 10톤 미만에서 300톤에 이르는 다양한 크기의 고인돌이 분포하고 있으며 탁자식, 바둑판식, 지상석곽형 등 다양한 형식의 고인돌이 분포하고 있다.

Hwasun Arena for Firsthand Education on Megalithic Culture, A total of 597 dolmens dot an area spanning some five kilometers along a valley named Bogeomjae, which straddles Hyosan-ri in Dogok-myeon and Daesin-ri in Chunyang-myeon, Hwasun County, South Jeolla Province.

Reported to academic circles rather recently in 1995, these dolmens were found buried under bushes in remarkably good condition. A survey on 35 dolmens at Jidong Village in Daesin-ri resulted in the discovery of diverse artifacts including stone implements and earthen vessels.

화순고인돌유적은 전라남도 화순군 도곡면 효산리와 춘양면 대신리 일대의 계곡을 따라 약 10㎞에 걸쳐 596기(고인돌 287기, 추정고인돌 309기)의 고인돌이 군집을 이루어 집중분포하고 있으며, 최근에 발견되어 보존상태가 양호하다. 또한 고인돌의 축조과정을 보여주는 채석장이 발견되어 당시의 석재를 다루는 기술, 축조와 운반방법 등을 확인할 수 있는 유적으로 평가된다.

These dolmens were probably built sometime between 800 B.C. and 500 B.C., as radiocarbon dating of charcoal retrieved from a burial cist pointed to 550 B.C. and thermoluminescence dating of earthenware to 770 B.C.

They include table, checkerboard and capstone dolmens. Scores of them weigh over 100 tons. One of them, named "Pingmae Bawi," meaning "stone hurling rock," is 7.3 meters long, 5 meters wide and 4 meters thick. Estimated to weigh some 280 tons, this is indisputably one of the largest dolmens in the world.

Gangwha : Table-type Dolmens in Aesthetic Forms, A total of 127 dolmens are scattered around the northern foot of Mt. Goryeo stretching over the five villages of Bugeun-ri, Samgeo-ri, Gocheon-ri,

Osang-ri and Gyosan-ri in Gwanghwa County, which belongs to the great Incheon metropolitan area. Seventy of them in comparatively better states are on the World Heritage List.

These dolmens characteristically lie on diverse terrain, including mountain bases, hills, flat lands and mountain ridges. They are located some 100-200 meters above sea level, notably on higher altitudes than most other dolmens around Korea, which are on average 300-350 meters above sea level.

강화고인돌유적은 인천광역시 강화군 부근리, 삼거리, 오상리 등의 지역에 고려산 기슭을 따라 160여기의 고인돌이 분포하고 있으며, 이곳에는 길이 6.399m, 높이 2.454m의 우리나라 최대의 탁자식 고인돌이 있으며 우리나라 고인돌의 평균고도보다 높은 해발 100m~200m까지 고인돌이 분포하고 있음.

Dolmens are among the most common types of prehistoric megalithic structures. Among other comparable monuments are the pyramids in Egypt and the Americas, Stonehenge in the United Kingdom, the Carnac menhir alignments in France, the moai statues of Easter Island in Polynesia, and the Tarxien Temples in Malta.

These prehistoric remains, differing in shape and function, are generally believed to have been used for interment of human remains, memorials, or ritual sites. Distinctively concentrated at the early phase of agricultural settlement, these stone structures, particularly dolmens, are highly valuable historical remnants.

They provide vital clues to the cultures, social structures and political systems as well as the spiritual world of prehistoric people. Dolmens have thus been objects of extensive academic interest and studies.

(4) Jeju Volcanic Island and Lava Tubes(2007)

A spectacular Geological Museum Jeju Island was created by the volcanic activities that went through four stages between 1.2 million and 250,000 years ago. With diverse and unique volcanic features and beautiful landscape stretching in every direction, the entire island is a virtual volcano museum.

Formed in the Quaternary Period of the Cenozoic Era, which is a relatively recent geological past, the initial volcanic landforms of Jeju Island have been well preserved, providing precious information about global volcanism.

제주도는 약 180만 년 전부터 역사시대에 걸쳐 일어난 화산활동으로 만들어졌다. 한라산 정상부에는 한라산 조면암과 백록담 현무암이 분포하며 한라산 조면암은 높은 점성을 갖고 돔상으로 솟아 한라산을 더 웅장하게 만들고 있다.

Some of the best examples of Jeju Island's volcanic landforms are Mt. Halla, its 368 parasitic cones, and the lava tubes formed by explosive eruptions of basaltic lava. Specifically, the mountain has the world's largest number of parasitic cones (called oreum in the Jeju dialect) to be derived from a single volcano.

These sites are highly regarded not only for their superb scenic beauty but also for their research value as examples representing the earth's geological history. In other words, the site's outstanding scenic beauty is not the sole condition for an inscription on the World Heritage List, but its exceptional geological and ecological values are also assessed as important prerequisites. As such, more weight is placed on the site's objective qualities, including its contributions to scientific research, rather than on aesthetic considerations, which can be inherently subjective.

세계유산으로 지정된 지역은 한라산, 성산일출봉, 거문오름 용암동굴계 등 3개이고, 거문오름용암동굴계는 지금으로부터 약 10~30만 년 전에 거문오름에서 분출된 용암으로부터 만들어진 여러 개의 용암동굴이며, 이 동굴계에서 세계자연유산으로 지정된 동굴은 벵뒤굴, 만장굴, 김녕굴, 용천동굴, 그리고 당처물동굴이다.

In 2007, UNESCO listed Jeju Volcanic Island and Lava Tubes as a World Natural Heritage in recognition of its landscape of surpassing natural beauty, unique volcanic landforms and ecology. Juju Volcanic Island and Lava Tubes, comprised of three sites – Mt. Halla Natural Reserve, the Geomunoreum Lava Tube System and Seongsan Sunrise Peak – is the first natural site in Korea to be placed on UNESCO's World Heritage List.

한라산은 남한에서 가장 높은 산으로서 화산활동에 의해 생성된 순상(방패모양)화산체이고, 성산일출봉은 제주도에 분포하는 360개의 단성화산체(cinder cones : 제주방언으로는 오름이라 함) 중의 하나이며, 해안선 근처에 뛰어난 경관을 제공하는 수성화산체이다.

Mt. Halla Natural Reserve – Unique Geography and Ecology: Jeju Island has an oval shape and is 70 kilometers from east to west and 30 kilometers from north to south. It is 1,847.2 square kilometers in area, about three times as large as Seoul, the capital city of Korea.

At the center of the island is Mt. Halla, a volcano rising 1,950 meters above sea level, and the mountain's gentle slopes descend from its peak all the way down into the sea, making the island look like one big mountain.

The area covering 151.35 square kilometers around the mountain (about 8.3 percent of the entire island) has been designated as a natural reserve.

Geomunoreum Lava Tube System: An Unimaginable Mystery: Jeju Island has over 90 percent of its land covered with basalt, a dark-colored rock of volcanic origin. Parasitic cones, distributed all over the island from Mt. Halla to the coastal areas, contribute to the volcanic landscapes unique to this island.

Seongsan Sunrise Peak Tuff Cone – A Key to Understand Hydrovolcanic Eruptions: Parasitic cones distributed all over Jeju Island are diverse in shape. Most of them are cinder cones, formed by an eruption from the ground. The volcanic products spewed out from a volcano, fell to the ground and accumulated in the form of rock fragments with numerous dark or reddish holes, called cinders or scoria.

Seongsan Sunrise Peak (179 meters above sea level), protruding from the coastline of Jeju Island at its eastern tip, is a typical hydromagmatic volcano created between 120,000 and 50,000 years ago by an underwater eruption from a shallow seabed. As the name Ilchulbong (Sunrise Peak) implies, sunrise viewed from here is a truly magnificent sight.

(5) Baekje Historic Areas(2015)

Baekje is one of the concurrently presenting ancient countries in Korean Peninsula(18 B.C–600 A.D.). Located in the mountainous mid-western region of the Republic of Korea. Tomb of King Muryeong (462–523) of Baekje Dynasty, a sixth-century royal mausoleum in Gongju, South Chungcheong, particularly the ornaments of the king's and the queen's crowns. The tomb in Gongju was accidentally found in 1971. Among the tombs from the Three Kingdoms era, it's the only tomb whose owner is clearly known.

백제는 기원전 18년부터 660년까지 700여 년간 존재한 한반도의 고대국가 중 하나이다. 백제역사유적지구는 공주시, 부여군, 익산시 등 3개 시 · 군의 8곳 문화유산으로 구성되어있다.

세부 등재지역을 살펴보면, 충남 공주시는 공산성(사적 제12호), 송산리 고분군(사적 제13호) 등 2곳, 충남 부여군은 관북리유적과 부소산성(사적 제428호와 사적 제5호), 능산리 고분군(사적 제14호), 정림사지(사적 제301호), 부여나성(사적 제68호) 등 4곳, 전북 익산시는 왕궁리유적(사적 제408호), 미륵사지(사적 제150호) 등 2곳이며, 백제역사유적지구는 5~7세기 한국, 중국, 일본의 고대 동아시아 왕국들 사이의 교류와, 그 결과로 나타난 건축기술의 발전과 불교의 확산을 보여주는 고고학 유적이다.

The Gongsanseong fortress and royal rombs at Songsan-ri in Gongju, the Busosanseong fortress and Gwanbuk-ri Administrative buildings, the Jeongnimsa Temple, the royal tombs in Neungsan-ri and the Naseong city wall in Buyeo, the royal palace at Wanggung-ri and the Mireuksa Temple in Iksan.

This property represents the historical tracts of relationships among east Asian ancient kingdoms of Korea, China, and Japan from 5th to 7th century and conclusively stands for the architectural development and the spread of Buddhism.

Through this property, the reputation of its capital, Buddhist temples, ancient tombs, architecture, and stone pagodas are seen to prove the culture, religion and the aesthetics of ancient kingdom Baekje period.

Baekje, Historic Areas of World Heritage, which display about 1,720 pieces of artifacts from the latter part of Baekje. The "Baekje Historic Areas" refer to a group of eight sites located in Iksan, North Jeolla and Gongju and Buyeo, South Chungcheong. The eight sites include heritage items like Buddhist temple sites, stone fortresses and groups of mausoleums.

One of the most important cultural heritage items of North Jeolla is the site of the Mireuk Temple (Korea's Historic Site No. 150) in Iksan. In a design never seen at the time in East Asia, the seventh-century temple consisted of three zones. Each zone had a stone pagoda and a temple.

(6) Namhansanseong Fortress(2014)

남한산성은 극동아시아 여러 지역의 영향을 바탕으로 다양한 군사 방어 기술을 종합적으로 구현하고 있는 조선왕조의 비상 시 임시 수도로서, 한국의 독립성 및 한국 역사상 다양한 종교 · 철학이 조화롭게 공존해온 가치를 상징하는 유산이다.

남한산성은 본성(한봉성과 봉함성을 포함)과 신남성(동서돈대)으로 구성된 연속유산으로 16세기에서 18세기에 이르는 기간 동안 동아시아 국가들 간 축성술과 도시 계획이 상호 교류한 증거가 되고 있으며, 7세기부터 19세기까지 축성술의 시대별 발달 단계와 무기 체계의 변화상을 볼 수 있고, 지금까지 주민들이 거주하고 있는 살아있는 유산으로서 가치를 보유한다.

7세기 초에 처음 만들어져 여러 차례 재건되었으며, 특히 17세기 청의 공격에 대비해 크게 중건되었으며, 중국과 일본의 영향을 수용하면서 서양식 무기 도입에 따른 성곽축조 기술의 변화를 종합한 군사 방어기술의 개념을 집대성하였다.

16세기와 18세에 이르는 기간 동안 동아시아의 한국과 중국 일본 간에 산성 건축술이 상호 교류한 중요한 증거이며, 남한산성은 국제 전쟁을 통해 동아시아 무기 발달과 축성술이 상호 교류한 탁월한 증거로, 조선의 자주권과 독립성을 수호하기 위해 유사시의 임시수도로서 기능할 수 있도록 계획적으로 축조된 유일한 산성 도시이다.

A mountain fortress that served as a temporary capital during the Joseon Dynasty, showing how the techniques for building a fortress developed during the 7th–19th centuries, located about 25km southeast of Seoul, underwent large-scale restructuring in 1626, during the reign of King Injo of the Joseon Dynasty.

The foundations of Jujangseong Fortress, built almost one thousand years earlier in 672, during the reign of King Munmu of Unified Silla, served as the base of the renovated structure. The defensive position of the fortress was reinforced by exploiting the rugged topography of the mountain (average height: at least 480m).

The defensive position of the fortress was reinforced by exploiting the rugged topography of the mountain (average height: at least 480m). The perimeter of its wall is about 12.3km. According to a record dating from the Joseon Period, about 4,000 people lived in the town built inside the fortress.

The fortress is also a result of the wide-ranging exchanges made and wars waged between Korea (Joseon), Japan (Azuchi- Momoyama Period), and China (Ming and Qing) during the 16th–18th centuries. The fortress is a "living record" of the changes in the way fortresses were built during the 7th–19th centuries.

(7) Haeinsa Temple Janggyeong Panjeon, the Depositories of the Tripitaka Koreana Woodblocks(1995)

대장경판은 고려 고종 때 대장도감에서 새긴 목판이고, 경(經) · 율(律) · 논(論)의 삼장(三藏)으로서 불교경전의 총서를 가리키는 말이며, 고려시대에 판각되었기 때문에 고려대장경이라 하며 또한 판수가 8만여 판에 이르고 8만4천 법문을 수록했다 하여 8만대장경이라고도 한다.

해인사 장경판전은 13세기에 만들어진 세계적 문화유산인 고려 대장경판 8만여 장을 보존하는 보고로서 해인사의 현존 건물 중 가장 오래된 건물이며 장경판전은 정면 15칸이나 되는 큰 규모의 두 건물을 남북으로 나란히 배치했다.

장경판전 남쪽의 건물을 수다라장, 북쪽의 건물을 법보전이라 하며 동쪽과 서쪽에 작은 규모의 동 · 서사간판전이 있으며, 건물을 간결한 방식으로 처리하여 판전으로서 필요로 하는 기능만을 충족시켰을 뿐 장식적 의장을 하지 않았고, 전 · 후면 창호의 위치와 크기가 서로 다르다.

통풍의 원활, 방습의 효과, 실내 적정 온도의 유지, 판가의 진열 장치 등이 매우 과학적이며, 합리적으로 되어 있는 점은 대장경판이 지금까지 온전하게 보존되어 있는 중요한 이유 중의 하나라고 평가받고 있음, 장경판전의 정확한 창건연대는 알려져 있지 않으나 조선 세조 3년(1457) 어명으로 판전 40여 칸을 중창하였고 성종 19년(1488) 학조대사가 왕실의 후원으로 30칸의 대장경 경각을 중건한 뒤 보안당이라 했다는 기록이 있으며, 광해군 14년(1622)에 수다라장, 인조 2년(1624)에는 법보전을 중수하였다.

장경판전은 가야산 중턱의 해인사에 위치한 관계로 서기 1488년 조선 초기에 건립된 후 한번도 화재나 전란 등의 피해를 입지 않아 보존 가치가 탁월한 팔만대장경이 고스란히 간직되어 있으며, 세계유일의 대장경판 보관용 건물이고 해인사의 건축기법은 조선 초기의 전통적인 목조건축 양식을 보이는데 건물 자체의 아름다움은 물론, 건물 내 적당한 환기와 온도 · 습도조절 등의 기능을 자연적으로 해결할 수 있도록 설계되어져 있으며, 이 판전에는 81,258장의 대장경판이 보관되어 있다.

글자 수는 무려 5천2백만 자로 추정되는데 이들 글자 하나하나가 오자 · 탈자 없이 모두 고르고 정밀하다는 점에서 그 보존가치가 매우 크며, 현존 대장경 중에서도 가장 오랜 역사와 내용의 완벽함으로 세계적인 명성을 지니고 있는 문화재이다.

Janggyeongpanjeon Depositories of Haeinsa Temple, the Printing Woodblocks of the Tripitaka Koreana, which was made during the Goryeo Period (918–1392), are housed in two depositories specially made for that purpose in 1488 at Haeinsa Temple.

As the oldest remaining buildings at the temple, the Tripitaka depositories are marked by the uniquely scientific and highly effective method of controlling ventilation and moisture to ensure the safe storage of the age-old woodblocks. The buildings were built side by side at the highest point (about 700m above sea level) in the precincts of Haeinsa Temple, which is located on the mid-slope of Gayasan Mountain at Hapcheon.

What makes these depositories so special is their unique design which provides effective natural ventilation by exploiting the wind blowing in from the valley of Gayasan.

Open lattice windows of different sizes are arranged in upper and lower rows on both the front and rear walls of the depositories to promote the optimum flow of air from the valley. Similarly, the floor, which was built by ramming layers of charcoal, clay, sand, salt and lime powder, also helps to control the humidity of the rooms.

(8) Historic Villages of Korea: Hahoe and Yangdong(2010)

한국의 씨족마을은 조선시대(1392~1910) 초기에 형성되기 시작하였고 조선 후기에는 전체 마을 중 약 80%를 점하게 되며, 오늘날까지 그 명맥을 유지하고 있으며, 한국에서의 씨족은 성씨와 본관을 같이 하는 부계혈연집단, 즉 조상을 같이 하는 동성동본인들과 다른 혈연집단에서 배우자로 들어온 여성들로 구성된 사회집단을 말한다.

씨족마을은 하나 혹은 소수의 씨족이 전체 주민구성의 다수를 차지하거나 마을의 의사결정에서 주도적 역할을 하는 마을을 말하며, 한국의 대표적 씨족마을이면서 양반마을인 하회와 양동은 모두 조선시대(1392~1910)에 양반문화가 가장 화려하게 꽃피었던 한반도 동남부(영남지방)에 위치하고 있고, 두 마을은 한국의 대표적인 마을 입지 유형인 배산임수의 형태를 띠고 있으며, 여름에 고온다습하고 겨울에 저온 건조한 기후에 적응하기 위한 건물의 형태와 유교 예법에 입각한 가옥으로 구성된다.

Hahoe and Yangdong(2010) were inscribed as the UNESCO World Heritage sites in 2010. Founded around the 15th century during the Joseon Dynasty (1392-1910), the two villages have well-preserved traditional architecture surrounded by natural environments that reflect the legacy of Confucian thoughts and principles.

Their residents also have maintained the Confucian lifestyle and other cultural traits of the distant past. In the Joseon Dynasty, it was one of the Confucian ideals for each clan of the noble class called yangban to create its own village in a place with auspicious geomantic properties and scenic beauty.

Therefore, many of the yangban families formed a community where the majority of its residents were relatives with the same last name. These communities contributed to having Confucian culture take root in the provinces. Hahoe and Yangdong are elite clan communities, which can be traced back to the noble families of the Joseon Dynasty.

하회는 하회마을과 병산서원으로 구성되어 있으며, 종가, 살림집, 정사와 정자, 서원과 서당, 그리고 주변의 농경지와 자연경관이 거의 완전하게 남아 있을 뿐 아니라, 유형 유산과 더불어 이들과 관련된 많은 의례, 놀이, 저작, 예술품 등 수많은 정신적 유산들을 보유하고 있다.

Hahoe is also home to many ancient books and documents, as well as other cultural relics. Some of them are national cultural properties, including Ryu Seong-ryong's war memoir mentioned above, A Collection of Treasure Books of the House of Ryu Seong-ryong,

A Collection of Treasure Relics of the House of Ryu Seong-ryong, and the masks used in the traditional mask dance handed down in the village. One of the village's intangible cultural properties, the Hahoe Mask Dance Drama (Hahoe byeolsingut talnori) is the oldest mask dance drama in Korea, and was performed by commoners.

Hahoe is famous for its natural environments which possess a charming harmony with its cultural landscape rooted in Confucianism. Where the Nakdong River meets Mt. Hwa, which rises 271 meters above sea level, the river changes its course and bends around a low hillock which is the seat of Hahoe, meaning the village "at a river's bend." Some liken the village to a lotus blossom floating on the water, and others describe it as resembling a gigantic yin-yang symbol (taegeuk) formed by the mountain and the river.

양동은 양동마을과 그 주변 관련 건축물인 동강서원, 옥산서원, 독락당으로 구성되어 있다. 종가, 살림집, 정사와 정자, 서원과 서당, 그리고 주변의 농경지와 자연경관, , 생산영역, 생활영역, 의식영역으로 구성되는 한국 씨족마을의 전통적인 공간구성을 기능적이고 경관적으로 온전하게 유지하고 있으며, 많은 유형 유산과 더불어 관련된 많은 의례, 놀이, 저작, 예술품 등 수많은 정신적 유산들을 보유하고 있다.

Yangdong is surrounded by Mt. Seolchang, which is located to the north of the city of Gyeongju. Described in terms of geomancy, the four ridges sloping down from the mountain top form the terrain in the shape of the Chinese character, and the houses are nestled on the valleys between the ridges.

Yangdong is also a treasure trove of ancient architecture. There remain as many as four houses built before the Japanese Invasions, which survived the widespread destruction that was caused by the war.

It is Hyangdan, which is the house of Yi Eon-jeok, built as the king's present when he was appointed as the governor of Gyeongsang Province. Concerned about his retainer's ailing mother, King Jungjong granted the house to Yi, so that he could take care of his mother while living with her there.

Visiting Korea's historical villages of Hahoe and Yangdong, one can catch a glimpse of "Korean" sensibilities and landscape, in which nature, geography, scenery, architecture, space, culture and people have interconnected relationships with one another to form a unique community. In the 21st century, wherein the concept of a village community is lost on most people, they are a valuable cultural heritage suggesting an "old and new" way of making today's towns and cities into cohesive communities.

(9) Royal Tombs of the Joseon Dynasty(2009)

조선시대의 왕릉은 조선시대의 국가통치 이념인 유교와 그 예법에 근거하여 시대에 따라 다양한 공간의 크기, 문인과 무인 공간의 구분, 석물의 배치, 기타 시설물의 배치 등이 특색을 띠고 있다.

특히 왕릉의 석물 중 문석인, 무석인의 규모와 조각양식 등은 예술성을 각각 달리하며 시대별로 변하는 사상과 정치사를 반영하고 있어서 역사의 흐름을 읽을 수 있는 뛰어난 문화유산에 속한다.

조선시대의 왕릉과 원은 강원도 영월의 장릉, 경기도 여주의 영릉과 녕릉 3기를 제외하고는 당시의 도읍지인 한양에서 40km 이내에 입지하고 있으며, 왕릉이 40기, 원이 13기, 총 53기가 있다.

조선시대(1392~1910) 왕실과 관련되는 무덤은 '능(陵)' 과 '원(園)' 으로 구분된다. 왕릉으로 불리는 능(陵)은 '왕과 왕비, 추존된 왕과 왕비의 무덤' 을 말하며, 원(園)은 '왕세자와 왕세자비, 왕의 사친(私親)의 무덤' 을 말한다.

조선시대의 능원은 600여년이나 되는 오랜 기간 동안 통치한 왕조의 능원제도의 특징을 갖고 있으며, 시대적 흐름에 따른 통치철학과 정치상황을 바탕으로 능원공간 조영형식의 변화, 관리공간 영역의 변화, 조형물 특성의 변화 등을 잘 반영하고 있는 독특한 문화유산이다.

Royal Tombs of the Joseon Dynasty(1392–1910) left behind a total of fortyfour tombs of its Kings and their Queen Consorts, most of which are located in and around the capital area including the cities of Guri, Goyang and Namyangju in Gyeonggi-do.

Some of these Royal Tombs are arranged in small groups in the Donggureung, Seooreung, Seosamneung and Hongyureung.

Donggureung A complex of Royal Tombs built for nine Joseon Kings and their seventeen Queens and Concubines.

Yeongneung The tomb of King Sejong and his consort Queen Soheon. Mongneung The tomb of King Seonjo and his consort Queen Inmok.

The Royal Tombs of Joseon are highly regarded as tangible heritage that reflect the values held by the Korean people, which were drawn from Confucian ideology and the feng shui tradition.

These historical remains are also valued highly for having been preserved in their original condition for anywhere from one to six hundred years, Of these, forty tombs are registered as UNESCO World Heritage Sites.

(10) Hwaseong Fortress(1997)

화성은 정조의 효심이 축성의 근본이 되었을 뿐만 아니라 당쟁에 의한 당파정치 근절과 강력한 왕도정치의 실현을 위한 원대한 정치적 포부가 담긴 정치구상의 중심지로 지어진 것이며 수도 남쪽의 국방요새로 활용하기 위한 것임. 화성은 규장각 문신 정약용이 동서양의 기술서를 참고하여 만든 「성화주략(1793년)」을 지침서로 하여, 재상을 지낸 영중추부사 채제공의 총괄아래 조심태의 지휘로 1794년 1월에 착공에 들어가 1796년 9월에 완공했다.

축성시에 거중기, 녹로 등 신기재를 특수하게 고안 · 사용하여 장대한 석재 등을 옮기며 쌓는데 이용하였으며, 일제 강점기를 지나 한국전쟁을 겪으면서 성곽의 일부가 파손 · 손실되었으나 1975~1979년까지 축성직후 발간된 "화성성역의 궤"에 의거하여 대부분 축성 당시 모습대로 보수 · 복원하여 현재에 이르고 있다.

성의 둘레는 5,744m, 면적은 130ha로 동쪽지형은 평지를 이루고 서쪽은 팔달산에 걸쳐 있는 중국, 일본 등지에서 찾아볼 수 없는 평산 성의 형태로 군사적 방어기능과 상업적 기능을 함께 보유하고 있으며 시설의 기능이 가장 과학적이고 합리적이며, 실용적인 구조로 되어 있는 동양 성곽의 백미라 할 수 있다. 또한 화성은 철학적 논쟁 대신에 백성의 현실 생활 속에서 학문의 실천과제를 찾으려고 노력한 실학사상의 영향으로 벽돌과 돌의 교축, 현안 · 누조의 고안, 거중기의 발명, 목재와 벽돌의 조화를 이룬 축성

방법 등은 동양성곽 축성술의 결정체로서 희대의 수작이라 할 수 있음. 사적 제3호로 지정 관리되고 있으며 소장 문화재로 팔달문(보물 제402호), 화서문(보물 제403호), 장안문, 공심돈 등이 있다. 화성은 1997년 12월 유네스코 세계문화유산으로 등재되었다.

Hwaseong Fortress(1997), Located in today's Jangan-gu of Suwon-si, Gyeonggi-do, Hwaseong is a large fortress (its walls extend for 5.7km) built in 1796 during the reign of King Jeongjo(1776-1800 A.D.) of the Joseon Dynasty.

Construction of the fortress was begun after the King moved the grave of his father, Crown Prince Sado, from Yangju in Gyeonggi-do to its current location near the fortress.

The fortification is elaborately and carefully designed to effectively perform its function of protecting the city enclosed within it.

The construction of the fortress and related facilities involved the use of scientific devices developed by the distinguished Confucian thinker and writer Jeong Yak-yong (1762- 1836), including the Geojunggi (type of crane) and Nongno (pulley wheel) used to lift heavy building materials such as stones.

(11) Changdeokgung Palace(1997)

창덕궁은 조선왕조 제3대 태종 5년(1405) 경복궁의 이궁으로 지어진 궁궐이며 창건시 창덕궁의 정전인 인정전, 편전인 선정전, 침전인 희정당, 대조전 등 중요 전각이 완성후 태종 12년(1412)에는 돈화문이 건립 되었고 세조 9년(1463)에는 약 6만2천평이던 후원을 넓혀 15만여평의 규모로 궁의 경역을 크게 확장했다.

창덕궁은 1610년 광해군 때 정궁으로 사용한 후 부터 1868년 고종이 경복궁을 중건할 때까지 258년 동안 역대제왕이 정사를 보살펴 온 법궁이었고, 왕들의 휴식처로 사용되던 후원은 300년이 넘은 거목과 연못, 정자 등 조원시설이 자연과 조화를 이루도록 함으로써 건축사적으로 또 조경사 적 측면에서 빼놓을 수 없는 귀중한 가치를 지니고 있다.

후원은 태종 5년(1405) 창덕궁을 창건할 때 후원으로 조성하였으며 창경궁과도 통하도록 하였음. 창덕궁 후원은 우리나라의 대표적인 전통 조원 시설로서 자연적인 지형에다 꽃과 나무를 심고 못을 파서 아름답고 조화 있게 건물을 배치하였다.

Changdeokgung Palace(1997) is one of the five Royal Palaces of Joseon (1392–1910), and still contains the original palace structures and other remains intact.

It was built in 1405 as a Royal Villa but became the Joseon Dynasty's official Royal Residence after Gyeongbokgung, the original principal palace, was destroyed by fire in 1592 when Japanese forces invaded Korea.

Thereafter it maintained its prestigious position until 1867, when Gyeongbokgung was and renovated and restored to its original status. Changdeokgung was listed as a UNESCO World Heritage Site in 1997.

(12) Jongmyo Shrine(1995)

종묘는 조선왕조 역대 왕과 왕비 및 추존된 왕과 왕비의 신주를 모신 유교사당으로서 가장 정제되고 장엄한 건축물 중의 하나이며, 태조 3년(1394) 10월 조선 왕조가 한양으로 도읍을 옮긴 그해 12월에 착공하여 이듬해 9월에 완공하였으며, 선조 25년(1592) 임진왜란 때 불타버려 광해군 즉위년(1608)에 다시 고쳐 짓고, 그 후 영조 와 헌종때 증축하여 현재 태실 19칸으로 되어 있다.

조선시대에는 정전에서 매년 춘하추동과 섣달에 대제를 지냈고, 영녕전에는 매년 춘추와 섣달에 제향일을 따로 정하여 제례를 지냈으나 현재는 전주이씨 대동종약원에서 매년 5월 첫째 일요일을 정하여 종묘제례라는 제향의식을 거행하고 있으며 제사 드릴 때 연주하는 기악과 노래와 무용을 포함하는 종묘제례악이 거행되고 있다.

종묘의 주전인 정전은 건평이 1,270㎡로서 동 시대의 단일 목조 건축물로는 세계에서도 그 규모가 가장 큰 건축물로 추정되며, 종묘의 건축 양식은 궁전이나 불사의 건축이 화려하고 장식적인데 반하여 유교의 검소한 기품에 따라 건립된 특수목적용 건축물이다.

Jongmyo Shrine(1995) is the royal ancestral shrine of the Joseon Dynasty (1392–1910).

It was added to the World Cultural Heritage list in 1995. Joseon Kings held memorial services with sinju for deceased kings and queens here.

A sinju is a piece of wood with the names of the dead. People believed that the souls of deceased kings and queens stayed inside of sinju.

They still do memorial services in Jongmyo on the first Sunday of May.

It was built to house eighty-three spirit tablets of the Joseon Kings, their Queen Consorts, and direct ancestors of the dynasty's founder who were posthumously invested with royal titles.

As Joseon was founded according to Confucian ideology, its rulers considered it very important to put Confucian teachings into practice and sanctify the institutions where ancestral memorial tablets were enshrined.

2) Memory of the World Register

세계 기록 유산이란 유네스코가 고문서 등 전 세계의 귀중한 기록물을 보존하고 활용하기 위하여 1997년부터 2년마다 세계적 가치가 있는 기록유산을 선정하는 사업으로 유산의 종류로는 서적(책)이나 문서, 편지 등 여러 종류의 동산 유산을 말하는데, 한국은 기록문화의 전통을 지닌 나라로 인식하고 있으며, 아시아의 어느 나라보다도 많은 세계에서 네 번째로 13개의 유네스코 지정 기록문화를 갖고 있다.

Korea is internationally recognized for the tradition of archival culture. Korea has 13 items recognized as UNESCO Memory of the World, more than any other country in Asia, and the fourth highest in the world. The

12 other documentary heritages include "Joseon Wangjo Sillok," a documentation of 472 years of the Joseon Dynasty (1392-1910);

"Hunminjeongeum Haerye," detailed explanations and examples of each letter of the Korean alphabet; "Seungjeongwon Ilgi," the world's longest record of Joseon kings' daily lives ; "Goryeo Daejanggyeong (Tripitaka Koreana)" ; "Donguibogam," a comprehensive medical book compiling 2,000 years of Eastern medicine knowledge; and "Nanjung Ilgi," a collection of diaries written by Admiral Yi Sun-sin during the seven-year Imjin War with Japan (1592-98).

(1) Baegun hwasang chorok buljo jikji simche yojeol (vol. Ⅱ), the second volume of "Anthology of Great Buddhist Priests' Zen Teachings"(2001)

「백운화상초록불조직지심체요절」(이하 불조직지심체요절이라 함)은 백운화상이 75세였던 고려 공민왕 21년(1372)에 노안을 무릅쓰고 선도(禪徒)들에게 선도(禪道)와 선관(禪觀)의 안목을 자각(自覺)케 하고자 함은 물론, 선풍(禪風)을 전등(傳燈)하여 법맥(法脈)을 계승케 하고자 저술한 것으로서, 그 제자 석찬과 달담이 비구니 묘덕의 시주를 받아 청주 흥덕사에서 1377년 7월에 금속활자로 인쇄하였다.

「불조직지심체요절」의 '직지심체'는 "직지인심 견성성불(直指人心 見性成佛)"이라는 수신오도(修身悟道)의 명귀에서 채록한 것으로 '참선하여 사람의 마음을 직시(直視)하면, 그 심성이 곧 부처님의 마음임을 깨닫게 된다'는 것이며 본서는 우리나라의 학승(學僧)들이 대교과(大敎科)를 마치고 수의과(隨意科)에서 공부하는데 사용되는 대표적인 학습서이다.

「불조직지심체요절」의 찬자(撰者)인 백운화상(白雲和尙)은 백운이 그의 호이며, 법명(法名)은 경한(景閑)이며, 고려 충렬왕 24년(1289)에 전라도 고부(古阜)에서 출생하여, 공민왕 23년(1374)에 여주(驪州)의 취암사(鷲巖寺)에서 77세를 일기로 입적(入寂)하였다. 이것은 독일의 구텐베르그보다 70여 년이나 앞선 것으로 1972년 유네스코가 지정한 "세계 도서의 해"에 출품되어 세계 최고(最古)의 금속활자본으로 공인된 것이다.

또한 활자 인쇄술에 적합한 먹, 즉 기름먹을 발명하는 계기가 되었으며, 한국이 혁신한 실용적인 활판 인쇄술은 동양 인쇄 사에 지대한 영향을 끼쳤고, 유럽등지로 전파된 것으로 보인다. 이 책은 이러한 가치를 인정받아 2001년 9월 유네스코세계기록유산으로 등재되었다.

"Jikji," the world's oldest extant book printed with movable metal type, was published at Heungdeok Temple in 1377 under the title of Evidence of Important Technological Advancement in the World's Printing History.

Korea has been campaigning vigorously that, although this Buddhist document had been limited to noblemen, the metal movable printing technique had been invented not by Gutenberg in Germany but here in Korea, in Cheongju. the significance of "Jikji" was recognized internationally when it was listed as part of Unesco's Memory of the World Program in 2001.

The international organization even established the Jikji Memory of the World Prize in 2004, a biennial award given to an individual or group who has contributed to preserving documents and promoting their heritage.

(2) Confucian Printing Woodblocks(2015)

유교책판은 조선시대 유학자들의 저작물을 간행하기 위해 판각한 책판으로, 305개 문중 · 서원 등에서 기탁한 718종 64,226장이다. 현재는 한국국학진흥원에서 보존, 관리하고 있으며, 유교책판은 선학과 후학이 책을 통하여 서로 소통하는 "Text Communication' 의 원형으로, 국가주도로 제작되어 종교적인 목적을 담은 한국의 기록유산인 팔만대장경과는 달리 유교책판은 국가가 아닌 각 지역의 지식인 집단들이 시대를 달리하여 만든 것이다.

수록 내용도 문학을 비롯하여 정치, 경제, 사회, 대인관계 등 다양한 분야를 다루고 있지만 모든 분야의 내용은 궁극적으로 유교의 인륜공동체를 실현하기 위한 공통성을 지니고 있으며, 유교책판은 저자의 직계 후손들이 길게는 550년, 짧게는 60년 이상을 보존해 온 기록물로, 모두가 출처가 분명한 진본이다.

유교책판의 일부는 이미 세계기록유산으로 등재된 한국의 조선왕조실록, 일성록, 승정원일기 등에 존재를 확인할 수 있는 기록이 나오며, 국가에서 만든 각종 '책판 목록집' 에도 대다수 유교책판의 존재가 기록되는 등, 국가의 공식 기록물을 통해서도 그 진정성을 확인할 수 있다.

This documentary heritage, collectively named the "Confucian Printing Woodblocks in Korea," comprises 64,226 hand-carved blocks used for printing 718 titles of words written during the Joseon Dynasty (1392–1910).

They have been entrusted by 305 family clans and Confucian academies.

Books from the Confucian Printing Woodblocks in Kroea were produced only after gathering opinion in the local community and gaining collective consensus, instances of which are rare in the history of the printing culture.

For this reason, revisions were made many times during production of the woodblocks, removing the possibility of mistakes or false content.

The inclusion of only refined content recognized through collective consensus has ensured authenticity of content.

This production process is attested to by Ganyeoksi ilgi, a detailed record of printing woodblock production.

(3) Printing woodblocks of the Tripitaka Koreana and miscellaneous Buddhist scriptures(2007)

고려대장경판(팔만대장경)의 제작은 한국이 13세기(1237–1248년)에 일구어낸 위대한 문화적 업적으로 학계에서 받아들여지고 있으며, 고려대장경판은 81,258 목판에 새긴 대장경판으로 아시아 전역에서는 유일하게 완벽한 형태로 현존하는 판본자료이다.

고려대장경보다 먼저 제작된 북송대장경과 고려 초조대장경 그리고 거란본대장경은 거의 전래되지 않고 있으며, 법원주림(法苑珠林), 일체경음의(一切徑音義)와 내전 수함음소(內典隨函音疎) 등은 고려대장경에만 수록되어 있고 다른 목록에는 보이지 않음. 현재 세계에서 가장 오래되고 가장 정확하고 가장 완벽한 불교 대장경판으로 산스크리트어에서 한역된 불교대장경의 원본과 같은 역할을 하고 있으며, 인도 및 중앙아시아 언어로 된 경전, 계율, 논서, 교리 및 불교와 관련된 역사적 기록물을 집대성하여 한역한 내용과 더불어 중국어가 원문인 일부 문헌을 선정하여 수록하고 있다.

그 엄청난 규모로 볼 때 이러한 대장경판의 제작은 상당한 국고 및 인력의 투입을 필요로 했을 것으로 보이고, 현재 해인사에 소장되고 있는 고려대장경판과 제 경판 87,000여장의 목판은 1098년부터 1958년까지의 오래 시간에 걸쳐 완성된 경판들로써 국가제작판과 사찰 제작판으로 나뉘며 국가제작판은 고려대장경으로 81,258판 5,200여 만자에 달하고, 사찰 제작판은 5,987판이다.

해인사는 11세기 초기부터 900년간 출판인쇄 문화를 선도하면서 한국의 불교문화를 이끌었던 곳이며 현재 해인사에서 소장하고 있는 경판은 그 다양한 역사를 보여주고 있고, 이곳의 경판은 중국에까지 그 천재성이 알려진 원효의 저술 등 한국의 위대한 고승들의 저술 등이 있으며 경전의 내용을 그림으로 표현한 판화가 시대별로 갖추어져 있는 등 세계에서 유일하고 희귀한 가치를 지니는 경판이 대부분임. 해인사 고려대장경판과 제경판은 2007년 6월 제8차 유네스코 기록유산 국제자문위원회(6.13~15, 남아공 프레토리아)에서 세계기록유산으로 등재되었다.

The Goryeo Daejanggyeong (Goryeo dynasty Tripitaka), known as the "Tripitaka Koreana" to the modern scholarly world, is a Korean collection of the Tripitaka (Buddhist scriptures).

Carved onto 81,258 wooden printing blocks in the 13th century, under commission by the Goryeo Dynasty of Korea (918–1392 CE), it is currently stored at Haeinsa Temple in the southwest of the Korean Peninsula.

It is often called the Palman Daejanggyeong ("Eighty-thousand Tripitaka") due to the number of the printing plates that comprise it.

Though the Tripitaka Koreana was a task commissioned by the Goryeo Dynasty to produce an edition of the Tripitaka in wooden printing blocks, there were also individual woodblocks of miscellaneous Buddhist scriptures commissioned directly by Haeinsa Temple.

With years of scribing dating from 1098 to 1958, there are 5,987 miscellaneous woodblocks that have been created and stored at Haeinsa Temple.

These miscellaneous scripture woodblocks, some of which are the only extant copy in the world, were created to supplement the Tripitaka.

The woodblocks of the Tripitaka Koreana and miscellaneous Buddhist scriptures show an outline of a complete "knowledge system" that produces and distributes knowledge.

The Tripitaka is a compilation of Buddhist literature including scripture, disciplinary manuals, commentary, doxography and history; based on this collection of information a unique system of scholastic research was established

(4) The Archives of the KBS Special Live Broadcast "Finding Dispersed Families"(2015)

〈KBS특별생방송 이산가족을 찾습니다〉 기록물은 KBS가 1983년 6월 30일 밤 10시 15분부터 11월 14일 새벽 4시까지 방송기간 138일, 방송시간 453시간 45분 동안 생방송한 비디오 녹화원본 테이프 463개와, 담당 프로듀서 업무수첩, 이산가족이 직접 작성한 신청서, 일일 방송진행표, 큐시트, 기념음반, 사진 등 20,522건의 기록물을 총칭. KBS는 1TV를 통해 1983년 6월 30일 밤 10시 15분부터 11월 14일 새벽 4시까지 방송

기간 138일, 방송시간 453시간 45분 동안 〈KBS특별생방송 이산가족을 찾습니다〉 를 생방송하였으며 이를 전량 녹화하였음. 〈KBS특별생방송 이산가족을 찾습니다〉 기록물은 전쟁의 참상을 전 세계에 고발하고 인권과 보편적 인류애를 고취시킨 생생한 기록이며, 이산가족을 찾겠다는 인파가 계속되는 여의도 광장과 KBS 주변은 세계인의 이목을 집중시켰다.

뉴질랜드 오클랜드 시에서 개최된 ABU(Asian Pacific Broadcasting Union)] 총회(1983.10)에서는 이산가족을 주제로 한 30분짜리 영어판 다큐멘터리가 상영되었으며, KBS 본관 중앙홀에서 마련된 기자실에서 전세계 25개국의 기자들이 상주하면서 상봉 소식을 실시간으로 전달하였고, 미국 ABC는 "나이트라인(Night Line)"을 통해 생중계하기도 했다.

The Archives of the KBS Special Live Broadcast "Finding Dispersed Families" comprises 20,522 records of live broadcasts by the Korean Broadcasting System of reunions of war-dispersed families from June 30 through November 14, 1983.

It holds 463 videotapes of 453 hours and 45 minutes of broadcasts, producers' journals, applications to participate, broadcast ephemera, audiotapes, and photographs.

The KBS Special Live Broadcast "Finding Dispersed Families" was aired daily on channel KBS1, beginning at 10:15 p.m. on June 30 and ending at 4 a.m.

On November 14, 1983, marking a total of 453 hours and 45 minutes of live broadcasting over 138 days.

The whole live broadcast was recorded. The 463 tapes of the original recordings, and other materials generated in course of broadcasting such as the posters carrying participants' capsule stories, cue sheets, programming schedules, radio recording materials, and photos are all authentic originals that have been preserved in the KBS archives.

Most of the records generated by the central government and local autonomous bodies have been preserved in the National Archives of Korea.

(5) Archives of Saemaul Undong(New Community Movement, 2013)

새마을운동 기록물은 대한민국 정부와 국민들이 1970년부터 1979년까지 추진한 새마을운동 과정에서 생산된 대통령의 연설문과 결재문서, 행정부처의 새마을 사업 공문, 마을단위의 사업서류, 새마을지도자들의 성공사례 원고와 편지, 시민들의 편지, 새마을교재, 관련 사진과 영상 등 약 22,000여 건의 자료를 총칭한다.

대한민국은 일본 식민지배와 한국전쟁에도 불구하고 괄목할 만한 경제성장과 민주화를 동시에 이룬 세계 유일의 국가로, 아프리카 등 많은 개발도상국들이 한국식 발전 모델을 학습하고 있다.

UN에서도 인정한 농촌개발과 빈곤퇴치의 모범 사례인 '새마을 운동'에 관한 역사적 기록물이다. 새마을운동기록물은 2013년 6월 유네스코 세계기록유산 국제자문위원회(6.18-21, 대한민국 광주)에서 세계기록유산으로 등재되었다.

The Archives of Saemaul Undong (literally, New Community Movement or New Village Movement) includes presidential speeches, government papers, village documents, letters, manuals, photographs and video clips related to Saemaul Undong conducted from 1970 to 1979 in the Republic of Korea.

South Korea today is a benchmarking model for many developing countries and is the only country in the world that has achieved rapid economic growth and democratization in the wake of colonial rule and war.

Saemaul Undong marked the first step in this remarkable journey. During 1970-1979, Korea's average farm household income jumped from $825 to $4,602, setting a milestone in poverty reduction.

The spirit of "Diligence, Self-help and Cooperation" spread widely among the rural population. The movement laid the foundation for Korea to grow into a major economy from one of the world's poorest countries.

The experience of the Korean people in this process is a valuable asset for humankind. Between 1970 and 2011, some 53,000 public officials and village leaders from 129 nations visited Korea to learn about Saemaul Undong. Archival materials included in this nomination have been used to inform programs emulating the movement in 157 villages in 18 countries.

(6) Nanjung Ilgi : War Diary of Admiral Yi Sun-sin(2013)

난중일기』는 원래 임진일기(1592년), 계사일기(1593년), 갑오일기(1594년), 을미일기(1595년), 병신일기(1596년), 정유일기(1597년), 속정유일기(1597년), 무술일기(1598년)로 구성되어 있었으나 현재는 1595년의 을미일기를 뺀 총7책이 보존되어 전해오고 있다.

『난중일기』는 이순신(1545~1598) 해군사령관이 임진왜란(1592~1598) 기간 중 군중(軍中)에서 직접 쓴 친필 일기이고 모두 8권의 책으로 구성되어 있으며, 임진왜란 발발(1592년 1월) 이후부터 이순신이 1598년 11월, 노량해전에서 전사하기 직전까지 7년의 기간을 망라하여 기록하고 있다.

전투상황에 대한 상세한 기록뿐 아니라 당시의 기후나 지형, 일반 서민들의 삶에 대한 기록도 전하고 있어 과거의 자연지형 및 환경, 서민의 생활상을 연구하는 중요한 자료로도 활용되고 있으며, 문장이 간결하면서도 유려하며, 현재까지도 대한민국 국민이 애송하는 시(詩)도 다수 포함되어 있어 문학사적 가치도 매우 높다. 2013년 6월 유네스코 세계기록유산 국제자문위원회(6.18-21, 대한민국 광주)에서 세계기록유산으로 등재되었다.

Nanjung Ilgi (War Diary of Admiral Yi Sun-sin), the handwritten journal of Admiral Yi Sun-sin, the Lord of Loyalty and Chivalry

(Chungmugong), of the Joseon Dynasty (1392–1910); 1 item, 7 volumes; National Treasure No. 76.Admiral Yi Sun-sin kept a daily journal over seven years from January 1, 1592 through November 17, 1598, recording his life in the military.

The diary consists of seven books, each covering roughly a year, and titled after the zodiac name of the year based on the Heavenly Stems in the Chinese calendar.

(7) Human Rights Documentary Heritage 1980 Archives for the May 18th Democratic Uprising against Military Regime, in Gwangju, Republic of Korea(2011)

5.18민주화운동 관련 기록물은 1980년 5월 18일부터 27일까지 대한민국 광주를 중심으로 전개된 민주화를 요구하는 시민들의 일련의 활동과 이후에 이 사건의 책임자처벌, 피해자 보상과 관련하여 기록되고 생산된 문건, 사진, 영상 등의 자료를 총칭한다.

주요소장처는 국가기록원, 육군본부, 국회도서관, 5.18기념재단 등이 있음, 5.18민주화운동은 한국의 민주화에 큰 전기가 되었을 뿐 아니라,1980년대 이후 동아시아 국가들의 냉전 체제를 해체하고 민주화를 이루는데 적지 않은 영향을 끼친 것으로 여겨져 왔고, 그런 세계사적 중요성을 인정받아 2011년 5월 유네스코 세계기록유산으로 등재되었다.

The events of May 1980 followed quickly upon the October 1979 assassination of President Park Chung-hee at the hands of the director of the KCIA (Korean Central Intelligence Agency), one of his closest colleagues.

The unforeseen death of a dictator who had taken control of the country following a military coup was expected to usher in an era of democracy long hoped for by the people of Korea.

Unfortunately, things unfolded differently. In the absence of authority, another military coup took place. Students and citizens from across the country were enraged by the situation and took to the streets in protest against the government.

On May 18th, 1980 the people of Gwangju passionately protested against the nationwide imposition of martial law. The new military government responsible for the coup dispatched special force paratroopers to Gwangju in order to suppress a peaceful protest led by university students and citizens.

The records are divided into three types. First, there are documents produced by the government institutions that came to power after 1980.

They include administrative documents of the central government as well as records of investigation and trial by military judicial institutes. These serve to demonstrate the nature of the government in and before 1980.

All the documents recorded by public officials during and after the incident as well as situation reports and compensation-related documents showing the severity of the damage are included.

Secondly, there are documents produced at the time of the May 18th Democratic Uprising (old statements, declarations, hand-written posters and reporters' notebooks) that reveal just how urgent and desperate the situation was. Particularly compelling are the photos by photographers and foreign correspondents that document the extent to which Gwangju was cut off from the outside world.

Thirdly, there are documents produced by the National Assembly and Supreme Court aimed at restoring the reputation of the people and discovering the truth about the incidents that took place during the time of the military government following the May 18th Democratic Uprising.

(8) Ilseongnok : Records of Daily Reflections(2011)

1760년(영조 36)에서 1910년(융희 4)까지 151년 동안의 국정 운영 내용을 매일매일 일기체로 정리한 국왕의 일기이고 임금의 입장에서 펴낸 일기의 형식을 갖추고 있으나 실질적으로는 정부의 공식적인 기록물이며 필사본으로 한 질만 편찬된 유일본이며 총 2,329책으로 구성되어 있고 모두 전하고 있으나 21개월분이 빠져있다.

정조는 '논어(論語)' 에서 증자(曾子)가 말한 '오일삼성오신(吾日三省吾身: 나는 날마다 세 가지 기준을 가지고 스스로에 대해 반성한다)' 에 깊은 감명을 받아 일찍부터 자신을 반성하는 자료로 삼기 위해 일기를 작성하였다고 한다.

정조가 왕위에 오른 후에는 규장각 관원들에게 명령하여 매일매일 일기를 작성한 다음 5일마다 일기를 정서하여 이를 국왕에게 올려 결재를 받도록 하였으며, 정조는 일성록이 자기 시대의 정치 사회적 상황을 확인하고 반성하는 근거 자료가 되기를 원했으며, 이를 위해 기존의 승정원일기와는 다른 방식으로 일성록을 편찬하도록 지시하였다.

일성록은 국정의 주요 현안들을 강(綱: 표제)과 목(目: 세부 사실)으로 나누어 기록하여 국정 운영에 참고할 내용들을 일목요연하게 찾을 수 있는 체재로 편찬되었으며, 이러한 과정을 거치면서 일성록은 정조의 개인 일기에서 공식적인 국정 일기로 전환하게 되었고, 책의 제목은 증자의 말을 인용하여 '일성록(日省錄)' 으로 했다.

일성록은 18~20세기 동 · 서양의 정치 · 문화적 교류의 구체적 실상과 세계사의 보편적 흐름을 담고 있다는 점에서 조선이라는 한 나라의 역사 기록물을 넘어서는 세계사적 중요성과 가치를 가지고 있다는 점을 인정받아 2011년 5월 유네스코 세계기록유산으로 등재되었다.

Ilseongnok is a chronicle of the king's activities and every aspect of state administration compiled in the form of a daily journal in the late Joseon period, covering all state affairs from 1760 (36th year of the reign of King Yeongjo of Joseon) to 1910 (4th year of the reign of Emperor Sunjong of the Korean Empire).

Iseongnok originated from Jonhyeongak Ilgi (diary), the diary kept by King Jeongjo from his youth, as the eldest son of the crown prince, during his days at the Jonhyeongak Hall where future kings were educated.

Profoundly impressed by Zengzi's remark in Noneo (The Analects of Confucius; Ch. Lunyu) saying, "Each day I examine myself on three counts," the monarch kept the journal from his early years to reflect on himself.

King Jeongjo continued to keep the journal after ascending the throne in 1776. But with the increasing amount of state affairs to handle he found it difficult to continue; so in 1783, the 7th year of his reign, he ordered the Royal Library officials to keep daily records and write out fair copies every five days for his approval.

It was not until 1785 that Ilseongnok adopted the style of description as we see it today. That year King Jeongjo instructed the Royal Library to compile a journal in a clear and well-organized style and format based on the records from his birth onwards, The Diary of Jonhyeongak, as well as Seungjeongwon Ilgi (The Diaries of the Royal Secretariat) compiled after his enthronement.

The compilation was named Ilseongnok (The Records of Daily Reflections) after the aforementioned remark by Zengzi, which had inspired him. With its publication, Ilseongnok was transformed from the king's personal diary to an official daily journal of state affairs.

(9) Donguibogam, Principles and Practice of Eastern Medicine(2009)

동의보감은 선조 30년(1597) 임금의 병과 건강을 돌보는 어의 허준(1539~1615) 선생이 선조의 명을 받아 중국과 우리나라의 의학 서적을 하나로 모아 편집에 착수하여 광해군 2년(1610)에 완성하고 광해군 5년(1613)에 간행한 의학 서적이며, 총 25권 25책으로 나무활자로 발행하였다.

허준은 선조 7년(1574) 의과에 급제하여 이듬해 내의원의 의관이 되었다. 1592년 임진왜란이 일어나자 왕을 모시고 의주까지 피난을 갔으며, 그 공을 인정받아 공신으로 추대되었으나 중인신분에 과하다는 여론이 일자 취소되었는데, 동의보감은 그가 관직에서 물러난 뒤 16년간의 연구 끝에 완성한 한의학의 백과사전격인 책이며, 허준 선생은 이외에도 중국의 의학서적을 번역하는 데에도 많은 업적을 남겼다.

동의보감은 모두 23편으로 내과학인 '내경편', '외형편' 4편, 유행병 · 곽란 · 부인병 · 소아병 관계의 '자편' 11편, '탕액편' 3편, '침구편' 1편과 이외에 목록 2편으로 되어 있고, 각 병마다 처방을 풀이한 체계가 정연한 서적이다.

우리 실정에 맞는 의서라 하여 동의보감이라 이름 하였으며, 훈련도감 자본으로 발행된 이 책은 중국과 일본에도 소개되었고, 현재까지 우리나라 최고의 한방의서로 인정받고 있으며, 제9차 유네스코 기록유산 국제자문위원회(2009.7월/바베이도스)에서 세계기록유산으로 등재되었다('09.7.31).

Donguibogam (hereinafter referred to as "Bogam"), literally meaning "Principles and Practice of Eastern Medicine," is an encyclopedic bible of medical knowledge and treatment techniques compiled in Korea in 1613.

It is edited by Heo Jun under the collective support of medical experts and literati according to the royal instruction.

The state initiated the synthesis of various medical knowledge and also the setting up and implementation of an innovative public health programme for the common people. In medical respect, Bogam successfully synthesized competing contemporary theories of medicine that had accumulated in East Asia for two millennia and went on to integrate medical knowledge and clinical experiences together in a single collection of volumes.

The work informs the evolution of medicine in East Asia and beyond. In terms of health care system, it developed the ideals of "preventive medicine" and "public health care by the state," which was virtually an unprecedented idea up to the 19th century.

Thus, it stands for the historical development of the knowledge and skills of medicine in East Asia and further reflects the human footprints of world medicine and culture. As such, the significance and importance of Bogam is incomparable to anything in the world.

(10) Uigwe, the Royal Protocols of the Joseon Dynasty(2007)

의궤는 조선왕조에서 유교적 원리에 입각한 국가 의례를 중심으로 국가의 중요 행사를 행사 진행 시점에서 당시 사용된 문서를 정해진 격식에 의해 정리하여 작성한 기록물이며, 같은 유교문화 군에 속하는 중국, 일본, 베트남 등에서는 의궤의 체계적인 편찬이 아직 확인되지 않고 있다.

의궤는 조선시대 600여 년에 걸쳐(1392~1910) 왕실의 주요 행사, 즉 결혼식, 장례식, 연회, 사신영접 등 뿐 아니라, 건축물 · 왕릉의 조성과 왕실문화 활동 등에 대한 기록이 그림으로 남아져 있어 600여 년의 생활상을 시각적으로 이해할 수 있는 귀중한 자료로 희소성을 가지고 있다.

총 3,895여 권의 방대한 분량에 이르는 의궤는 왕실의 주요한 의식이 시기별, 주제별로 정리되어 있어서, 조선왕조 의식의 변화 뿐 아니라 동아시아 지역의 문화를 비교연구, 이해하는 풍부한 내용을 담고 있다.

특히 반차도, 도설 등 행사모습을 묘사한 시각 콘텐츠는 오늘날의 영상자료처럼 당시의 모습을 입체적으로 생동감 있게 보여주고 있는데, 예컨대 정조의 능행도(陵幸圖)는 전 여정을 15.4m에 걸쳐 표현하고 있으며, 이런 형태(시각중심 visual-oriented)의 기록유산은 뛰어난 미술장인과 사관의 공동 작업을 통해서만 만들어질 수 있다는 점에서 독특한 성격을 지니고 있음. 한 마디로 의궤는 장기간에 걸쳐 조선왕조의 주요 의식을 방대한 양의 그림과 글로 체계적으로 담고 있으며 이러한 유형은 동서양 전 세계적으로 유례를 찾아볼 수 없다는 점에서 매우 뛰어난 기록유산의 가치(outstanding value of documentary heritage)를 지니고 있다.

A unique form of documentary heritage, the "Uigwe" is a collection of Royal Protocols of the over 500 year-long Joseon Dynasty (1392 –

1910), that both records and prescribes through prose and illustration the major ceremonies and rites of the royal family.

The exquisite value of the Uigwe lies within its rarity, in that it captures so many details of so many different aspects of the life of the royal family.

Documenting not only the records of all the procedures, protocols, formalities and requirements needed to conduct important ceremonies such as weddings, funerals, banquets and receiving foreign missions, it also includes details on the construction of royal buildings and tombs as well as other various cultural activities of the royal family.

Categorized by time and theme and comprised of over 3,895 books, the Uigwe makes it possible to understand the changes that took place over time in royal ceremonies and allows for detailed comparisons with the other contemporaneous East Asian cultures.

In particular, the pictorial materials, such as "Banchado" and "Doseol" illustrate the rituals and ceremonies of the time with a sophistication and vividness that matches the visual materials of the present day.

(11) Seungjeongwon Ilgi, the Diaries of the Royal Secretariat(2001)

승정원은 조선 정종 대에 창설된 기관으로서 국가의 모든 기밀을 취급하던 국왕의 비서실이라 할 수 있는 곳으로, 1623년(인조1) 3월부터 1894년(고종31) 6월까지 272년간 승정원에서 처리한 국정 기록과 승선원, 궁내부, 비서감, 규장각으로 명칭이 바뀌면서 1910년(융희 4)까지 총 3,243책의 기록이 남아 있다.

승정원일기는 조선왕조 최대의 기밀 기록인 동시에 사료적 가치에 있어서 조선왕조실록, 일성록, 비변사등록과 같이 우리의 역사와 문화를 세계에 자랑할 만한 자료이며, 또한 세계기록유산으로 등재된 조선왕조실록을 편찬할 때 기본 자료로 이용하였기 때문에 실록보다 오히려 가치 있는 자료로 평가되고 있음은 물론, 원본 1부밖에 없는 귀중한 자료로 국보 제303호(1999.4.9)로 지정되어 있으므로 인하여 세계 최대 및 1차 사료로서의 가치를 인정받아 2001년 9월 유네스코세계기록유산으로 등재됐다.

승정원일기는 일기 식으로 한달에 1책씩 작성하는 것을 원칙으로 하였으나 후기로 올수록 내용이 많아져 한 달에 2책 이상이 되는 경우도 있으며, 조선 건국 초부터 정리되었으나 조선전기분(朝鮮前期分)은 임진왜란 등의 병화(兵火)로 대부분 소실되었고 현재는 3,243책만이 남아있어 국사(國史)연구뿐만 아니라 한국의 정치, 경제, 사회, 외교, 문화, 군사 등 모든 학문 연구에 필수적인 자료이다.

또한 17세기부터 20세기 초까지 일기로 300년간의 국문학의 변천과정을 확인할 수 있는 국문학적 가치가 인정되고 있으며, 288년간 매일의 날짜 정보를 기록한 것으로서 특히 조선왕조실록의 날짜는 60갑자로만 표기되어 있어 오늘날 우리가 쓰는 태양력으로 환산하는 데 많은 혼란을 겪고 있으나 승정원일기는 60갑자와 수시 력 역법의 일자를 동시에 표기하고 있어 역사의 기초자료가 되고 있으며, 또한 전통적인 유교사회 내부로부터 자생적인 천주교 수용이 민중들 사이에 어떻게 전개되었으며 이에 대한 정치권의 대응 등을 자세히 살필 수 있다.

Seungjeongwon, the Royal Secretariat of the Joseon Dynasty, was responsible for keeping Seungjeongwon Ilgi, the Diaries of the Royal Secretariat, a detailed record of the daily events and official schedules of the court, from the Joseon Dynasty's first king, Taejo, to its 27th and last, Sunjong.

But through the vicissitudes of time, only 3,243 diaries are extant. The extant diaries have detailed information on 288 years of the Joseon Dynasty, from March 12, 1623 (the 1st year of the 16th king, Injo) to August 29, 1910 (the 4th year of the 27th king, Sunjong). Seungjeongwon Ilgi has the largest amount of authentic historic recordings and state secrets of the Joseon Dynasty.

Also, it had served as the primary source to the Annals of the Joseon Dynasty, thus, its historic value is even greater than that of the Annals.

It was designated as National Treasure No. 303 in April, 1999 and registered as Memory of the World in September 2001.

Its content contains the entire picture of Seungjeongwon, a pivotal office in a royal court, taking care of not only important national events but also simple routines as well.

The king's appointments including gyeongyeon, or discussions with scholars on the Confucian and other Chinese classics, meetings with court functionaries, administrative acts, and affairs in the queen's inner palace were listed in the preface to a monthly diary.

The names of the royal secretaries and of the scribes are recorded in every day's diary. Underneath the list are recorded the names of daily deputy officials and their attendance or absence.

(12) The Annals of the Joseon Dynasty(1997)

조선왕조실록은 조선왕조의 시조인 태조로부터 철종까지 25대 472년간(1392~1863)의 역사를 연월일 순서에 따라 편년체로 기록한 책으로 총 1,893권 888책으로 되어 있는 오래되고 방대한 양의 역사서이다.

조선왕조실록은 조선시대의 정치, 외교, 군사, 제도, 법률, 경제, 산업, 교통, 통신, 사회, 풍속, 미술, 공예, 종교 등 각 방면의 역사적 사실을 망라하고 있어 세계적으로 그 유례가 없는 귀중한 역사 기록물이며, 역사기술에 있어 매우 진실성과 신빙성이 높은 역사기록이라는 점에서 의의가 크다.

조선왕조실록의 기초자료 작성에서 실제 편술까지의 편수 간행작업을 직접 하였던 사관은 관직으로서의 독립성과 기술에 대한 비밀성을 제도적으로 보장받았으며, 실록의 편찬은 다음 국왕 즉위한 후 실록청을 개설하고 관계관을 배치하여 편찬하였으며 사초는 군주라 해도 함부로 열람할 수 없도록 비밀을 보장함으로써 이 실록의 진실성과 신빙성을 확보하였다.

실록이 완성된 후에는 특별히 설치한 사고(史庫)에 각각 1부씩 보관하였는데, 임진왜란과 병자호란을 거치면서 사고의 실록들이 병화에 소실되기도 하였으나 그때마다 재

출간하거나 보수하여 20세기 초까지 정족산, 태백산, 적상산, 오대산의 4사고에 각각 1부씩 전하여 내려왔다.

정족산, 태백산 사고의 실록은 1910년 일제가 당시 경성제국대학으로 이관하였다가 광복 후 서울대학교 규장각에 그대로 소장되어 현재에 이르고 있으며, 오대산 사고의 실록은 일본으로 반출하여 갔다가 관동대지진으로 소실되어 현재 27책만 남아 있다.

적상산본은 구황궁 장서각에 소장되어 있다가 1950년 한국전쟁 당시 북한이 가져가 현재 김일성종합대학에 소장되어 있으며, 1984년 서울대학교 규장각에 함께 보관되어 있는 조선왕조실록 정족산본 및 태백산 본을 분리하여 안전하게 보관하고 있다.

조선왕조실록은 정족산본 1,181책, 태백산본 848책, 오대산본 27책, 기타 산엽 본 21책을 포함해서 총 2,077책이 일괄적으로 국보 제 151호로 지정되어 있으며, 1997년 10월에 유네스코 세계기록유산으로 등재되었다.

실록편찬시 이용되는 자료는 정부기관에서의 보고 문서 등을 정리해 둔 춘추관시정기, 전왕 재위시의 사관들이 작성해 둔 사초(史草), 승정원일기, 의정부등재, 일성록 등 정부 주요기관의 기록과 개인의 문집 등이었다.

특히 사초는 사관들이 국가의 모든 회의에 빠짐없이 참가하여 왕과 신하들이 국사를 논의, 처리하는 것을 사실대로 기록하는 동시에 그 잘잘못 및 인물에 대한 비평, 그리고 기밀사무 등을 직필(直筆)하였으며, 조선시대에는 사법(史法)이 매우 엄하여 사관이외에는 아무도 볼 수가 없었으며, 기록의 진실성을 확보하기 위해서 왕까지도 보지 못하게 하였다.

The Annals of the Joseon Dynasty cover more than 470 years of the history of the dynasty, from the reign of King Taejo (1392–1398), the founder, to the reign of King Cheoljong (1849–1863).

With the kings as the central figures, the annals are daily records of the overall history and culture of the Joseon Dynasty, covering politics, military affairs, the social system, law, economics, industry, transportation, communications, customary arts, crafts, religion, etc.

The annals of a given king were definitively compiled only when his successor ordered it.

The materials were collected from Sacho, or Draft History, Sijeonggi, or Daily Records, Seungjeongwon Ilgi, or the Diaries of the Royal Secretariat, Uijeongbu Deungnok, or the Documents of the State Council, Bibyeonsa Deungnok, or Records of the Border Defense Council, Ilseongnok, or Daily Records of the Royal Court and Important Officials, etc.

Of these, Draft History and Daily Records were the most important sources. The main authors of Draft History were two historiographers, two assistant historiographers and four censors.

These writers always participated in every national conference and kept records of the actual details of national affairs under discussion between king and officials. Sometimes they made character sketches of persons who had done good or evil deeds.

The Daily Records were placed in the custody of the Office for Annals Compilation (Chunchugwan).

Nobody was allowed to read Draft History and Daily Records except historiographers. Even the king was not excepted.

Any historiographer who disclosed the contents of the annals was severely punished as a felon. The regulations and ordinances governing historiography were very strict.

The annals were printed and then preserved in the historical archives under rigorous management. There are a total of 2,077 books in these four editions of the Annals of the Joseon Dynasty, all of the highest value for history.

(13) Hunminjeongeum Manuscript(1997)

훈민정음(해례본)은 1446년 음력 9월에 간행된 1책의 목판본으로, 새로 만든 문자 '훈민정음' 의 창제 목적과 이 문자의 음가 및 운용 법, 그리고 이들에 대한 해설과 용례를 붙인 책이다.

세종이 직접 작성한 '예의(例義)' 부분과 정인지(鄭麟趾)를 비롯하여 신숙주(申叔舟) · 성삼문(成三問) · 최항(崔恒) · 박팽년(朴彭年) · 강희안(姜希顔) · 이개(李塏) · 이선로(李善老) 등 집현전 8명의 학자들이 만든 '해례(解例)' 두 부분으로 구성되어 있으며, 그 동안 이 책의 서명을 문자 이름인 훈민정음과 똑같이 훈민정음(訓民正音)이라고 부르거나, 또 해례가 붙어 있고 훈민정음(언해본)과 구분하기 위해서 '훈민정음 해례본' 또는 '훈민정음 원본' 등으로 명명해 온 것이다.

국보 제70호로 지정되어 있는 훈민정음(해례본)은 국보 제71호로 지정되어 있는 동국정운권1, 6과 함께 경상북도 안동시 와룡면 주촌의 이한걸(李漢杰) 씨 댁에 전래되던 것인데, 1940년에 발견될 당시 원 표지와 첫 두 장이 떨어져 나가고 없었는데 그 후 보충하여 끼워 넣는 과정에서 실수가 있었다.

세종 서문의 마지막 글자 '이(耳)' 가 '의(矣)' 로 잘못 씌어지고, 구두점과 권성이 잘못되었거나 빠진 것도 있으며, 이 책에는 구점(句點; 右圈點)과, 두점(讀點; 中圈點) 및 파음자(破音字)의 성조를 표시하는 권성(圈聲)도 정확하게 표시한 책임. 구두점과 권성을 다 표시한 것은 성리대전(性理大全(1415년)의 체재와도 일치하며, 최근에 이 책 외에 또, 다른 훈민정음(해례본) 한 책이 경북 상주에서 발견된 바 있다.

Korea's official script is Hangeul, the unique Korean alphabet. This name, a compound of han, meaning "the Korean people" or "great" and geul, meaning "letters," was given to it early in the 20th century. The creator of hangeul was King Sejong the Great (reigned 1418–1450), the fourth king of the Joseon Dynasty.

Sejong was concerned that Chinese characters, until that time used to write Korean, were a writing system for representing Chinese, a language completely different in structure from Korean, and were therefore hard for Koreans to learn and use.

In the twelfth lunar month of 1443, he completed development of a writing system suitable for representing Korean, which he called Hunminjeongeum, "Proper sounds to instruct the people." Hunminjeongeum was an alphabet formed of 28 letters.

Today's hangeul uses only 24 of these, having dropped four. This orthography not only represents the Korean language perfectly but also is easy to learn and use. It is recognized as being both original and scientific.

Sejong himself wrote a preface clarifying the origin and the purpose of the new alphabet and giving brief examples and explanations of each of its letters, while he had the scholars of the Jiphyeonjeon, or "Hall of Worthies," give detailed explanations and examples of them.

The resulting work was published in the ninth lunar month of 1446, and the new alphabet was widely made known to the public. The work's title was the same as the then name of the alphabet, Hunminjeongeum.

The recently discovered complete edition is known as the Haerye Edition of Hunminjeongeum (Haerye referring to the explanations and examples of the Jiphyeonjeon scholars, which were missing in the previously known editions). The extract publication date is not clear. But in the Annals of King Sejong, the official record of his reign, it is noted that the book was published in the ninth month of 1446, and the scholar Jeong In-ji's so, or "postface," which appears in the volume, was written in the first ten days of the ninth lunar month of 1446, so we can judge that it was published by the tenth day of that month.

3) Intangible Heritage of Humanity

무형문화유산이란 2003년 유네스코 무형문화유산 보호 협약(Convention for the Safeguarding of Intangible Cultural Heritage)에 의거하여 문화적 다양성과 창의성이 유지될 수 있도록 대표목록 또는 긴급목록에 각국의 무형유산을 등재하는 제도이며, 2005년까지 인류구전 및 무형유산걸작이라는 명칭으로 유네스코 프로그램 사업이었으나 지금은 세계유산과 마찬가지로 정부 간 협약으로 발전됐다.

It was also around this time that concerns rose about rapid globalization and discussions took place around Samuel Huntington's thesis on the clash of civilizations.

As a result, people called for cultural diversity and this naturally led to an interest in intangible cultural heritage.

Korea and Japan were among the few countries that introduced a system to identify and preserve intangible cultural heritage. Korea has had a regulation on intangible heritage since 1962, modeled after Japan's system.

(1) Royal ancestral ritual in the Jongmyo shrine and its music (2001) : 종묘제례(2001)

프랑스 파리에서 열린 유네스코 회의에서 종묘제례 및 종묘제례악이 우리나라 첫 인류무형문화 유산으로 등재됐으며, 종묘제례(宗廟祭禮)란 조선 왕조 역대 왕과 왕비 및 추존된 왕과 왕비의 신주(神主)를 모신 종묘에서 행하는 제향 의식임. 종묘제례악은 이러한 제향 의식이 거행되는 도안 연주되는 기악과 노래, 춤을 말한다.

Gods, or supernatural beings, are not recognized in Confucianism, but instead ancestral spirits are venerated as objects of divine worship.

As an absolute monarchy that upheld Confucianism as its ruling ideology, the Joseon Dynasty placed utmost importance on worshipping the spirits of royal ancestors.

Therefore, Jongmyo which housed the spirit tablets of past kings and queens was the loftiest pantheon, and the rites performed at this royal shrine were the state events of primary importance.

(2) Pansori epic chant(2003) : 판소리(2003)

판소리는 한 명의 소리꾼과 한 명의 고수(북치는 사람)가 음악적 이야기를 엮어가며 연행하는 장르이며, 장단에 맞추어 부르는 표현력이 풍부한 창(노래)과 일정한 양식을 가진 아니리(말), 풍부한 내용의 사설과 너름새(몸짓) 등으로 구연(口演)됐다.

Since ancient times, the Korean people have been renowned for their enjoyment of song and dance. Pansori, or the epic chant of Korea, is a genre of indigenous traditional music that has stirred the hearts of Koreans for ages with its passionate, mournful sounds.

Pansori is often compared to Western operas, such as "Aida," "Carmen" or "La boheme," but in contrast to the spectacular stage of a Western opera, created by a large number of performers including a dance troupe, a chorus and a symphony orchestra, and embellished by elaborate costumes and lighting, the stage of a pansori has just a solo singer holding nothing more than a single folding fan and who appears along with a drummer carrying a single drum.

(3) Gangneung Danoje Festival(2005) : 강릉단오제(江陵端午祭, 2005)

강릉단오제는 단옷날을 전후하여 펼쳐지는 강릉 지방의 향토 제례 의식이다. 4주 동안 계속되는 이 축제 때는 단오굿, 민요 오독떼기, 관노가면극, 시 낭송 및 다양한 민속놀이가 열린다.

Dano is the fifth day of the fifth month according to the lunar calendar. Ancient Koreans viewed dates that had two repeating odd numbers as being particularly auspicious. On these holidays, people played fun games and prepared dishes in accordance with the season.

In particular, dano was the day in which the cosmic yang energy (positive, male energy) was strongest and was considered the biggest holiday along with the New Year's Day and the Harvest Moon Festival (chuseok).

Most of all, the "Double Fifth Day" was closely connected with farming.

It was roughly around the time when the grains had been planted in the field, and when rice planting in the paddy was completed and the hectic spring farming was basically finished.

After completing the preparations for one year of farming, a commemorative service was held to pray for a bountiful harvest and to take a break and enjoy playing games. This was called "Danoje," meaning the Double Fifth Festival.

(4) Ganggangsullae(2009) : 강강술래(2009)

우리나라의 대표적인 민속 예술의 하나로 풍작과 풍요를 기원하는 풍속의 하나로, 주로 음력 8월 한가위에 연출된다.

밝은 보름달이 뜬 밤에 수십 명의 마을 처녀들이 모여서 손을 맞잡아 둥그렇게 원을 만들어 돌며, 한 사람이 '강강술래' 의 앞부분을 선창(先唱)하면 뒷소리를 하는 여러 사람이 이어받아 노래를 부르며, 이러한 놀이는 밤새도록 춤을 추며 계속되며 원무를 도는 도중에 민속놀이도 곁들인다.

The full moon rises 12 times in a year. The moon is largest at the first full moon in the lunar New Year(daeboreum) and the harvest moon that rises in the eighth lunar month during the Korean thanksgiving holidays (hangawi, or chuseok).

It is only on this day that regardless of class or social status, men and women of all ages can all enjoy the day as a single group. Villagers enjoy the holiday that starts on the lunar New Year's Day, going around to each house playing music.

On this day, men play the farmers' band music to increase the festive mood, and women hold hands and skip together in a traditional circle dance (ganggangsullae).

Under the bright full moon the women taste the feeling of freedom and pray for a bountiful harvest in the year ahead or celebrate the joy of the harvest. The circle dance, which combines song and dance, is Korea's representative pastime for women in a group. On these moonlit nights many find it impossible to stay indoors. "Kwaeng-geurang kwaeng kwaeng kwae kwaeng kwaeng kwaeng dudu dida dudu diung.

(5) Namsadang Nori(2009) : 남사당놀이(2009)

'남자들로 구성된 유랑광대극' 으로서 원래 유랑예인들이 널리 행하던 다방면의 한국 전통 민속공연이고, 공연은 날이 어두워지면 놀이판으로 잡은 넓은 마당에 횃불을 올리고 시작했으며, 풍물, 버나(대접 돌리기), 살판(땅재주), 덧뵈기(탈놀음), 어름(줄타기), 덜미(꼭두각시놀음) 등을 공연했으며 지금은 전문 극단에 의해 그 명맥을 이어가고 있다.

During the Joseon Dynasty (1392-1910), there were nomadic troupes of entertainers called namsadang, who traveled across the nation and engaged in a wide array of performances, including singing, dancing, playing musical instruments, acrobatic feats, mask dances and puppet plays.

They were very popular among commoners who seldom had an opportunity for entertainment or an outlet to relieve the weariness of their hardworking lives.

A namsadang troupe was composed of 40-50 individuals, including the leader (called mogabi or kkokdusoe), planner (gombaengisoe), chief of each performance part (ddeunsoe), training performers (gayeol), beginners (ppiri), advisors (jeoseungpae), and porters who carried props and installations.

Mostly, children from poor families or runaways joined the troupe to become performers, and although the troupe consisted of lower-class people like poor peasants and orphans, it operated under strict organizational rules.

In general, the performances of a namsadang troupe took place at the village square with the repertoire consisting of the farmer's band music (pungmul), a dish-spinning show with rhetoric and singing (beona), acrobatics on the ground (salpan), tightrope walking with rhetoric and singing (eoreum), a four-act mask drama (deotboegi), and a puppet play (deolmi). Each of these separate acts was conducted one by one seamlessly over the course of a long program.

(6) Yeongsanjae(2009) : 영산재(靈山齋, 2009)

한국 불교문화의 중심 요소인 영산재는 부처가 인도의 영취산에서 법화경을 설법하던 모습을 재현한 것이며, 하늘과 땅의 영가(靈駕)와 모든 성인(聖人)을 맞아들이는 의식에서 시작하여 부처의 영적 세계의 사고방식을 표현하는 봉송(奉送) 의례로 마무리된다.

"All living beings must die, and all those who meet must part," says a widely-quoted Korean proverb. Humans are mortal.

In Buddhism, it is believed that the dead can be freed from anguish and suffering by understanding Dharma, or the laws of the Buddha, even after death.

The Rites of Vulture Peak (Yeongsanjae) are a combination of exorcism, memorial service and Dharma celebration, which prays for posthumous enlightenment.

The rites are served on the 49th day after a person's death because Buddhists believe that the fate of the deceased for the next life is determined in the 49 days that follow death.

(7) Jeju Chilmeoridang Yeongdeunggut(2009) : 제주 칠머리당 영등굿(2009)

제주시 건입동 칠머리 당에서 열리는 이 굿은 제주도 전역에서 이루어지는 유사한 굿 가운데 대표적인 의식이고, 바다의 평온과 풍작 및 풍어를 기원하기 위해 음력 2월에 제주에서 시행하는 세시풍속이며 제주의 마을 무당들은 바람의 여신(영등 할망), 용왕, 산신 등에게 제사를 지낸다.

It is nearly impossible to discuss Korean culture without mentioning the shamanic rituals called gut.

Even in modern times, any attempt to have a genuine understanding of Koreans and their culture requires some amount of knowledge about the age-old shamanic tradition, which involves the "disentangling" of knots,

or conflicts; the knots between humans and nature, the knots between people, and the knots that exist within our inner selves. It aims to help people reconnect with their true nature and inner vitality.

A set of rites to entertain this goddess of the wind is recorded in the 15th-century geography book, Survey of the Geography of Korea (Dongguk yeoji seungnam), as a religious event for fishing communities; it shows that the faith in the goddess of the wind existed in the Joseon era or even earlier.

The rites were held in many villages all over Jeju Island until the mid-20th century, but now the ritual custom has almost disappeared from the entire island except for in a very small number of fishing towns.

(8) Cheoyongmu(2009) : 처용무(處容舞, 2009)

궁중 연례에서 악귀를 몰아내고 평온을 기원하거나 음력 섣달그믐날 악귀를 쫓는 의식인 나례에서 복을 구하며 춘 춤이 처용무이다.

궁중 무용의 하나이며, 동해 용왕의 아들로 사람 형상을 한 처용이 노래를 부르고 춤을 추어 천연두를 옮기는 역신으로부터 인간 아내를 구해냈다는 한국 설화를 바탕으로 한 처용무는 동서남북과 중앙 등의 오방을 상징하는 흰색 · 파란색 · 검은색 · 붉은색 · 노란색의 오색 의상을 입은 5명의 남자들이 추는 춤이다.

The Dance of Cheoyong (Cheoyongmu) was derived from a legendary folk tale about a mythical character named Cheoyong.

It is a mask dance that has been passed down for over a thousand years from the Silla Kingdom (57 B.C.–A.D. 935). Also called the Dance of Cheoyong in the Five Directions (Obang cheoyongmu) and noted for its majestic and vigorous movements, this is the only form of Korean traditional court dance performed by dancers wearing masks.

The folk tale is set in Silla during the reign of King Heongang (r. 875–886). Cheonyong, the son of a dragon, met the king on the beach in Gaeunpo (today's Ulsan) and joined his entourage. He married a Silla woman and lived in Sorabeol, the capital city which is today's Gyeongju.

One day, he came home to find his wife in bed with a stranger. Surprisingly, Cheoyong just turned around and left the room, dancing and singing a song of his own composition.

(9) Gagok, lyric song cycles accompanied by an orchestra(2009) : 가곡(2010)

가곡(歌曲)은 소규모 국악 관현 반주에 맞추어 남성과 여성들이 부르던 한국 전통 성악 장르이고, 가곡은 시조 및 가사와 함께 정가(正歌)에 속하며 예전에 가곡은 상류 계층이 즐기던 음악이었지만, 오늘날에는 전국적으로 널리 알려진 성악곡이 됐다.

Gagok refers to a genre of Korean vocal music composed from traditional three-line poetry (sijo) and accompanied by an ensemble of native instruments, consisting of a twelve-stringed, or else six-stringed, zither (gayageum or geomungo), a large, or else small, bamboo flute (daegeum or sogeum), a two-stringed zither (haegeum) and a two-sided drum (janggu).

In the Joseon Dynasty (1392–1910), vocal music was roughly divided into two kinds according to the class of people who enjoyed them.

First, aristocrats and literati enjoyed three genres of songs composed from poetry.

The term "sijo" mentioned above refers not only to the poetic genre itself but also the songs composed from the poetry – the songs with simple melodies and rhythms, which were often sung without accompaniment.

On the other hand, if the same poetry was set to more sophisticated songs accompanied by an ensemble it was called gagok. Lastly, songs composed from the prose-poetry named gasa were longer and had more complicated melodies.

(10) Daemokjang, traditional wooden architecture(2010) : 대목장(2010)

대목장(大木匠)은 한국의 전통 목조 건축, 특히 전통 목공 기술을 가지고 있는 목수를 말하며, 그들은 전통적인 한옥에서부터 궁궐이나 사찰과 같은 기념비적 목조 건축물에 이르는 역사적 건축물의 유지보수와 복원, 재건축을 담당함. 대목장은 건축물의 기획 · 설계 · 시공은 물론 수하 목수들에 대한 관리감독까지 전체공정을 책임지는 장인

A house is where a family lives. But it also serves as a marker of its owner's social status and wealth. That seems to explain why many palaces, residences of noble families, and Buddhist temples were built to be more majestic and imposing than the others. In the past, all the Korean houses, whether it was a royal palace, a Buddhist temple or a commoner' house, were wooden structures.

The construction of a traditional wooden building goes through a number of processes. First, the construction begins with the purchase of timber, layout planning and structural designing. Next, the wood is cut into various beams and columns, and the framework is completed.

Then, the walls are put up, the roof is covered with tiles, and some parts of the surfaces are painted with colorful designs. Naturally, larger houses need heavier wooden beams and roofs, and the frameworks also have to be stronger.

Traditional woodworking techniques, including the skill to connect wooden beams, require a long period of training to master. Also the carpenter should have a comprehensive knowledge of various tools and the ability to use them skillfully. Therefore, skilled carpenters are produced through decades of apprenticeship and field experience.

(11) Falconry, a living human heritage(2010) : 매사냥(2010)

'매사냥' 이란 매나 기타 맹금(猛禽)을 길들여서 야생 상태에 있는 사냥감을 잡도록 하는 전통 사냥이며, 매사냥꾼들은 비록 그 배경이 서로 다를지라도 매를 훈련하고 돌보는 방법, 사용하는 도구, 유대감을 형성하는 과정 등의 보편된 가치, 전통, 기술을 공유한다.

Unlike other forms of hunting, falconry is an indirect method of hunting that uses a trained falcon.

It involves domesticating a falcon so that it captures wild prey. In order to engage in falconry, the falcon must first be hunted and captured and then it must go through the process of being domesticated. Falconry's original purpose began with hunting, but after going through a long period of history, it also came to have the additional purpose of sport.

According to a record in "Biographies (Yeoljeon)" of the History of the Three Kingdoms (Samguk Sagi), King Jinpyeong (r. 579–632) of the Silla Kingdom became so enraptured by falconry that he neglected matters of state, and as a result the state official Kim Hu-jik requested that after his death, his body be buried by the roadside along King Jinpyeong's hunting route to make the king realize the error of his ways.

This was because the king had lost himself to hunting. Falcon hunters often declare that, "The person who has never experienced the joy of capturing and domesticating a falcon cannot comprehend the feeling of accomplishment experienced when the falcon you have raised like it was your own child completes its first hunt. Falconry enables one to have a rapport with nature, and it is the best way to build great character."

(12) Jultagi, tightrope walking(2011) : 줄타기(2011)

널리 알려진 놀음의 하나로 대부분의 나라에서는 단지 곡예기술에 중점을 두고 있는데, 한국의 전통 공연예술인 줄타기는 음악 반주에 맞추어 줄타기 곡예사와 바닥에 있는 어릿광대가 서로 재담을 주고받는다는 점에서 독특하다.

줄타기 곡예사는 간단한 동작으로 시작하여 점점 더 어려운 묘기를 부리는데 무려 40가지나 되는 줄타기 기술을 몇 시간 동안이나 공연한다.

Tightrope walking is a widespread form of entertainment that in most countries focuses purely on acrobatic skill. The traditional Korean performing art of Jultagi is distinctive in that it is accompanied by music and witty dialogue between the tightrope walker and an earthbound clown. Jultagi is performed outside.

The tightrope walker executes a variety of acrobatic feats on the rope, along with jokes, mimicry, songs and dance, while a clown engages the tightrope walker in joking banter, and a team of musicians plays music to accompany the entertainment. The tightrope walker starts with simpler feats, gradually moving to more difficult acrobatics, displaying some forty different rope techniques in a performance that can last several hours.

Today, tightrope walking performers are frequently invited to local festivals that take place throughout the country, particularly in spring and autumn. Currently, transmission of tightrope walking in Korea is centred on the Jultagi Safeguarding Association in Gyeonggi-do Province.

(13) Taekkyeon, a traditional Korean martial art(2011) : 택견(2011)

유연하고 율동적인 춤과 같은 동작으로 상대를 공격하거나 다리를 걸어 넘어뜨리는 한국 전통 무술, 우아한 몸놀림의 노련한 택견 전수자는 직선적이고 뻣뻣하기보다는 부드럽고 곡선을 그리듯이 움직이지만, 엄청난 유연성과 힘을 보여줄 수 있다.

발동작이 손만큼 중요한 역할을 한다. 부드러운 인상을 풍기지만, 택견은 모든 가능한 전투 방법을 이용하며 다양한 공격과 방어 기술을 강조하는 효과적인 무술이다.

Taekkyeon is a traditional Korean martial art that makes use of fluid, rhythmic dance-like movements to strike or trip up an opponent.

The graceful movements of a well-trained Taekkyeon performer are gentle and circular rather than straight and rigid, but can explode with enormous flexibility and strength.

The feet play as important a role as the hands. In spite of its gentle impression, Taekkyeon is an effective martial art highlighting a broad variety of offensive and defensive skills employing all available fighting methods.

It also teaches consideration: a skilled Taekkyeon practitioner can rapidly dominate an opponent, but a true master knows how to make an opponent withdraw without incurring damage.

As a part of seasonal farming-related traditions, Taekkyeon serves to facilitate community integration, and as a sport accessible to all plays a major role in promoting public health.

Taekkyeon is also practised by a great number of people as a daily activity. There are approximately fifty recognized practitioners of Taekkyeon at present, and the Korean Taekkyeon Association plays a significant role in the transmission and promotion of this traditional martial art.

(14) Weaving of Mosi(fine ramie) in the Hansan region(2011) : 한산모시(2011)

충청남도 서천군 한산 지역에서 만드는 모시로, 이 지역은 여름 평균 기온이 높으며 해풍으로 인해 습하고 토양이 비옥하여 다른 지역에 비해서 모시가 잘 자라서 품질이 우수하므로, 이 때문에 한산모시는 모시의 대명사로 불린다.

'한산(韓山) 모시 짜기'는 전통적으로 여성이 이끄는 가내 작업인데 어머니가 딸 또는 며느리에게 기술과 경험을 전수하고, 또 모시 짜기의 전통은 마을의 정해진 장소에서 이웃과 함께 모여서 일함으로써 공동체를 결속하는 역할을 하였다.

Weaving of Mosi in Hansan is transmitted by middle-aged women in the township located in Chungcheongnam-do province, Republic of Korea.

The region boasts fertile land and sea winds that allow ramie plants to thrive. Weaving ramie cloth involves a number of processes, including harvesting, boiling and bleaching ramie plants, spinning yarn out of ramie fibre, and weaving it on a traditional loom.

Ramie cloth is comfortable in hot summer weather and is used to produce a variety of clothing from dress suits and military uniforms to mourning garments.

The whiteness of the bleached ramie fabric, as well as its refined quality and neatness, makes it suitable for high–end clothing as well as for clothing for ordinary people.

Weaving of Mosi traditionally takes place in the form of women–led family operations in which mothers transmit techniques and experience to their daughters or daughters–in–law.

(15) Arirang, lyrical folk song in the Republic of Korea(2012) : 아리랑(2012)

한국의 서정민요로, 2012년에 유네스코 인류무형문화유산으로 등재된 아리랑은 역사적으로 여러 세대를 거치면서 한국의 일반 민중이 공동 노력으로 창조한 결과물이다.

단순한 노래로서 '아리랑, 아리랑, 아라리오' 라는 여음(餘音)과 지역에 따라 다른 내용으로 발전해온 두 줄의 가사로 구성되어 있으며, '한국의 서정민요 아리랑' (Arirang, lyrical folk song in the Republic of Korea)이라는 이름으로 등재됐다.

북한도 2014년 '조선민주주의인민공화국 아리랑 민요' (Arirang Folk song in the Democratic People' s Republic of Korea)로 유네스코에 등재하여, 아리랑은 한민족의 노래에서 세계인의 문화유산이 됐다.

Arirang is a popular form of Korean folk song and the outcome of collective contributions made by ordinary Koreans throughout generations. Essentially a simple song, it consists of the refrain 'Arirang, arirang, arariyo' and two simple lines, which differ from region to region.

While dealing with diverse universal themes, the simple musical and literary composition invites improvisation, imitation and singing in unison, encouraging its acceptance by different musical genres.

Experts estimate the total number of folk songs carrying the title 'Arirang' at some 3,600 variations belonging to about sixty versions.

A great virtue of Arirang is its respect for human creativity, freedom of expression and empathy. Everyone can create new lyrics, adding to the song's regional, historical and genre variations, and cultural diversity. Arirang is universally sung and enjoyed by the Korean nation.

At the same time, an array of practitioners of regional versions, including local communities, private groups and individuals, actively lead efforts for its popularization and transmission, highlighting the general and local characteristics of individual versions.

Arirang is also a popular subject and motif in diverse arts and media, including cinema, musicals, drama, dance and literature. It is an evocative hymn with the power to enhance communication and unity among the Korean people, whether at home or abroad.

(16) Kimjang, Making and Sharing Kimchi in the Republic of Korea(2013) : 김장(2013)

김장은 한국 사람들이 춥고 긴 겨울을 나기 위해 많은 양의 김치를 담그는 것을 말하며, 김치는 한국 고유의 향신료와 해산물로 양념하여 발효한 한국적 방식의 채소 저장식품을 일컫는데, 역사적 기록에 의하면 760년 이전에도 한국인의 식단에는 김치가 있었다고 한다. 김장은 한국인의 자연환경에 대한 이해를 통합한 음식 문화로, 지역 생태계를 잘 반영하고 있다.

Kimjang, making large quantities of Kimchi to sustain Koreans through the long winter months, has been an essential part of preparing for the long harsh seasons.

A variety of socio-cultural entities also practice Kimjang for diverse purposes; sharing with less privileged neighbours, promoting cooperation among members, or educating the time-honoured tradition to the young. All Koreans are thus part of the one large Kimgjang community, which transcends regional and socio-economic boundaries within Korean society.

Over time, Koreans have developed methods that best fit their specific natural conditions. The specific methods and ingredients used in Kimjang are considered an important family heritage, typically transmitted from a mother-in-law to her newly married daughter-in-law.

The preparation of Kimjang follows a yearly cycle. In spring households procure shrimp, anchovy and other seafood for salting and fermenting. In summer, they buy sea slat for the brine. In late summer, red chilli peppers are dried and ground into powder. Late autumn is Kimjang season, when communities are collectively make and share large quantities of Kimchi to ensure that every household has enough to sustain it through the long, harsh winter.

(17) Nongak : Community Band Music, Dance, and Rituals in the Republic of Korea(2014) : 농악(2014)

농악은 공동체 의식과 농촌 사회의 여흥 활동에서 유래한 대중적인 공연 예술로 2014년에 유네스코무형문화유산으로 등재됐다.

농악은 타악기 합주와 함께 전통 관악기 연주, 행진, 춤, 연극, 기예 등이 함께 어우러진 공연이라고 말할 수 있으며, 각 지역의 농악 공연자들은 화려한 의상을 입고, 마을 신과 농사 신을 위한 제사, 액을 쫓고 복을 부르는 축원, 봄의 풍농 기원과 추수기의 풍년제, 마을 공동체가 추구하는 사업을 위한 재원 마련 행사 등, 다양한 마을 행사에서 연행되며 각 지방의 고유한 음악과 춤을 연주하고 시연한다.

Nongak originated from communal rites and rustic entertainments that promoted harmony as people gathered to pray for peace and prosperity.

It has evolved into a representative performing art genre of Korea, widely performed and enjoyed by all Koreans.

Nongak has been practiced for various purposed, such as appeasing gods, chasing evil spirits and seeking blessings, praying for a rich harvest in spring, celebrating the harvest in autumn festivals, and professional entertainment.

Any joyful community event was never complete without music and dance performed by the local band clad in colourful costumes. The music frequently uses uneven beasts of complex structures like simple three-time, compound time, and simple time and compound time.

Small hand-held gongs and hourglass drums play the main beats, while large gongs and barrel drums create simple rhythmic accents.

(18) Tugging rituals and games(2015) : 줄다리기(Tugging rituals and games, 2015)

줄다리기는 동아시아와 동남아시아의 벼농사 문화권에서 찾아볼 수 있는 전통 의식이자 놀이이며, 줄다리기의 명칭은 캄보디아에서는 '테안 프롯(Lbaeng Teanh Prot)', 필리핀에서는 '푸눅(Punnuk)', 한국에서는 '줄다리기', 베트남에서는 '깨오 꼬(K?o co)' 라고 부른다.

줄다리기는 여러 공동체가 풍작과 번영을 기원하는 마음을 담아 연행하는 전통이며, 줄다리기는 사회적 결속과 연대를 도모하고 함께 즐기는 여흥이고, 새롭게 시작된 농경 주기를 알리는 표식이기도 한다.

줄다리기는 서로 마주보고 서서 양쪽 끝에서 줄을 자기 쪽으로 잡아당기는 형식으로 행해지며, 이 놀이는 경쟁적인 놀이가 아니므로 이기고 지는 승부에 연연하지 않고, 공동체의 안녕을 위해서 연행한다는 것 때문에 이 활동을 통해 공동체의 구성원은 협력의 중요성을 되새기게 된다.

Juldarigi or Tugging Rituals, a traditional performance originated in the community centered society, has been practiced focusing on the plenty and abundance as harvest blessings with strong bondinghood among neighbors of East-Southern Asia countries. Community members encourage the connection and social memberships while practicing Juldarigi and which also mean the farming season has began.

Tugging Rituals and Games play in two teams by pulling the string against each other. Albeit it seems competitive game, it is often a part of a ritual that represents harmony and solidarity among community men.

The entire process is led by the elder who have responsible for having the young generations participate in this game in order to strengthen the communityship.

Juldarigi or Tugging Rituals rooted from the various regions of East-Southern Asia shares the common features such as pulling the string against, however it has reflected clearly the authenticity and originality.

(19) Culture of Jeju Haenyeo(Women Divers, 2016) : 제주해녀(2016)

인류무형문화유산에 등재된 제주 해녀문화는 '물질' 뿐만 아니라 공동체의 연대의식을 강화하는 '잠수굿', 바다로 나가는 배 위에서 부르는 노동요인 '해녀노래' 등으로 구성된다. 무형유산위원회는 제주 해녀문화에 대해 지역의 독특한 문화적 정체성과 문화적 다양성을 보여주고, 안전과 풍어를 위한 의식, 선배가 후배에게 전하는 잠수기술과 책임감, 공동 작업을 통해 거둔 이익으로 사회적 응집력을 높이는 활동 등이 무형유산으로서 가치가 있다고 평가했다.

The Culture of Jeju Haenyeo exists throughout Jeju Island. And it includes the practitioners of diving work which are called hanyeo in general or jamnyeo or jamsu; Muljil, the diving work transmitted from a mother to a daughter and from a mother-in-law to a daughter-in-law; jamsugut, a shamanistic ritual for the goddess of the sea; and Haenyeo Norae(or Haenyeo Song).

A Jeju haenyeo has her mental map of sea, including the reefs and the habitat for the shellfish. By repeated diving over a long time, such a map and the knowledge have been acquired.

On average, Jeju haenyeo hold their breath for one minute which diving then meters deep underwater to gather marine products. Based on the diving skills, the Jeju haenyeo community is classified into three types: the upper – skilled called sanggun, the middle – skilled called junggun, and the lower–skilled called hagun.

The culture of Jeju haenyeo contributes to the advancement of women's status in Korean society, a male–centre Confucian society. Furthermore, it raises global awareness of the importance of ICH for sustainable development.

The nature of Jeju haenyeo culture such as the substainability of diving work, consideration for the weak, commitment to common good, and its ecological aspects is a good example for sustainable development of human societies.

UNESCO recognised its social cohesion and cultural continuity for communities concerned and its internal awareness of the importance of women's work as intangible cultural heritage.

And the culture of Jeju Haenyo encourages intercultural dialogue between haenyeo communities and other communities, which have similar practices. In this context the culture of Jeju Haenyeo inscribed on the Representative List of the Intangible Cultural Heritage of Humanity on December 1, 2016.

Tourism Guide Quiz

1. Introduce "Donguibogam" briefly.

2. What is 'pansori'?

3. List Intangible Heritages designated by UNESCO.

4. Introduce some festive events on Jeongwol Daeboreum.

5. Introduce Haeinsa Temple, mainly focusing on Tripitaka Koreana.

수행 Tips : The ability to raise 4차 산업혁명과 여행 · 관광산업의 미래변화에 대한 사례

4차 산업혁명과 여행 · 관광산업의 미래

4차 산업혁명은 우리 삶의 방식, 일하는 방식, 서로 연관되는 방식을 속도(Velocity)와 범위(Scope), 충격(Impact)이라는 기술적 측면으로 변화시킬 것이다. 인류의 산업혁명 1차 산업혁명 18세기에 증기기관과 기계화, 2차 산업혁명 19세기 말에 전기와 대량생산 체제, 3차 산업혁명 20세기 후반에 컴퓨터와 인터넷 그리고 정보화 시대, 그리고 4차 산업혁명은 현재 첨단 정보통신기술이 고도의 지능화를 더한 혁신적인 변화를 일으키는 산업혁명, 스마트혁명을 말한다. 즉 사물인터넷(IoT), 빅데이터, 인공지능(AI), 가상현실(VR), 증강현실(AR), 클라우드 서비스 등의 첨단 ICT를 기반으로 한 핵심요소들을 응용함으로써 사회 · 경제 · 문화 전반적으로 새로운 차원으로 진입하게 된다.

관광 · 여행 산업측면에서 그동안 여행사가 관광객에게 숙박 · 음식 · 교통 · 체험 · 쇼핑 · 의료 등을 매개했지만, 향후 그 자리를 플랫폼과 정보가 대신하며, VR · AR을 활용한 관광안내, 숙박 리뷰 플랫폼, 소셜다이닝 중개 플랫폼 등의 신규 관광 사업이 증가할 것이다. 항공예약 정보 등을 여행 시기에 맞게 자동으로 통보해 주는 기능도 향후 기술적용 수준에 따라서 그야말로 혁명적인 서비스로 발전할 가능성이 크다. 이미 구글트립(Goole Trips)은 전 세계 도시에 대한 가이드서비스를 제공하는 것은 물론 구글이용자 개인별 위치 히스토리등을 활용해 식당이나 여행지 등을 맞춤형으로 추천한다. 현재 일본에서는 로봇이 객실 안내 등의 업무를 맡는 '로봇호텔'이 등장하고 있다.

관광 · 여행 산업영역에서 4차 산업혁명의 빠르게 진화하고 있는 기술은 플랫폼 경제, 사물인터넷, 빅데이터 부문 등에서 주된 변화가 일고 있다. 대표적인 글로벌 플랫폼 여행기업인 에어비앤비, 우버, 트립어드바이저 등이 '챗봇(Chatbot)' 같은 첨단 ICT를 도입하거나 다른 플랫폼 기업과의 제휴를 통해서 꾸준히 영역을 확장하고 있다. 여행객 소비패턴 및 기호분석에 빅데이터를 활용하는 사례도 점차 증가되고 있으며, 개인의 취향과 필요에 맞는 여행지와 여행스타일, 음식, 액티비티를 안내하는 것은 물론 그에 필요한 항공과 호텔 등도 조회부터 구매까지 원스톱으로 처리하고 있다. 향후 챗봇을 활용한 여행상담 서비스가 상용화 단계로 접어들고 있다는 점에서도 미래 여행 · 관광산업의 한 단면을 유추해 볼 수 있다.

그러나 4차 산업혁명의 영향이 여행 · 관광산업에 모두 긍정적인 것만은 아니다. 무엇보다도 부정적인 요소로 지적하고 있는 점은 바로 일자리 감소다. 자동화는 결국 전통적 개념의 일자리를 상당 부분 감소시킬 것이라는 우려다. 세계경제포럼에서도 인공지능과 로봇의 영향으로 2020년까지 약 510만 개의 일자리가 감소할 것으로 예측하고 있다. 그러나 "옛날을 보는 것은 지금을 살피는 것만 못하고 남에게서 구하는 것은 자신에게서 반추하는 것만 못하다(일성록 서문)"의 뜻을 새기며 정보통신 세계최고의 강국 우리도 ICT와 융 · 복합을 통한 여행 · 관광산업의 새 비즈니스 모델개발 등 미래를 위한 투자와 노력을 펼쳐야 할 때이다.

–You have to make hay while the sun shines. –

Unit 7

Tourist Attractions

Domestic Tour Guide English

Unit 7

Tourist Attractions

1) Korean Folk Village(KFV) : 한국민속촌

■ 역사와 전통, 문화가 살아 있는 공간

조선시대 캐릭터를 접목한 전통문화 테마파크인 한국민속촌은 역사와 문화가 공존하는 전통문화 테마파크이며, 1974년 문을 연 이래 지금까지 생생한 문화 체험이 가능한 자연 속의 전통문화 관광지다.

조선시대 각 지방의 실물 가옥을 이건 · 복원해 배산임수 지형에 자리한 촌락을 재현, 99만㎡(약 30만 평) 부지에 차별화된 조선시대 공간을 갖추었다.

전통 공간 재현에 머물지 않고 사또와 포졸, 거지, 악사 등 살아 움직이는 조선시대 캐릭터를 도입해 관람객과 소통하고, 놀이 공간에 호러 테마 전시와 체험 존을 조성해 이색적인 재미를 느낄 수 있으며, 40년간 한국의 민속 체험 관광 명소이자 아이들의 학습 현장으로 사랑받았으며, 새로운 즐거움을 선사하는 전통과 자연, 문화의 복합 테마 관광지이다.

Photo 7-1 Korean Folk Village, Credit, KFV.

Lying in a spacious site of 990,000m^2 and in nature-given geomantic location 'facing water and backgrounded by mountains', Korean Folk Village (KFV) is a village from the Joseon period composed of real houses relocated from provinces of the country.

Reconstructed through a long survey of houses remaining in different parts of the country and authentication by specialists, it is a real village from the Joseon period that unfolds in seasonal transformation scenes from everyday folk culture meticulously collected.

The village was created with common people's houses and aristocrats' houses relocated or restored from different parts of the country such as south, middle, north, and islands. It presents the real life from old Joseon life, which includes gwana (provincial government office), seowon and seodang (the educational institutions), hanyakbang (the medical institution), Buddhist temples and seonangdang (the religious buildings), and the fortune-teller's place. Visitors can meet various bamboo ware exuding an artisan's tact including items for daily life such as sewing box, Dutch wife, and basket as well as furniture, stationery, and playthings.

At the pyrography workshop, visitors can appreciate the process of drawing or writing on wood or paper with hot instruments as well as various pyrography. (Demonstration of pyrography).

2) Jeju Jeolmul Natural Recreation Forest : 제주절물자연휴양림

■ 장애물 없는 관광자원 부문

제주절물자연휴양림은 침엽수림이 우거져 삼림욕하기 좋으며, 길에 보편적 디자인(universal design, 장애의 유무나 연령 등에 관계없이 모든 사람들이 편하고 안전하게 이용할 수 있도록 설계하는 것)을 적용하여 교통 약자를 동반한 가족이나 단체 등이 함께 즐길 수 있도록 시설 편의를 제공하고, 산림 휴양 관광지가 온 국민이 편리하고 안전하게 숲의 혜택을 누릴 수 있는 장소로 인식되도록 나눔길을 조성하였다.

건강산책로와 함께 만남의길, 생이소리길, 너나들이길, 삼울길 등 5개 코스, 총 7km 구간에 '다함께 무장애 나눔길'을 설치, 휠체어나 유모차 이동이 수월하며, 산책 중에 쉬었다 갈 수 있는 간이 쉼터와 추락 방지 턱 등 편의 시설도 설치하였다.

제주절물자연휴양림 다함께 무장애 나눔길 산림 복지에서 소외된 장애인, 노약자, 임산부 등 교통 약자가 편리하고 안전하게 숲의 혜택을 누리게 하는 데 목적을 두어, 일정 구간마다 쉼터, 추락 방지 턱, 수목 표찰, 야외 탁자, 평상, 벤치 등 다양한 편의 시설을 조성해 휠체어나 유모차 등을 이용하기 편리하다.

<u>Photo 7-2</u> Jeju Jeolmul Natural Recreation Forest, Credit, Jeju City

With a total area of 300 hectares, Jeju Jeolmul Natural Recreation Forest, is mainly occupied by 30-to-45-year-old cedars: 100 hectares of natural forest, 200 hectares of artificial forest. In harmony with the cool breeze blowing in from the sea, on the trail built in a planted area of cedars and Japanese black pines, In the shade, visitors can feel a chill even in mid-summer. Cedars, the dominant trees in the forest have been planted since the mid-60s, at the same time scrub was removed.

As the well-built cedar plantation was developed into a natural recreation forest, it became the most famous rest area for most of the people who are visiting nation wide. There are various facilities that allow visitors to spend some quality time with their families or lovers: trails, a water spring, a pond, a public lawn, a woodcraft experience center, sports facilities, amusement facilities for children, and accommodations, etc.

In the case of the trail, it has a gentle slope without stairs that the elderly and children can use comfortably. The disabled can use wheelchairs if they are accompanied by guardians. Jeolmul Oreum, a parasite volcano, is located at an altitude of 697 meters, and one hour is enough time to hike to the top and walk back.

At the top, visitors can see a horseshoe-shaped crater from the observatory; also take in a grand view of Musuchon Stream, the largest stream in Jeju in the west: and see Jeju-si in the north. There is walking around about 2.3 kilometer-long photo is located at an altitude of 697meters, visitors can enjoy an unobstructed view of surroundings at the Oreum Observatory.

3) GyeongWonRu(慶源齋) Embassador : 경원재 앰배서더

■ 전통의 멋과 최상의 서비스를 제공하는 국내 최초 5성 한옥 호텔

고풍스런 전통미를 뽐내는 경원재 앰배서더는 특급 호텔 서비스가 접목된 국내 최대 규모의 한옥 호텔이다. 최근 호텔 최고 등급인 별 다섯 개를 획득해, 국내 한옥 호텔 최초로 5성 호텔, '한반도의 시간을 산책하다' 라는 콘셉트 아래 고려와 조선 시대 전통 건축양식으로 지은 경원재 앰배서더는 대한민국을 대표하는 명장들이 참여하여 한옥의 완성도를 높였다.

외부는 고풍스러운 건축미를 자아내고, 내부는 전통 한옥의 단점을 보완하고 호텔의 현대적인 편리함을 접목해 격조 있는 숙박 시설을 제공, 높은 현대 건축물 사이에서 고즈넉한 멋을 뽐내며 전통과 현대가 어우러진 한옥 호텔 경원재 앰배서더는 객실 30실, 영빈관 '경원루' 와 한식당 '수라', 연회장 '아리랑' 등으로 구성되었다.

한옥 호텔의 특징을 살려 전통 혼례를 진행하여 우리 민족 고유의 혼례 문화를 보존 · 계승하고, 나아가 동서양의 문화가 어우러진 결혼식 문화를 창조하는 데 앞장서면서 전통 혼례의 메카로 자리 잡았으며, 숙박만 하는 일반 호텔을 넘어 한옥, 한식, 한복 등을 체험할 수 있는 문화 공간으로 활용되면서 내국인 투숙객은 물론 외국인에게도 만족도가 높다.

모든 방문객을 대상으로 명장들의 작품을 직접 둘러보는 '스탬프 투어' 프로그램과 한복 체험 프로그램을 진행, 우리 문화에 대한 폭넓은 이해와 학습의 기회를 제공한다.

Photo 7-3 GyeongWonRu(慶源齋) Embassador Hotel, credit, GyeongWonRu

GyeongWonRu(慶源齋) built in the architectural style, Jusimpo(柱心包) of the Goryo Dynasty, exudes the beauty and pride of the Korean people.

This facility will accommodate business conferences, meetings, weddings and other large VIP gatherings.

With its woodlands, lakes, and lawns, the Songdo Central Park is a beautiful patch of nature in an urban landscape. Enjoy jogging and biking in the Central Park in accordance with an instructional map and get a breath of fresh air. Visitors from around the world, as well as, our native Koreans can bask in the ancient royalty of our Korean heritage.

Gyeongwonjae is equipped with a traditional Korean–style exterior, combined with the advantages of modern facilities including 30 luxurious rooms.

Experts in ancient architecture spent their time to restore the legacy of the past, Deluxe King Rooms featuring 'Ink wash painting" wallpaper, incorporating modern amenities for current day conveniences,

Deluxe Numaru is suitable for both family and business purposes with effective spacing. One double & one single beds add comfort to your stay,

the Ondol Room is a traditionally designed guestroom with a touch of Korea's own design.

Experience the authentic Korean style accommodation at our Ondol Room, Twelve Deluxe Suites featuring colorful and a unique pattern of beddings for sleeping on the floor (Ondol). These Suites allows one to experience a tradition of the past while enjoying a comfortable rest, Two Royal Suites are located separate from the Deluxe Rooms and Deluxe Suites, which will provide a quiet and private ambience.

4) N Seoul Tower : N서울타워

도심 속 로맨틱 아일랜드로 입지를 굳힌 남산서울타워는 예로부터 백년해로의 길지로 널리 알려진 남산(262m) 정상에 위치한 높이 236.7m의 탑으로, 해발 480m 위치에서 서울시를 360도 파노라마 뷰로 조망할 수 있는 최고의 전망을 자랑한다.

외국인이 선택한 관광 명소 1위로 꼽힌 바 있는 서울의 상징이자, 영원한 사랑을 꿈꾸는 전세계 연인들의 로맨스 성지이다.

연인들을 위한 로맨틱한 체험 콘텐츠 '사랑의 자물쇠'와 '하트 의자'가 큰 인기rk 있으며, 가족들을 위한 캐릭터 체험 전시관으로 '헬로키티아일랜드'와 '쎈토이뮤지엄&쇼룸' 등이 있다.

또한 서울 전경을 바라보며 즐길 수 있는 미슐랭 스타쉐프가 선사하는 고품격 프렌치코스 '엔그릴' 30여 종의 한식뷔페와 전통적인 한식 정찬 '한국' 등 특별한 다이닝이 갖추어져 있는 특별한 젊음과 낭만이 함께하는 곳이다.

Photo 7-4 Namsan(N)Seoul Tower, credit, seoul city

Namsan(N)Seoul Tower was built in 1969 as Korea's first integrated transmission tower beaming television and radio broadcasts across the capital. Since opening to the public in 1980, it has become a much-loved Seoul landmark.

The tower's main attractions include multi-colored digital art projected onto the tower at night, a digital observatory, a roof terrace, the HanCook restaurant, the n.Grill restaurant, and the Haneul (Sky) Restroom.

Namsan Seoul Tower's mountain surroundings on Namsan Mountain have made it a popular place to unwind for locals and tourists alike.

Seoul has a number of viewing platforms where visitors can enjoy the nighttime cityscape or gaze out onto the Hangang (River) but the tower's Digital Observatory is unique, offering an astonishing 360 degree panorama over the city, and 32 LCD screens recounting the 600-year history of Seoul. That is why the observatory is so popular and such a source of pride. Situated on top of the N Plaza, the Roof Terrace is a spacious wooden viewing deck whose exotic atmosphere makes it very popular with lovers. A recent attraction for courting couples is "Locks of Love," thousands of padlocks attached to the fence by romantic Seoulites symbolizing their undying affection.

5) Dongdaemun Design Plaza(DDP) : 동대문디자인플라자(DDP)

뉴욕타임즈가 뽑은 '2015년 꼭 가봐야 할 명소 52곳'에 선정된 동대문 DDP(동대문디자인플라자)는 '디자인 · 창조산업의 발신지'를 모토로 하는 복합문화공간이다.

DDP는 컨벤션, 전시, 공연, 패션쇼 등이 상시 이뤄지는 공간으로 세계 최대 규모의 3차원 비정형 랜드마크 건축물이고, 지하 3층, 지상 4층 규모의 DDP는 알림터, 배움터, 살림터, 디자인장터, 동대문역사문화공원의 5개 시설로 구성되어 총 15개 공간이다.

알림터는 디자인 창조산업의 신제품과 트렌드를 소개하는 공간, 배움터는 전시를 통해 지식을 전파하는 공간, 살림터는 다양한 최신 트렌드 상품을 접할 수 있는 공간으로 꾸며져 있다.

동대문역사문화공원은 새로운 이벤트와 만나고 쉬고 향유하는 열린 시민공원이며, 2015년 인스타그램 국내 최다 장소태그이고, 2015년 페이스북 국내 사용자에게 가장 인기있는 장소 5위, 'SBS별에서 온 그대, KBS2프로듀사, MBC그녀는 예뻤다' 촬영지이다.

Photo 7-5 Dongdaemun Design Plaza (DDP), credit, seoul city

DDP selected as one of the "Top 52 Places to Visit in 2015" by the New York Times, Dongdaemun Design Plaza (DDP) is the newest and most iconic landmark of the Korean design industry.

Located at the center of the Dongdaemun area, the DDP will serve as a key venue for design-related shows and conferences, exhibitions, and other events and gatherings. Designed by world renowned architect, Zaha Hadid, DDP is the world's largest atypical architecture. The DDP is comprised of five halls: Art Hall, Museum, Design Lab, Design Market, and Dongdaemun History and Culture Park.

The Art Hall is the primary launch pad for the Korean creative industry. The hall is a key venue for conventions, trade shows, exhibitions, fashion shows, concerts and performances.

The Museum Hall brings together Korean design and global trends. The Museum Hall is comprised of five sections: Design Playground, Design Dulle-gil(trail), Design Museum, Design Exhibition Hall, and the Design Rest Area. The Design Lab serves as an incubator for rising Korean and international creative product designers.

The Dongdaemun History & Culture Park is the newest park in downtown Seoul. The park gives a glimpse of how the area was once used as a military training ground during the Joseon dynasty. The park seamlessly extends onto the rooftop of DDP, making it a truly unique park in Korea.

There was most Instagram tagged location in Korea in the year 2015 and included in the list of the top 5 most popular places according to Korean Facebook users in 2015, also Was the filming location for the SBS drama "You Who Came from the Stars," the KBS2 drama "Producer," and the MBC drama "She Was Pretty."

6) Cheonggyecheon Stream : 청계천

종로구와 중구 사이를 가르는 10.84km의 하천. 청계천이라 하지만 청계천에는 무수히 많은 이야기가 농축되어 있는데, 그것은 600년 수도 서울이 가지는 역사이기도 하고, 서울 시민 개개인이 가진 소소한 추억이기도 한 장소이다.

2003년 7월부터 2005년 9월까지 청계천은 엄청난 변신을 도모한 청계천은 복개한 청계천로와 삼일로 주변 5.84km 구간을 복원하고 총 22개의 다리를 설치하는 등 시민들의 쉼터로 탈바꿈하기 위한 대대적인 공사 끝에 재탄생되었으며, 청계광장을 중심으로 각종 문화행사 등이 열리면서 지금은 광장의 역할도 하고 있으며, 최근에는 예술 공간으로서의 역할도 훌륭히 해내고 있다.

Photo 7-6 Cheonggyecheon Stream, credit, seoul city

광교 갤러리와 청계창작스튜디오 같은 창작 무대에서는 예술가들의 감성을 만날 수 있고, 주말에는 거리 예술가들의 공연이 펼쳐지는 곳이며, 청계천은 스물두 개의 다리가 놓인 5.84km 전 구간이 물길 따라 새로운 풍경을 드러내지만, 그 가운데 특별히 '청계8경' 이라 불리는 명소가로는 청계광장과 광통교, 정조반차도와 패션광장(문화의 벽), 청계천 빨래터와 소망의 벽, 존치교각(터널분수)과 버들습지 등은 청계천에서 놓쳐서는 안 될 비경일 뿐 아니라 각별한 의미의 장소이다.

Cheonggyecheon is an 11 km long modern stream that runs through downtown Seoul. Created as part of an urban renewal project, Cheonggyecheon is a restoration of the stream that was once there before during the Joseon Dynasty(1392~1910).

The stream was covered with an elevated highway after the Korean War(1950~1953), as part of the country's post-war economic development.

Then in 2003, the elevated highway was removed to restore the stream to its present form today. The stream starts from Cheonggye Plaza, a popular cultural arts venue, and passes under a total of 22 bridges before flowing into the Hangang (River), with many attractions along its length. Cheonggyecheon's turbulent history is on display at the Cheonggyecheon Museum which opened in September 2005.

The museum offers visitors the chance to learn about the many changes the stream has seen, including being buried underground and being restored. The story is told with the help of a scale-model and period photographs. Admission is free.

7) Seoul City Wall : 서울 한양도성

한양도성은 1396년 현재 서울의 도심부를 감싸고 있는 백악 · 낙타 · 목멱 · 인왕의 능선을 따라 처음 축조된 이후 여러 차례 개축되었으며, 평균 높이 약 7~8m, 전체 길이 약 18.6km에 이르며, 현존하는 세계의 도성 중 가장 오랫동안 도성 기능을 수행했다. 한양도성에는 4대문과 4소문이 있으며, 4대문은 숙정문 · 흥인지문 · 숭례문 · 돈의문이며, 4소문은 창의문 · 혜화문 · 광희문 · 소의문이다.

한양도성길은 창의문에서 혜화문에 이르는 백악 구간, 혜화문을 지나 흥인지문까지 이어지는 낙산 구간, 흥인지문에서 장충체육관에 이르는 흥인지문구간, 장충체육관에서 남산공원까지 이어지는 남산 구간, 백범광장을 지나 돈의문 터까지 이르는 숭례문 구간, 마지막으로 돈의문 터에서 창의문까지 이어지는 인왕산 구간으로 나누어진다.

Photo 7-7 The Seoul City Wall, credit, seoul city

The Seoul City Wall was originally built in 1396, surrounding Hanyang (present-day Seoul) during the Joseon Period (1392–1987).

The wall stretches for 18.6km along the ranges of Bugaksan (Mt.), Naksan (Mt.), Namsan (Mt.), and Inwangsan(Mt.), and stands at average height of 7~8m.

The Seoul City wall consisted of eight gates which were originally built between 1396–1398, but only six remain today.

The North, South, East, and West gates of the wall are known as the "Four Great Gates" (Sukjeongmun, Heunginjimun, Sungnyemun, Dongeuimun), while the Northwest, Northeast, Southwest, and Southwest gates are known as the "Four Small Gates" (Changuimun, Hyehwamun, Gwanghwamun, Soeuimun).

8) Hongdae : 홍대거리

서울의 밤은 안전하고 화려 함, 예술적인 분위기와 다양한 문화, 어두운 밤이 달빛을 거두어가는 새벽에도 그 빛을 잃지 않는 네온사인 빛으로 많은 젊은이들과 외국인들을 강한 힘으로 끌어들이고 있는 서울의 밤을 느껴 볼 수 있는 곳이다.

라이브 공연이 뿜어내는 에너지와 다양한 문화를 음미하고 싶다면, 1년, 365일 인디밴드의 공연이 이어지는 라이브클럽과 바가 있으며, 특별히 다른 젊음의 쇼핑장소가 있는 홍대거리이다.

홍대와 상수동 구석구석의 작은 공연이 열리는 카페와 바에는 다양한 장르의 음악을 라이브로 들려주는 개성 강한 인디아티스트의 공연을 즐기기 위해 많은 이들이 몰려들며, 작은 공간에서 뮤지션들과 같이 교감하며 즐기는 음악에는 비길 수 없는 매력이 있으며, 서울의 젊음과 열정을 즐기고 싶다면, 다양한 음악과 춤, 사람을 만날 수 있는 클럽이 있는 곳이다.

Photo 7-8 Hongdae Street, credit, seoul city

Hongdae is the scene where Korean culture, both pop and indie, manifests, especially at night. More information on planning a Sangam day trip can be soon found at K-stars and their K-style if the Korean Wave has washed over you, then there's no better place to tread the path of such tastemakers as Hongdae, the live-wire district of music and art culture.

Whether you've come on your own or with equally eager friends, the ever-trending university area remains the only place in Seoul where you can transition from daytime exploring to nighttime adventures just as easily as you shuffle through your K-Pop playlist.

Across the street and around the corner is a three-story store aptly named Around the Corner. Its multi-designer displays only cover two floors, but the smaller selection gives customers room to consider the subtler hip-hop motifs and mixed prints that punctuate the street wear-filled racks.

Remember, just because Hongdae is more casual and "free" than, say, Gangnam or Apgujeong, doesn't mean fashion doesn't matter. The vibe you can see from the stores and the people on the streets, is effortless with an edge of the true Hongdae touch.

9) Gwanghwamun Square : 광화문광장

조선 태조는 1394년에 도읍을 한양으로 옮기고 정국인 경복궁을 지었으며, 궁의 정문인 광화문 앞 길의 좌우에 의정부를 포함해 육조 관아 거리, 한양 최고의 길을 건설했으며, 2009년 그 길이 다시 열렸다.

광화문에서 청계광장에 이르는 광장이 들어선 것이며, 종로구 세종로에 위치한 광화문광장은 크게 광화문에서 청계천 방향으로 '광화문의 역사를 회복하는 광장', '육조 거리의 풍경을 재현하는 광장', '한국의 대표 광장', '시민들이 참여하는 도시문화 광장', '도심 속의 광장', '청계천 연결부'로 나뉨. 개별 공간의 특성을 바탕으로 역사성을 부활하고 문화와 휴식의 공간으로서 기능을 갖는다.

특히 '한국의 대표광장'은 세종대왕 동상이 자리해 광장의 구심점 역할을 하고 있고, 오가는 사람들의 발길로 항상 떠들석한 광화문 광장이지만 밤에는 고요하고 아름다운 야경 명소가 되고 있으며, 인왕산 자락을 배경으로 600년을 내려온 서울 경관의 중심이기에 야경뿐만 아니라 우리 민족의 얼과 역사까지도 느낄 수 있다.

Photo 7-9 Gwanghwamun Square, credit, seoul city

Gwanghwamun Square is located on Sejong-ro in Jongno-gu and is vast in size. Gwanghwamun Square stretches out from Gwanghwamun Gate, towards Cheonggyecheon Stream, and is divided into 6 sections: "Recovering the History of Gwanghwamun Gate Plaza," "Reenacting Yukjo Street Plaza," "Korea Main Plaza," "Civil Participation Urban Culture Plaza," "Downtown Plaza" and "Cheonggyecheon Stream Connector."

In 2009, the square was redeveloped into a space of historical revival, culture, and relaxation. The focal point of the square is the statue of King Sejong the Great. During the day, the square is always busy with people but at night it is a tranquil and beautiful tourist attraction.

Gwanghwamun Square, with Inwangsan Mountain just behind it, is not just a beautiful tourist locale. The square has over 600 years of history and it is a place where the spirit of the Korean nation can be felt.

10) Lotte World Adventure : 롯데월드 어드벤처

롯데월드 어드벤처는 실내 어드벤처와 호수공원인 실외 매직 아일랜드로 나뉘어 있으며, 롯데월드에 들어서면 가장 먼저 만나는 곳이 어드벤쳐이며, '작은 지구 마을' 을 테마로 조성된 어드벤처는 거대한 돔 형태의 실내 테마 파크로 날씨나 계절의 제약을 받지 않아 좋다.

이곳에는 22종의 놀이 기구가 설치되어 있고 시즌별로 리우삼바카니발, 할로윈파티, 크리스마스 축제 등이 펼쳐지며, 석촌호수 가운데 자리한 매직 아일랜드에는 총 17종의 놀이 기구가 있는데 그 중에서도 자이로스윙, 자이로드롭, 아틀란티스 등은 짜릿한 스릴을 느낄 수 있는 인기 최고의 놀이 기구가 설치되어 있고, 매직 아일랜드 호수에서 뱃놀이를 즐길 수 있으며, 석촌 호수를 유유히 떠가는 제네바 유람선이나 단둘이서 오붓하게 백조보트를 타면서 낭만적인 시간을 가질 수 있다.

Photo 7-10 Lotte World Adventure, credit, Lotte World

Opened in 1989, Lotte World Adventure is a major recreation complex located in downtown Seoul.

It consists of Indoor Adventure, the world's largest indoor theme park, an outdoor theme park called Magic Island, a luxury hotel, the Korean Folk Museum, shopping malls, department stores, sports facilities and a movie theater, all in one place.

Indoor Adventure is the world's largest indoor theme park and hosts a dazzling variety of seasonal festivals and parades all year round and features 22 different rides.

Magic Island, the outdoor theme park of Lotte World, is an artificial island located in the middle of Seokchon Lake and boasts 17 different rides including the high-altitude free-fall thrill ride, the Gyro Drop.

11) Bomun tourism area : 보문관광단지

■장애물 없는 관광자원

1971년 정부에서 수립한 경주종합개발계획사업의 일환으로 종합휴양지 조성을 목적으로 개발된 보문관광단지는 경주지역의 역사적 특성을 살려 고대와 현대가 잘 어우러지도록 조성하여 전 지역이 온천지구 및 관광특구로 지정되어 있다.

특급호텔과 국제회의시설, 각종 레저 및 휴양시설, 사이버관광 안내시스템과 각종 기반시설 등 세계 관광객들이 언어와 문화의 장벽을 느끼지 않고 안락하게 체류할 수 있도록 관광인프라가 완비되어 각국 정상들이 찾는 세계수준의 관광단지로 동해안 감포 관광단지의 연계 개발과 더불어 한국관광산업의 1번지로서 뿐만 아니라 국제적인 종합관광휴양단지로 자리매김 하고 있다. 사계절 관광객이 이용할 수 있는 온천형 관광지로 개발하고 우아하고 정취 있는 전통적 이미지가 창출될 수 있는 내륙형 관광 휴양지로 개발하기 위해 꾸준히 노력하고 있다.

사이버 관광안내시스템과 각종 기반 시설 등 사이버 관광안내시스템과 각종 기반 시설 등 관광인프라가 완비된 국제적인 종합관광휴양단지이다. 연간 800만 명 이상의 관광객이 방문하는 종합관광휴양단지, 보문호를 주변으로 보문호반길, 경관교량(물너울교), 수상공연장, 보문호 유람선 및 오리배 운영 등 체험거리와 정기적인 축제, 공연 등 다양한 볼거리 제공, 장애인을 포함한 남녀노소 누구나 보문호의 멋진 전경을 감상하며 몸과 마음을 힐링할 수 있는 새로운 '열린 관광지' 명소이다.

Photo 7-11 Bomun tourism area, credit, gyeongju City

International convention halls at Bomun Lake Resort offer you exquisite services. The convention halls of all international luxurious hotels at Bomun Lake Resort are equipped with a full range of latest facilities enough to hold a variety of international conventions, seminars, exhibitions and performances.

Accommodate up to 2,000 people at once, and a 6-language simultaneous interpretation system and the latest audio-visual equipments are furnished. It accommodates up to 1,000 people (Convention hall is equipped with a 5-lahguage simultaneous interpretation system.

The Gyeongju World Culture Expo Park will put on various cultural programs for visitors on the themes of vivid culture and hands-on experience in Korean history. Small, beautiful gardens within Bomun Lake Resort help you enjoy the romantic adventure and pleasure of travel.

These gardens are also ideal for fun with family, lover or friend. If you walk around the garden path, your feeling will be much better and more relaxed. Located at the entrance of Bomun Lake Resort, this garden is surrounded by low rolling hills and pine forests, where you can feel like you are walking through a peaceful forest deep in mountains.

12) Jeju Global Geopark : 세계 지질 공원

지질공원이란 과거로부터 배우고 익혀서 지속가능한 미래를 만들어나가는 것(2010년 유럽지질공원 총회에서 정의된 지질공원의 의미하며, 지질공원이란 인간에 의해 만들어진 인공적인 공원이 아니며, 지질공원은 과학적 중요성, 희귀성, 아름다움을 지닌 지질 현장으로서 지질학적 중요성뿐만 아니라 생태학적, 고고학적, 역사적, 문화적 가치도 함께 지니고 있는 지역으로 보전, 교육 및 관광을 통하여 지역경제의 발전을 도모하고자 조성했다.

제주는 뛰어난 경관을 자랑할 뿐만 아니라 약 180만 년 전부터 1천 년 전까지 화산활동의 흔적이 원형 그대로 보존돼 있어 학술적으로 연구가치가 매우 높은 지역, 이런 가치를 인정받아 2010년 섬 전체가 유네스코 세계지질공원으로 인증됐고 그 중에서도 특히 경관이 아름다운 한라산 · 만장굴 · 성산일출봉 · 서귀포층 · 천지연폭포 · 중문대포주상절리 · 산방산 · 용머리해안 · 수월봉 등 9곳이 핵심지질명소로 지정돼 세계지질공원 네트워크(GGN)에 가입돼 있으며, 2014년 3월, 우도 · 비양도 · 선흘곶자왈이 추가돼 핵심지질명소는 총 12으로 늘어났다.

특히 한라산은 한라산은 1,950m의 높이를 자랑하는 한라산은 남한에서 가장 높은 산으로 세계지질공원과 함께 생물권 보전지역과 세계자연유산으로도 등재돼 있는 제주의 보물이며, 정상부에는 깊이 108m, 너비 550m의 백록담 분화구가 있으며 약 40여 개의 오름과 천태만상의 영실기암 등 파괴되지 않은 화산지형을 관찰하는데 최고의 장소, 현재 정상을 오를 수 있는 관음사, 성판악 탐방로 외에도 어리목, 돈내코, 영실, 석굴암, 어승생악 탐방로 등 7개의 탐방로가 개방돼 있다.

Photo 7-12 Jeju Global Geopark, credit, Jeju City

Geopark is to learn from the past and make a sustainable future(The definition of a geopark as defined at the 2010 Europe Geopark General Assembly). Geopark is not an artificial park made by humans. Geopark is a geological site with scientific importance, rarity, and beauty.

In addition to their geological importance, Geoparks also embrace ecological, historical, and cultural values. Geoparks have been created to promote the regional economy through preservation, education, and tourism.

Jeju Global Geopark, Besides the magnificent landscape, Jeju is also of great significance in terms of academic research, as there are traces of volcanic activities occurring from 1.8 million years to one thousand years ago in their original states.

Such value was recognized by UNESCO and the entire Jeju Island was designated as a UNESCO global geopark in 2010.

In particular, nine places with majestic landscape – namely, Hallasan Mountain, Manjanggul Cave, Seongsan Ilchulbong Peak, Seogwipo Stratum, Cheonjiyeon Waterfall, Jungmun Daepo Columnar Jointed Lava, Sanbangsan Lava Dome, Yongmeori Tuff Ring, and Suwolbong Peak – have been designated as main geological sites and listed in the Global Geopark Network (GGN).

Now there are 12 main geological sites in total listed by the GGN, after Udo Island, Biyangdo Island, and Seonheul Gotjawal(Gotjawal : a unique forest in Jeju)were added to the list since March 2014.

13) HILTON HOTEL BUSAN : 힐튼호텔 부산

해외 휴양지가 부럽지 않은 동부산 해안에 위치한 '도심형 리조트' 힐튼 부산은 아름다운 해안절경과 산을 배경으로 한 레저, 회의 및 컨벤션, 웨딩을 위한 완벽한 공간이다.

현대적인 10층 건물은 천혜의 환경과 조화를 이뤄 평온한 휴식과 다채로운 경험을 제공, 310개의 객실에서는 안락함을, 4개의 레스토랑과 바에서는 세계적인 맛과 멋을 즐길 수 있다.

부산 최대 면적의 연회장에서는 성공적인 회의 및 이벤트를, 부산의 유일한 웨딩 채플에서는 극적이고 로맨틱한 웨딩을 경험 할 수 있으며, 호텔 그 자체뿐만 아니라, 호텔 주변의 유명한 역사 문화 관광지와 편의시설인 해동 용궁사, 송정 해수욕장, 국립부산과학관, 롯데 프리미엄 아울렛을 방문하여 이곳의 문화와 멋을 즐길 수 있다.

Photo 7-13 HILTON HOTEL BUSAN, credit, HILTON HOTEL

Located 15 minutes away from Haeundae Beach and 25 minutes from the BEXCO and Centum City areas, Hilton Busan is situated on the Eastern shore of the city. Sitting right on the ocean coastline and surrounded by natural settings, this unique location makes our hotel a true getaway destination, on the doorstep of the Busan megalopolis.

A unique urban hotel by the sea at HILTON BUSAN, The ultimate business and leisure destination in Busan, Hilton Busan offers a unique, urban retreat right on the seafront.

There is 10-story hotel boasts indoor and outdoor dining venues, swimming pools, a health club, meeting and event space and more. Explore Busan's famous beaches and soak up the local culture at nearby shops, temples, museums and attractions.

Whether conducting business, keeping up with a fitness routine or looking to spend quality time with your family, our Hilton hotel is here to make the most of your stay by offering the services you need, the amenities you expect, and the extras you deserve. There are designed with comfort and convenience in mind; providing a place to unwind or to catch up on work. Explore the various types of rooms, explore the amenities, and choose the space that's right for you.

14) Museum of Silhak(Practical Learning) : 실학박물관

실학은 17~19세기의 세계사적 변화를 가장 선진적으로 대변하고 체계화한 사상으로서, 조선후기라는 시대적 배경 아래에서 개혁성과 현실 지향성을 지니며 발생하고 발전하였으며, 오늘날 한국학 연구의 뿌리도 실학에서 그 연원을 찾을 수 있으며, 경기도는 실학이 태동하고 성장 · 발전했던 곳일 뿐만 아니라 실학 관련한 문화유산을 가장 많이 보유한 지역이다.

따라서 한강유역을 중심으로 경기도 곳곳엔 실학자들이 생활터전으로 삼고 학문을 연구했던 유적지가 많이 남아 있으며, 이것이 바로 실학 대학자이신 다산 정약용 선생의 생가 옆에 실학박물관이 자리한 연유이다.

실학박물관은 실학 및 실학과 관련된 유 · 무형의 자료와 정보를 수집 · 보존 · 연구 · 교류 · 전시하며 지역 주민에게 교육과 정보, 다양한 프로그램을 통한 즐거움을 제공하는 다목적 차원의 문화복합공간으로서의 역할을 하고 있는 대한민국 유일의 실학관련 박물관이다.

Photo 7-14 Museum of Silhak, credit, Gyeonggi-do

Practical Learning occurs Ginny said the reforms and real orientation under the historical background of ideas as a representation and organizing the world-historical changes of the 17th and 19th centuries, the most advanced, and has developed Joseon. The roots of today's Korean studies can also find the origin in practical science.

Gyeonggi-do is a practical science is quickening, and growth and development as well as gotil who held the most cultural heritage related to practical science area. Gyeonggi silhakja around the Han River are a lot of sites that remain samgo research studies in life grounds.

This is also a very practical science museum is located next to the birthplace of condensed practical science teacher college jayisin Dasan Jeong. This museum is the tangible and intangible resources and information collection, preservation, research, exchanges and exhibitions, and education and information, and versatile dimensional cultural complex space serves as the providing pleasure through a variety of programs to local residents related to practical science and practical science Practical Learning of the only domestic construction is related to the museum.

The practical science museum will spread out to new practical science movement many people who experience air easily fold the practical science in their lives through research, exhibitions, and various educational programs.

15) Suwon Hwaseong Cultural Festival : 수원화성문화제

조선 제22대 정조대왕의 효심과 부국강병의 원대한 꿈으로 축성된 세계문화유산 수원화성에서 수원의 대표적인 전통문화관광축제인 '수원화성문화제'가 매년 가을에 개최, 수원화성문화제의 하이라이트인 정조대왕 능행차를 필두로 혜경궁 홍씨 진찬연 등의 재현행사이며, 수원천에서 아름답게 펼쳐지는 수원사랑등불축제 등 다채로운 공연과 체험행사로 국내외 관광객들의 눈과 귀를 즐겁게 해 줄 '수원화성문화제' 2017년 가을, 과거와 현대가 조화롭게 어우러진 문화예술의 고장 수원에서 각종 먹을거리, 볼거리 등도 마음껏 즐기고 조선시대의 모습도 생생히 체험, 문화체육관광부 지정 2017 문화관광 유망축제로 선정됐다.

Photo 7-15 Suwon Hwaseong Cultural Festival, credit, Suwon-City

Korea first 22 tank Maharaja of piety and rich gangbyeong won a major heritage tourism festival in Suwon in the consecration to the Dream World Heritage Hwaseong Fortress of Suwon Hwaseong Cultural Festival 'in the come be held in the fall of every year.

Led by highlighting the virtue Great performance by all means of Suwon Hwaseong Cultural Festival hyegyeonggung Hong jinchanyeon such reproduction events, and colorful performances and experience events such as the beautiful unfolding Suwon Love Lantern Festival in Suwoncheon give delight to the eyes and ears of the domestic and foreign tourists Suwon Hwaseong Cultural festival " 2017 autumn and various food from broken neck of the past and modern culture and art blend harmoniously, unlimited attractions also enjoy hope to see it also vividly experience state of the Joseon Dynasty. Cultural specified, Sports and Tourism 2017 Cultural chosen tourism as a promising festival.

16) The Westin Chosun Seoul : 신세계조선호텔

古한 터가 福을 더해드리는 호텔 웨스틴 조선 호텔, 서울 웨스틴조선호텔은 예로부터 양택 대명당으로 알려져 있으며, 지금의 서울 웨스틴조선호텔 자리는 과거 고종황제가 천신께 제를 올리던 '환구단' 이 자리하고 있던 만큼 최고의 명당 터로 바이어나 사업가들도 거래를 성사시키려면 서울 웨스틴조선호텔에서 만나라는 말도 있다.

100년 역사가 스며든 대한민국 최초의 연회 공간, 그랜드 볼룸은 행사 성격 및 규모에 맞게 두 곳으로 나누어 독립적으로 사용할 수 있으며 연회 스타일로 최대 450명까지 수용이 가능, 환구단의 아름다움을 만끽할 수 있는 2층 연회장은 최대 250명의 연회가 가능한 오키드룸과 각종 모임 및 회의에 편리한 4개의 별실로 이루어져 있다.

한편 호텔 웨스틴 조선호텔의 상생경영전략에 의한 휴가활성화 제도 및 프로그램을 통하여 임직원들에게 충분한 휴식과 업무스트레스를 해소할 수 있는 기회를 제공하고, 이를 통하여 직장 만족도 증대 및 업무 생산성을 향상시키기 위한 올바른 휴가문화를 촉진하여 관광산업 발전 및 지역경제 활성화에 노력하고 있다.

Photo 7-16 The Westin Chosun Seoul, credit, Chosun Hotel

It has been almost a century since our hotel was first established in 1914 and for all these years, the Westin Chosun Seoul has long been synonymous with luxurious accommodation and first-class service in Korea.

The Westin Chosun Seoul is located in the heart of Seoul, where Prince Ko-Jong was known to perform a traditional ceremony (Jesa) to honor his ancestors. Since the beginning, this splendid hotel was used to house guests of state, dignitaries, foreign officials, as well as being the center of political, economic, and social gatherings.

At the end of the Japanese occupation in 1945, President Syngman Man Rhee proceeded to change the hotel's name to "Chosun Hotel" from the Japanese name "Chosen Hoteru". Soon after Independence Day, the hotel was at the center of a series of historic events, such as the U.S. occupation during the Korean War, the invasion of Incheon Beach and the establishment of the 3rd Republic.

In 1979, the world famous Westin International Hotel group invested in The Chosun Hotel, leading to our current name, The Westin Chosun Seoul. In 1995, Shinsegae took over The Westin Chosun Seoul, making it the first hotel in Korea to be 100 % locally owned. Grand banquet hall and 6 mid-sized banquet halls equipped with state-of-the-art equipment fitness center, swimming pool, sauna, business center, beauty salon, barber shop, sundry shop, flower shop.

17) The Upo Ramsar Wetland : 우포늪

경상남도 창녕 우포늪은 우리나라 최대의 자연늪지이다. '늪' 이라고 하면 가장 규모가 큰 우포늪뿐만 아니라 목포, 사지포, 쪽지벌 등 네 개의 늪을 모두 아우르며, 둘레는 7.5㎞에 전체면적은 2,314,060m²임. 이곳에 늪지가 처음 형성되기 시작한 것은 1억 4,000만 년전며, 공룡시대였던 중생기 백악기 당시에 해수면(海水面)이 급격히 상승하고 낙동강 유역의 지반이 내려앉아, 낙동강으로 흘러들던 물이 고이게 되면서 곳곳에 늪지와 자연호수가 생겨났다.

현재 진리에는 그 당시 것으로 추정되는 공룡발자국화석이 남아있으며, 늪의 바닥에는 수천만 년 전부터 숱한 생명체들이 생멸(生滅)을 거듭한 끝에, 억겁을 세월을 간직한 이 부식층이 있기에 우포늪은 '생태계의 고문서', 또는 '살아있는 자연사박물관' 이라고 불린다.

1960년대 초에 백조도래지(천연기념물 제15호)로 지정됐다가 급격한 개발로 인해, 백조 수가 급감하자 천연기념물 지정이 취소되었으나, '생태계 보호지역' (1997년)과 '람사조약' 에 의한 국제보호습지(1998년)로 지정된 이후로는 예전의 생태계가 빠르게 되살아나고 있다.

우포늪은 생태계 보전지역으로 자연환경보전법 적용을 받고 있어 낚시, 논우렁 채취 등을 금지하고 있으며, 현재 우포늪 일대에는 430여 종의 식물이 분포하고, 우리나라 전체 식물종류의 10%에 해당되며, 수생식물의 종류는 우리나라 전체의 50~60%를 차지한다.

Photo 7-17 The Upo Ramsar Wetland, credit, Changnyeong-Gun

It is recognized and protected under the Ramsar Convention held in March, 1998 and the Ramsar List of Wetlands of International Importance and it was designated as a Wetland Protected Area in February, 1999 and as a Natural Reserve (No.524) in January, 2011 by the Ministry of Environment and in February, 2012, the natural wetland areas around the Upo Wetland that need rehabilitation was designated as a wetland rehabilitation zone (62,940m^2).

Wetland Protected Area has an area of 8.547km^2 and the Natural Reserve has an area of 3.438km^2. The area of submerged part of Upo Wetland is approximately 2.313km^2. There are two competing views about the origin of Upo Wetland. One says that the Wetland was created 140 million years ago and the other says that it was created in B.C 4,000 which is about 6,000 years ago.

However, in the sedimentary rocks near the Upo Weltand, footprints of a dinosaur which existed approximately 110 ~ 120 million years ago, fossilized raindrop patterns, insect fossils have been found and the claim that the wetland was created 140 million years ago is regarded as the more probable one.

Upo Wetland is a vast wetland full of beautiful aquatic vegetation that includes cattails, irises, reeds, water rice, water chestnuts, hornworts, arrowheads and thorn lotuses, Yellow Floating Heart lotuse, and summer migratory birds such as the Pheasant-Tailed Jacana, Grey Heron, Night Heron and winter migratory like the Whooper Swan, Falcated Duck, Eurasian Spoonbill, Bean Goose. Resident birds like the Little Grebe, Eurasian Eagle-Owl, Daurian Redstart and Common Kestrel can be found as well.

18) Suncheon Bay : **순천만습지**(구 순천만자연생태공원)

순천시 교량동과 대대동, 해룡면의 중흥리, 해창리 선학리 등에 걸쳐 있는 순천만 갈대밭의 총 면적은 약 15만 평에 달하며, 순천 시내를 관통하는 동천과 순천시 상사면에서 흘러 온 이사천의 합수 지점부터 하구에 이르는 3㎞ 쯤의 물길양쪽이 죄다 갈대밭으로 뒤덮혀 있다.

순천만 갈대 군락지는 국내 최대 규모이며, 39.8km의 해안선에 둘러싸인 21.6㎢의 갯벌, 5.4㎢의 갈대밭 등 27㎢의 하구 염습지와 갯벌로 이루어진 순천만 일대에 갈대밭만 무성한 게 아니며, 가까이 다가가 보면 물억새, 쑥부쟁이등이 곳곳마다 크고 작은 무리를 이루어 자리 잡고 있다.

하구의 갈대밭 저편에는 불그스레한 칠면초 군락지도 들어서 있고, 이곳은 흑두루미, 재두루미, 황새, 저어새, 검은머리물떼새 등 국제적인 희귀조이거나 천연기념물로 지정된 11종이 날아드는 곳으로 전 세계 습지 가운데 희귀 조류가 가장 많은 지역으로 알려져 있으며, 이와 같은 희귀조류 이외에도 도요새, 청둥오리, 혹부리오리, 기러기 등을 포함해 약 140종의 새들이 이곳 순천만 일대에서 월동하거나 번식하고 있다.

Photo 7-18 Suncheon Bay, credit, Suncheon City

Suncheon bay is located to the East on the Korean south cost. The administrative area of Suncheon Bay is more than 75km², and the total area of exposed land during ebb tide is 12km². Suncheon Bay A wetland region connectiong land and sea, Wetlands, including "swamps," "marshes" and "bogs', is an area of transition connecting sea and land.

It is sometimes referred to as the "swirl of life" or the "lungs of the earth" because of the rich abundance of life filling it. The Suncheon Bay wetland expands over the area where the Dong-cheon and Isa-cheon rivers meet. These two rivers contribute all the components needed to form the wetland. A recent increase in their flowing-slope has added a current that is increasing the development of the wetland.

As a saltwater wetland, Suncheon Bay is extremely unique to the Korean Peninsula and is therefore named as a preservation area in light of ecological development and protection. A bed of reeds and suede japonica provides a habitat for migratory birds. This results in a beautiful sight that charms tourists and lures them to experience the wetland.

19) Jeonju Hanok village : 전주 한옥마을

전주한옥마을은 전주시 풍남동과 교동에 위치해 있고, 한국의 전통 건물인 한옥(韓屋)이 800여 채나 밀집되어 있으며 빠르게 변화는 도시 속에 옛 것을 그대로 간직한 전주한옥마을은 한국의 옛 전통을 맛볼 수 있는 곳으로 유명하다.

전주한옥마을의 멋은 무엇보다도 한옥의 아름다운 특징이고 멋이고, 한옥의 구조는 크게 안채와 사랑채로 나누어져 있으며 안채는 여인들이 머무는 곳으로 규수방이 있고, 사랑채는 남자들이 사용하던 곳으로 선비방으로 되어 있다.

한옥의 특징은 온돌방인데, 한국은 주로 앉아서 생활하기 때문에 바닥에 온돌을 깔며, 온돌의 구조는 방 밖에 아궁이(함실)을 만들고 구들(아궁이 안쪽)밑으로 불을 때면 온돌이 따뜻하게 데워지고, 여름에는 시원하고 겨울에는 따뜻하다는 것이 온돌의 가장 큰 특징인데, 이곳에 가면 한옥생활체험관이 따로 마련되어 있다.

Photo 7-19 Jeonju Hanok village, credit, Jeonju City

The first place the Japanese stayed was outside of West Gate, around Jeonjucheon River, near present Daga-dong. Outside of West Gate was usually a residential area for the lower classes or tradespeople.

At the time, the inside and outside of the castle had a clear difference of the social class. The castle was existed to represent the difference of the social class. Koreans began to form the Korean-style house village around Gyo-dong and Pungnam-dong as the repulsion against the extension of Japanese's power before and after 1930.

This was the consciousness of a conflict against Japanese houses and the expression of national pride. Korean-style houses of Gyo-dong and Pungnam-dong formed in 1930's were contrasted with Japanese-style and directed the strange city color harmonizing with the western style.

Jeonju is a city where the 2002 FIFA World Cup was held. Taking this opportunity, the city has been promoting Hanok village construction project since the event.

There are also a variety of historic sites, such as Gyeonggijeon, Jindong Catholic church, Pungnam-dong, Omokdae, Hyanggyo, Gyeonhwon site of an ancient castle, Namgosanseong, etc. along with various traditional culture facilities like Traditional Culture Center, Crafts Exhibition Hall, Luxury Goods Store and so on.

Therefore, many specialists and citizens are pointing out the importance of governmental administration of Jeonju Hanok to preserve the history and tradition of urban housing culture of Korea.

20) Hoengseong SoopCheWon : 국립 횡성 숲체험원

국립횡성숲체원은 하늘 높이 뻗은 잣나무 숲과 자작나무 숲이 아름다운 전문적인 '산림복지서비스를 제공하는 공공기관' 으로 청태산 해발 850m에 위치하고 있으며, 숲을 통해 느끼는 자연의 가치는 사람이 느낄 수 있는 감성 이상의 행복과 희망을 갖게 하고, 모든 사람들에게 소중한 경험시키고자 국립횡성숲체원은 더 많은 사람들에게 이러한 산림의 특별한 가치를 누리게 해주고자 만들어진 편안한 숲속의 쉼터이다.

숲에 존재하는 다양한 환경요소, 자연물 등을 이용하여 활용하여 인체의 면역력을 높이고, 신체적 정신적 건강을 회복시키는 산림복지서비스를 제공하고 있다.

산림복지는 산림을 국민복리 증진에 적극 활용하기 위해 도입된 새로운 정책적 개념이며, 산림문화 · 휴양, 산림치유 및 교육 등의 서비스를 창출、제공함으로써 국민의 복리 증진에 기여하기 위한 경제적 · 사회적 · 정서적 지원과 관련된 활동으로, 이 개념을 실현하기 위하여 운영되고 있는 것이 국립 횡성 숲체험원이다.

Photo 7-20 Hoengseong SoopCheWon, credit, The Korea Forest Service in KOREA.

National Forest Healing Center is a forest welfare complex that is established to improve people's health and increase quality of life by using abundant forest resources of the Baekdudaegan Mountain Ridge.

National Forest Health Center not only provides a forest healing service, but also educates manpower specializing in forest healing, develops products related to forest healing, and expands the culture of forest healing.

It is Korea's first recreational facility owned by Korea Forest Welfare Institute which focuses on forest education.

It has been built to be environment-friendly byaiming at user's safety and convenience and by considering the efficiency of facility management, it has developed programs to customize to all ages and types.

It has been established to perform various functions such as improving people's awareness about the importance and value of our forest and actualizing social unification.

Tourism Guide Quiz

1. Recommend one of the best tourist attractions representing Changnyeong-Gun.
2. Explain Korean Folk Village.
3. Introduce Seoul City Wall briefly.
4. Recommend one of the best attractions near Suncheon City.
5. Introduce Gwanghwamun Square.

수행 Tips : The ability to raise 한국관광 100선 사례

2017 한국관광 100선 선정결과, 자료출처 : 한국관광공사

지역		관광지
수도권	서울(11)	서울 5대 고궁 ***
		명동거리 **
		북한산 국립공원***
		롯데월드
		북촌한옥마을 ***
		홍대거리
		동대문디자인플라자 & 동대문시장 **
		인사동 ***
		이태원 관광특구
		남산 N서울타워 ***
		광장시장 **

지역		관광지
수도권	경기(11)	수원화성 ***
		용인 한국민속촌***
		광명동굴
		용인 에버랜드 **
		양평 두물머리***
		포천 국립수목원*
		과천 서울랜드 & 서울대공원
		연천 한탄강관광지**
		파주 DMZ
		가평 아침고요수목원**
		파주 헤이리예술마을**
	인천(2)	차이나타운* & 송월동동화마을
		송도 센트럴파크

지역		관광지
충청권	대전(2)	장태산 자연휴양림**
		계족산 황톳길**
	충북(3)	단양팔경***
		괴산 산막이 옛길**
		청주 청남대
	충남(5)	공주 공산성
		공주 무령왕릉**
		태안 안면도***
		서천 국립생태원**
		서산 해미읍성**
호남권	광주(2)	광주 대인예술시장
		광주 양림동 역사문화마을
	전북(6)	전주한옥마을***
		마이산*
		완주 삼례문화예술촌
		임실 치즈마을**
		군산시간여행**(근대문화유산)
		부안 변산반도**
	전남(9)	순천만습지*** & 순천만국가정원
		담양 죽녹원**
		신안 홍도
		청산도
		장흥 정남진 토요시장
		여수 오동도** & EXPO 해양공원

지역		관광지
호남권	전남(9)	강진 가우도
		보성 녹차밭***
		곡성 섬진강 기차마을***
경상권	부산(4)	감천문화마을**
		부산 원도심 스토리투어
		국제시장 & 부평깡통시장
		태종대***
	대구(2)	방천시장 & 김광석 다시 그리기길**
		대구근대골목***
	울산(4)	영남 알프스
		태화강 십리대숲
		대왕암공원
		간절곶*
	경북(7)	울릉도 & 독도***
		경주 불국사 & 석굴암***
		경주 동궁과월지 & 첨성대**
		안동 하회마을***
		울진 금강송 숲길
		포항운하 & 죽도시장
		영덕 대게거리
	경남(8)	진주성***
		합천 해인사***
		창녕 우포늪***
		통영 동피랑마을**

지역		관광지
경상권	경남 (8)	거제 바람의 언덕
		남해 독일마을**
		통영 소매물도***
		거제 해금강***
강원권	강원 (12)	설악산***
		평창 대관령**
		춘천 남이섬***
		오대산**
		삼척 대이리 동굴지대*
		고성 DMZ
		강릉 커피거리**
		홍천 비발디파크 & 오션월드
		속초해변
		강릉 경포대***
		원주 뮤지엄 산(SAN)**
		인제 원대리 자작 나무 숲 **

지역		관광지
제주권	제주 (12)	한라산***
		성산일출봉**
		올레길***
		우도***
		쇠소깍**
		제주절물자연휴양림
		섭지코지**
		비자림 & 사려니숲 길**
		서귀포 매일올레시장
		돌문화 공원
		지질트레일
		에코랜드 테마파크

2017년 신규(■, 33개),
* 2013년, 2017년 2회 선정지 (5개) ,
** 2015년, 2017년 2회 선정지(32개),
*** 2013년부터 3회 연속 선정지(30개)

Unit 8

Korean Food

Domestic Tour Guide English

Unit 8

Korean Food

오랜 옛날부터 한국인들은 '밥이 보약' 이라는 속담에 따라 음식이 약과 같은 기능을 수행할 수 있다는 신념을 견지해 왔다. 음식을 어떻게 먹고 소비하는가에 건강과 병을 얻을 수 있다는 믿음과 생각은 음식이 도움이 되지 않을 때 약을 사용한다는 기본적인 원리로, 한국 전통 의술 발전에 결정적인 역할을 했다.

Since ancient times, the Korean people have maintained a belief that food and medicine have the same origin and hence perform the same function, following the adage that 'food is the best medicine'.

They believe that health and illness alike come from the food they consume and how they eat it, and this idea has played a crucial role in the development of traditional Korean medicine whose basic principle is that we should use medicine only after food has failed.

1) Fermentation of Food : 발효 음식

한국 전통음식을 이해하는데 키워드중의 하나는 발효이며, 오랜 기간 저장되어져 영양적 특성과 맛을 증가시킬 수 있도록 성숙을 돕는 변형과정을 말한다. 전통 발효음식을 대표한다 할 수 있는 한국의 된장, 고추장, 간장 등은 어떤 장소에서든 몇 달부터 여러 해 동안 발효시킨다. 발효의 정도는 레스토랑이나 집에서 요리할 때 양념과 맛을 내는 핵심요소이다.

One of the key words to understanding traditional Korean food is fermentation, a metabolic process that helps food to 'mature' so that it has improved taste and nutritional properties and can be stored for a longer period.

The Korean foods that best represent the tradition of fermentation developed in Korea include doenjang (soybean paste), ganjang (soy sauce), Gochu-jang (chili paste) and jeotgal (salted seafood), whose fermentation can take anywhere from several months to several years.

The degree of fermentation is a key factor in the taste and flavor of food cooked at home and in restaurants

2) **Doenjang**(Soybean Paste) **and Ganjang**(Soy Sauce)

한국 전통음식의 가장 중요한 두가지 품목은 간장과 된장이며, 그것들을 만들기 위해서는 충분히 요리될 때까지 끓이거나 물에 흠뻑 젖도록 하는 것이 필요하다. 장을 만드는데 주 원료는 콩이며, 콩을 삶아 쪄서 메주로 만들어 발효시킨 후 소금물에 우려낸 것이 간장이고, 우려내고 남은 메주를 으깨 소금 간하여 다시 발효 시킨 것이 된장이다.

Two of the most important items of traditional fermented food in Korea are doenjang and ganjang. To make them, it is necessary to soak soybeans in water and boil them until fully cooked.

Then, they must be pounded and ormed into brick-shaped lumps, and left to dry and ferment. Then, they are placed in salted water in a large pot along with dried red chili and heated charcoal, which help remove impurities and odor during the fermentation process.

The beans thus prepared are then left for about two to three months until they become fully fermented.

This product should then be divided into two, solids and liquid, of which the former needs to be brewed for over five more months and the latter for over three months to develop a full flavor and taste. Just like wine, soy sauce tends to have a richer flavor and taste when brewed for a longer period.

3) **Gochu-jang**(Red Chili Paste)

메주가루에 찹쌀, 소금을 넣어 발효시킨 것을 '고추장'이라 하는데, 고추장은 한국 전통양념의 하나이다. 콩엿기름,소금,코추분말, 쌀분말, 보리대맥, 밀가루, 보리 엿기름을 혼합하여 발효시키는 것이며, 고추장은 한국인의 가장 오래된 중요한 전통 양념 중의 하나이다.

고추는 수백 여년 전에 소개된이후 뜨겁거나 짜릿함을 좋아하는 사람들의 기호식품이었으며 고추와 고추장은 흔히 한국인의 열정적인 성격과 강렬한 상징으로 간주되기도 한다.

Gochujang (chili paste) is a traditional Korean condiment made by fermenting a mixture of soybean malt, salt, and chili pepper powder with a blend of powdered rice, barley, flour, and malted barley.

Gochujang has long been one of the most important traditional condiments among Korean people, whose palates have evolved towards a preference for hot and spicy foods since they were introduced to chili several hundred years ago.

Chili and gochujang are now often regarded as a symbol of the vibrant, energetic disposition of Korean people.

4) **Jeotgal**(Salted Seafood)

젓갈(소금으로 절인 해산물) 다양한 해산물(멸치, 새우, 굴, 대합)들이 소금 및 다른 양념들과 홉합시킨 후 차가운 곳에서 발효시켜 만든다.

Jeotgal (salted seafood) is made by mixing one of a variety of seafood (such as anchovy, shrimp, oyster, or clam) with salt, or with other condiments in addition to salt, and fermenting it in a cool place.

They say that a longer period of fermentation makes it tastier. The tradition of making fermented fish sauce yielded several special delicacies including sikhae, which is made by fermenting fish mixed with rice and condiments.

5) Kimchi

현재 전 세계적으로 한국 음식의 대표적인 것으로 평판받고 있는 김치는 발암 물질의 반대론자자들에게도 영양가치로 칭찬받고 있을 뿐만 아니라 다양한 조미료와 미각으로 자극을 창조하는 수많은 변화현상에 찬미하고 있다.

Now beginning to gain a worldwide reputation as a representative food of Korea, kimchi has been praised for its anti-carcinogenic properties and nutritional value, as well as numerous variations that create excitingly diverse flavors and tastes.

The most common type of kimchi is made by mixing salted white cabbage with kimchi paste made of chili powder, garlic, spring onion, Korean radish ginger, fish sauce and other ingredients like fresh seafood.

Kimchi is normally eaten after fermenting it for several days although some prefer mugeunji (ripe kimchi) which is fully fermented for over one year.

전통적으로 각 지역에서 생산물의 혼합에 따라 다양한 변화를 가져오는데, 서울의 경우 근정(왕조김치)김치, 보쌈김치, 총각김치, 깍두기 등이 있으며 전라도 지방의 경우 잘 알려진 고들빼기 김치, 갓김치 등이 있다.

The ingredients of kimchi vary according to each region and its special local produce and traditions. Seoul, for instance, is famous for gungjung kimchi (royal kimchi), bossam kimchi (wrapped kimchi), chonggak kimchi (whole radish kimchi), and Kkakdugi (Diced Radish Kimchi), while Jeolla-do (Jeolla Province) is well known for its godeulppaegi kimchi (Korean lettuce kimchi) and gat kimchi (leaf mustard kimchi).

In 2006, a US health magazine, Health Magazine, selected kimchi as one of the five healthiest foods on earth.

6) Bibimbap

비빔밥(문자그대로 믹스된 쌀)은 요리전 다른 합성물과 잘게썬 고기, 신선한 계절 채소, 볶은 달걀, 지어진 쌀과 함께 믹스되어 만들어지는 음식이며, 유네스코는 전주비빔밥과 관계된 전주를 '미식도시'로 지정했다. 전주시는 매년 가을에 한국을 넘어 세계 미식가들을 위하여 비빔밥 축제를 개최하고 있다.

Bibimbap (literally "mixed rice") is essentially a dish of cooked rice served after mixing it with an assortment of fresh and seasoned vegetables, fried egg, minced raw beef and other ingredients before cooking.

The dish is closely related with Jeonju, a UNESCO-designated "City of Gastronomy," where food-related festivals, including the Bibimbap Festival, are held every autumn, attracting gastronomes from across Korea and beyond.

Bibimbap has recently begun to attract worldwide attention for its nutritional balance, which is said to help keep those who eat it free from geriatric diseases, and is now generally cited as one of the three most representative dishes of Korean cuisine along with kimchi and bulgogi.

7) Bulgogi

불고기는 한국전통음식으로 문자그대로 '불로익힌 고기' 이며, 다양한 조미료, 달콤한 간장소스와 함께 양념장에 소고기와 돼지고기를 조금씩 자른 후 재워둔 후 불로 익힌 음식이다.

Bulgogi, which literally means "fire meat", refers to a traditional Korean dish made by grilling beef or (rarely) pork after shredding or slicing it and marinating it in sweet soy sauce mixed with a great variety of condiments.

It is one of the rare meat dishes to have developed in Korea, where people were generally more accustomed to eating vegetable dishes, and has won many enthusiasts outside the country.

Bulgogi has recently been adopted by fast-food restaurants in Korea, resulting in the emergence of bulgogi hamburgers and pizzas.

8) **Tteok**(Rice Cake)

떡 또는 한국의 떡은 쌀 분말에 다른 곡류들과 접착성 있게 정리되어 만들어지며, 때로는 식사대용으로 먹기도 한다.

Tteok, or Korean rice cake, refers to a range of sticky cakes made by steaming powdered rice with other grains, usually beans, or by pounding boiled rice into different shapes and textures.

While tteok was sometimes eaten as part of a meal, it was more often one of a variety of special foods served at special family or communal occasions such as birthday parties, wedding receptions, memorial services and traditional holidays. Rice is the main ingredient of tteok, but it is often mixed with other grains, fruits, nuts and herbs such as mugwort, red bean, jujube, soybean and chestnut.

Korean people in the past assigned various symbolic meanings to tteok and made and ate it according to those meanings. They made (and still make) baekseolgi (white steamed rice cakes), for instance, on the first birthday of a baby as it symbolizes a long life, and they made patsirutteok (steamed red bean and rice cake) whenever they started a business as its red color was believed to help repel evil forces.

9) **Juk**(Porridge)

죽은 한국스타일 죽으로 다양한 곡물들로 만들어지며, 소아나 나이 지긋한 사람들에게 흔히 공급되고 있으나, 소화에 문제가 있거나 아픈 사람들이 찾기도 하는데, 최근 죽집들이 한국에 많이 나타나기 시작했다.

Juk is a Korean-style porridge made of various grains that is usually served to children, the elderly, or people suffering from digestive problems. In recent years juk houses have begun to appear in many parts of Korea.

They usually prepare the dish with a wide range of ingredients, mostly grains and vegetables, and it has also been developed into numerous varieties, some of which are now served at small specialty diners.

10) Noodles

한국인들은 국수음식을 널리 보급시킨 사람들 중의 하나라고 할 수 있는데, 잔치국수가 그 하나이며, 결혼식에서 손님들에게 뜨거운 멸치 살코기 국물로 조리되어 대접한다.

Korean people have developed a wide range of noodle dishes that are full of symbolic meanings. One such dish is janchi guksu (literally "banquet noodles"), which is served in a hot anchovy broth to the guests at a wedding reception, (hence the name).

This dish is so closely related with the idea of a happy marriage in Korea that a question such as "When can we eat noodles?" would readily be understood to mean "When do you plan to get married?". It is also eaten to celebrate birthdays because it symbolizes a long, healthy life.

Korean people also have a long established tradition of eating naengmyeon (cold buckwheat noodles), served in either cold beef broth (Pyeongyang naengmyeon) or with a spicy chili sauce (Hamheung naengmyeon).

11) **Hanjeongsik**(Korean Table d'hote)

한정식은 다른 말로 한국의 세트 음식메뉴라고 할 수 있으며, 원래 쌀밥, 수프 그리고 장소에 따라 셋에서 다섯가지 보조음식(대부분 채소)으로 구성된다.

Hanjeongsik, otherwise known as the Korean set meal, originally consisted of cooked rice, soup, and anywhere from three to five, (largely vegetable,) side dishes.

As people are gradually becoming better off due to the thriving national economy, today's set meal tends to be much more luxurious with tens of new dishes, meat and fish included, although the three basic dishes, i.e. rice, soup, and kimchi, still remain.

Two cities in the southwestern part of Korea, Jeonju and Gwangju, are particularly famous for this traditional Korean meal.

12) **Korean Temple Cuisine**

한국의 불교도의 사찰음식은 그들만의 전통요리법으로 채소를 혼합하여 훌륭한 음식을 창조했는데, 스님들과 비구니들의 건강을 유지하고 단백질을 공급할 수 있도록 개발한 것이다.

Korean Buddhist temples have maintained their own culinary traditions, creating a wonderful range of vegetable dishes and ingredients and developing recipes to provide the proteins and other substances required for the monks and nuns to remain healthy.

Temple foods are now enthusiastically received by vegans and other people who follow special diets for health-related reasons.

13) Alcoholic Beverages

알코올음료의 다양성은 기념식이나 기억해야 할 의식, 축제, 휴가 기간 동안 공동사회에 필요한 것으로 개발되어 왔다. 현재 한국에는 300여 가지의 전통음료가 잔존하고 있는데, 서울의 문배주, 송절주, 경기도 광주의 산성소주, 강원도 홍천의 옥성주 등이 그것이다.

A wide variety of alcoholic beverages have been developed across different parts of Korea to meet the needs of local communities during holidays, festivals, memorial rites and other commemorative occasions.

Currently some 300 traditional beverages have survived, including Munbaeju (wild pear liquor) and Songjeolju (pine knot liquor) in Seoul; Sanseong Soju (distilled liquor) in Gwangju of Gyeonggi-do; Hongju (red liquor) and Leegangju (distilled liquor) in Jeolla-do; Sogokju (rice wine) in Hansan of Chungcheong-do; Insamju (ginseng liquor) in Geumsan; Gyodong Beopju (rice liquor) and Andong Soju (distilled liquor) in Gyeongju of Gyeongsangbuk-do; and Okseonju (distilled liquor) in Hongcheon of Gangwon-do.

오늘날 한국에서 가장 전통있는 알코올음료 중의 하나는 막걸리인데, 다른 이름으로 농주, 탁주, 동동주로 알려져 있기도 하다.

One of the most popular traditional alcoholic beverages across Korea today is makgeolli (rice wine), which is also known by other names such as nongju (farmer's wine), takju (cloudy wine) and dongdongju (rice wine).

It is made by a process in which steamed rice, barley or wheat is mixed with malt and left to ferment, and has an alcohol content of 6–7%, making it a fairly mild drink. It has recently begun to fascinate connoisseurs and health-conscious young consumers across many parts of the world, resulting in the opening of makgeolli brewery schools and the appearance of well-trained sommeliers.

Another hugely popular alcoholic beverage of Korea is soju which is made by adding water and flavoring to alcohol extracted from sweet potatoes and grains. With an alcohol content that varies but is significantly higher than makgeolli, it is much appreciated by ordinary citizens across Korea and is rapidly gaining enthusiasts outside Korea.

Tourism Guide Quiz

1. Tell me how to make Gochu-jang (Red Chili Paste).
2. Explain a fermentation of food in Korea.
3. Introduce makgeolli (rice wine) briefly.
4. What is your favorite liquor? Why?
5. Introduce Korean Temple Cuisine.

수행 Tips : The ability to raise 온고지신(溫故知新)

문화예술 공간으로 재탄생되고 있는 오래된 숙박 공간

역사와 함께했던 지역의 오래된 여관들은 대부분 교통의 요지에 자리 잡고 있다. 숙박업의 특성상 일찌감치 사람들이 많이 오가는 곳에 자리를 잡았기 때문이다. 이런 옛날 여관들이 새 옷을 갈아입고 이름을 문화 공간, 전시회장, 게스트하우스로 변신 중이다. 그 대표적인 사례 중의 하나가 종로구 통의동 보안여관이다.

1930년대 경복궁 돌담길 건너편에 통의동 3번지에 세워져 시인 서정주, 소설가 김동리, 함형수와 함께 머물며 시 동인지 '시인부락'을 펴냈던 곳이기도 하다. 보안여관은 1930~40년대 지방에서 올라온 젊은 문학청년 예술가들이 투숙하던 곳이다. 보안여관은 2004년까지 숙박업소였지만 이후 복합 문화예술 공간으로 변했다.

문화예술 공간을 운영하는 회사가 부지를 매입해 기존건물의 모습을 간직한 채 이곳에서 다양한 전시회를 열고 있다. 지금도 보안여관엔 절반정도 뜯어진 꽃무늬 벽지, 부서진 벽과 먼지 낀 창틀이 그대로 남아 있다. 최근엔 가수 서태지가 '소격동' 뮤직비디오를 보안여관에서 촬영하기도 했다.

또한 한국을 대표하는 소설가 조정래의 '태백산맥'은 전남 보성군 벌교가 무대다. 소설 속의 남도여관은 전남 보성군 벌교읍에 자리 잡은 보성여관을 모델로 했다. 보성여관도 1930~1940년대가 배경이며, 상업 중심으로 일본인이 많이 오갔던 곳이다.

보성여관은 지금기준으로 5성급 호텔, 투숙객은 주로 일본인이었으므로 2층엔 다다미방이 남아 있다. 이후 숙박업소로 이용, 1980년대 후반부턴 가게로 이용되다가 2004년 문화재로 등록되었다. 현재는 리모델링 사업을 거쳐 지금은 카페, 소극장, 갤러리로 쓰이고 있으며 총 7개는 숙박도 가능하다.

강남구 신사동 신사역 근처의 신사장도 지어진지 40년이 넘은 곳으로 2013년까지도 숙박업소로 쓰였지만 이후 재단장을 통하여 복합 문화공간으로 사용하고 있다. 영화 '오늘의 연애'를 이곳에서 촬영하기도 했던 장소이다.

벽체와 콘크리트 벽은 그대로 남겨 오래된 공장 같은 느낌을 주고, 1층은 카페로 쓰이고 2~3층은 강연회, 콘서트, 작품 전시회 등을 여는 공간으로 활용한다. 또 패션브랜드 캘빈클라인, 운동화 브랜드 컨버스, 화장품 브랜드 랑콤 등이 이곳에서 제품 개점파티를 열기도 하였다. 이러한 지역은 한국의 전통 숙박과 옛 모습에서 향수를 느끼고자 하는 내·외국인 고객들이 요즈음 많이 찾는 곳이다.과거에 관하여 배우고 가슴에 품어야 한다는 온고지신(溫故知新)이란 말이 있다.

– History repeats itself. By searching the old, learn the new. –

Unit 9

Industrial Toursim in Korea

Unit **9**

Industrial Toursim in Korea

한국은 전례 없는 경제성장을 이루어 평자는 "한강의 기적"을 이루었다고 일컫는데, 한국전쟁 3년 동안 국가 산업시설의 대부분이 파괴되었으며, 자본과 자연자원이 전혀 없었다.

South Korea has achieved economic growth at an unprecedented speed. Observers called what the country has accomplished the "Miracle of the Hangang River", as most of the country's industrial facilities were destroyed during the three-year-long Korean War, and the country was devoid of capital and natural resources.

Figure 9-1 한국의 5대 수출품과 수출액

자료출처 ; 산업자원부

1960년대 초기에 국가는 경제발전계획으로 수출지향정책을 추진하였는데, 주요 수출 품목은 주로 원자재와 소규모 공장에 의한 경공업분야였다.

In the early 1960s, the country pushed ahead with export-oriented economic development plans. At first, the country's major export items were mainly light industrial products manufactured in small factories, or raw materials.

1970년대에는 국가는 중화학산업 상품수출에 기반하여 중화학 산업시설에 투자하였다. 현재 국제경쟁력을 자랑하는 화학, 철강, 조선업과 같은 많은 기업들을 갖고 있다. 강한 경쟁력의 기반이 그 시기에 만들어졌다.

In the 1970s, the country invested in heavy chemical facilities and laid the basis for the export of heavy industrial products.

At present, the country has a number of industries that boast solid international competitiveness, such as the shipbuilding, iron/steel, and chemical industries. The foundation of such strong competitiveness was built around that time.

국가는 중위권 국가 순위의 동기가 된 1988년 서울 올림픽을 유치했으며, 국제 대중매체들은 대만, 싱가포르, 홍콩과 함께 아시아의 4마리 용중의 하나라로 불렀다.

The country hosted the 1988 Seoul Olympic Games, which provided the country with the momentum to join the ranks of semi-advanced countries. The international mass media called the country one of the four Asian tigers, along with Taiwan, Singapore, and Hong Kong.

1996년 12월에 대부분 선진국들로 구성된 OECD의 29번째 국가로 가입하였다.

1960년대에 한국의 수출량은 3천2백80만 달러였으나, 2013년에는 5천5백96억달러에 달하였다. 1948년 1인당 GDP(국민총생산량)은 얼마 안 되는 60달러에 비하여 2013년에는 2만6천205달러가 되었다.

In December 1996, the country became the 29th country to join the OECD, which is largely composed of advanced countries.

In 1960, South Korea's exports amounted to US$ 32.8 million; but by 2013 they reached US$ 559.6 billion. In 1948 GDP per capita was a paltry US$ 60; whereas in 2013 it was US$ 26,205.

Figure 9-2 한국의 GDP와 GNI

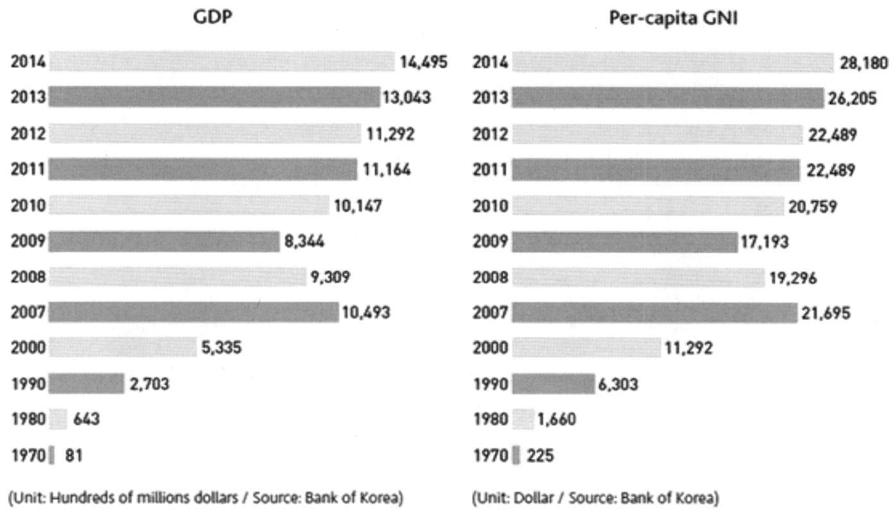

자료출처 ; 한국은행

한국은 부족한 자본과 자원구조에서 성장주도의 대기업 집단 경제구조에 의한 수출주도형 구조였다. 대기업들은 산업을 지배하였으며, 국가의 경제구조는 외부 조건에 민감한 수출과 수입에 크게 의존되었다.

South Korea gradually established an export-oriented economic structure centered on large businesses in the process of pursuing growth as a country with insufficient capital and resources.

Conglomerates came to dominate industry, while the country's economic structure became heavily reliant on exports and imports, leaving it susceptible to external conditions.

1997년 11월 IMF(국제통화기금)에 의한 긴급원조를 통한 외환위기에 직면하였다. 그것은 빠른 경제성장 구조체제하에서의 첫 국가적 시련이었다.

In November 1997, a foreign exchange crisis hit the country, forcing it to turn to the IMF for a bailout. It was the first ordeal the country had had to face after years of rapid economic growth.

Figure 9-3 한국의 해외 무역량

자료출처 ; IMF

2년만에 한국은 IMF체제에서 벗어나 경상수지 균형을 맞추었고 전 성장률을 회복했다. 그 과정에서 IMF로부터 빌려온 자금을 갚기위한 정부의 금모으기 캠페인에 350만의 국민들이 참여했다. 227톤의 금이 모아졌으며, 세계인들은 국가 채무를 갚는데 한국 국민들의 자발적인 참여에 놀라워했다.

In only two years, the country regained its previous growth rate and price levels as well as a current account balance surplus.

In the process, some 3.5 million people joined in the campaign to collect gold to help the government repay the fund borrowed from the IMF.

A total of 227 tons of gold were collected. The world marveled at the Koran people's voluntary participation in the determined effort to repay its national debts.

외환위기를 탈출하기 위한 노력을 하면서 한국은 세계 경제와 재정시스템에 대한 채택으로 부수적인 효과를 얻었다.

While making concerted efforts to extricate itself from the foreign exchange crisis, the country benefitted from certain ancillary effects, such as the adoption of the globalized economic and financial system.

그러나 재구성 중에 정부의 재정 지출과 이익 불균형과 같은 어두운 면도 있었다. 경제 위기 후 한국경제는 견고한 성장을 지속하고 있다.

However, the restructuring process also had its dark sides. The government's fiscal expenditure increased and the income imbalance deepened. After overcoming the economic crisis, the South Korean economy continued to record solid growth.

2010년에 한국은 세계 7대 수출국가로 부상하였으며, 2011년부터 2013년까지 국가의 수출과 수입량이 1조 달러를 유지하고 있는데, 세계 9번째의 연간 1조달러 국제무역국가에 해당한다. 2014년 12월 기준으로 한국의 외환보유고는 3,636억달러, 단기해외부채 31.7%로 유지하고 있어 외환교환위기에 충분한 균형을 유지하고 있다. 이러한 좋은 경제 결과는 국가 신용등급을 상승시키고 있다.

By 2010, South Korea had emerged as the world's 7th largest exporting country. From 2011 to 2013, the total volume of the country's exports and imports stood at US$1 trillion. Thus, the country became the world's 9th country to attain the target of US$1 trillion in annual foreign trade.

The country's foreign currency reserves stood at US$363.6 billion as of the end of December 2014, and the country is in a sufficiently stable position to cope with a foreign exchange crisis, with the percentage of its short-term foreign debts being 31.7% in 2014. The country's sovereign credit rating has risen in recognition of the dazzling economic results recorded by the country.

■ Sophisticated Information Society(세련된 정보화 사회)

한국은 정보 커뮤니케이션 기술을 선도하고 있는 활력 있는 나라이다. CDMA와 WiBro상용화의 세계 제1의 국가로 2011년 이 기술에 기초하여 전국적인 네트워을 구축하고 있다. 이 세련되 정보화 기술은 정부의 혁신을 포함하여 다양한 사회 각 분야의 변화를 이끌어 왔다.

South Korea is a leading powerhouse in information and communication technology. It is a country full of dynamism.

It became the first country in the world to commercialize the CDMA and WiBro technologies and established a nationwide network based on the use of these technologies in 2011. These sophisticated information and communication technologies have led to changes in diverse social sectors, including the innovation of government administration.

SNS를 통하여 국민들은 유용한 정보를 얻고 상호소통을 하며 정부의 불편사항을 보고하여 공적구성원으로서의 사용도 한다. e-정부와 관련된 기술 수출은 2002~2012년 사이에 8억7천3백18만달러를 기록하고 있으며, UN의 193개국에 대한 e-정부 평가에 있어 세계 1위를 위치하고 있다.

With the help of such advanced technologies, the procedures for reporting a baby's birth, moving home or registering a person's death are handled more efficiently. Under the Social Networking Service (SNS), people now use an interactive communication system in which the government provides useful information to people while members of the public can report cases of inconvenience to the government.

The country exported e-government-related technologies worth US$873.18 million between 2002 and 2012.

In the biennial e-government evaluation conducted by the UN, South Korea ranked No. 1 in terms of comprehensive scores in 2010 and 2012 among the 193 countries evaluated.

카카오톡을 통한 3천만 명, 스마트 폰 유저, SNS와 다른 PoP Cast는 커뮤니케이션에 새로운 분야로 확대되고 있어, 정보전달과 연예분야와 같은 것과 같이 고유기능을 더하여 사용되고 있다.

The number of Kakao Talk subscribers stands at 300 million worldwide. It is used by most South Korean smart phone users. Pop Cast, another form of SNS, is establishing a new area in the communication (broadcasting) sector. Now, SNS even exerts an influence in politics through the formation of public opinion, in addition to its inherent functions such as the delivery of information or entertainment.

1) 한국 농어촌공사 : Korea Rural Community Corporation(KRC)

한국농어촌공사는 1908년 창립 이래 한 세기 넘는 시간 동안 국민의 먹을거리 생산기반을 확충하고 농어촌 생활환경 개선에 주도적인 역할을 해온 농정 최일선 기관, 기후변화에 따른 재해대비, 세계화에 대응한 경쟁력 강화 등 변화하는 시대적 환경에 맞게 농어업 · 농어촌 발전을 뒷받침해가고 있는 공기업이다.

과학적인 재해대응과 농정변화에 맞는 생산기반 관리 등 농정의 변화를 주도 · 실행하고 간척지 활용, 농어촌 공간의 재창조 등 미래사업 창조로 농어업의 지속 성장을 위한 혁신을 이루고 있는 기업이다.

투명하고 공정한 경영, 정부 · 유관기관과의 협업경영 · 열린 경영을 지향하며, 고객중심의 영농서비스를 통해 농어촌의 삶의 질을 높이는데 힘쓰고 있는 국민의 기업. 환경 친화적으로 능어촌정비사업과 농지은행사업을 시행하고 농업기반시설을 종합관리하며 농업인의 영농규모적정화를 촉진함으로써 농업생산성의 증대 및 농어촌의 경제. 사회적 발전에 이바지함을 목적으로 하고 있는 글로벌 공기업이다.

청렴윤리가 확고히 자리매김할 수 있도록 제도를 마련하고 다양한 청렴윤리 활동을 펼치고 있으며, 특히 UN Global Compact에 가입 후 인권, 노동, 환경, 반부패관련분야에서 국제사회 수준의 윤리경영 실천도 솔선수범하고 있는 공기업이다.

Photo 9-1 Korea Rural Community Corporation(KRC), credit, KRC

Korea Rural Community Corporation(KRC) has fulfilled its responsibilities to develop, maintain and manage agricultural production infrastructure for over a century since its foundation in 1908, focusing on the production of Korea's staple food, rice. The corporation has also been leading large-scale national projects including the world's largest Saemangeum reclamation project.

Recently, they are raising the nation's status and role abroad by undertaking agriculture and rural village development projects in foreign countries. In particular, KRC is emerging as a globally-competitive and symbolic rural community development public enterprise.

Its competitiveness centers on talented manpower and technical knowhow on rural infrastructure development. They are overseas consulting services and international agriculture cooperation projects, including the Second Saemaeul Movement targeting developing countries, are good examples.

KRC will direct all of its efforts to become the best public enterprise in the world to meet the expectation of customer including farmers and townsmen through self-regulation and creative activity, harmony between the environment and development, and the realization of advanced technology.

KRC fosters and manages the country's food production foundation with clean water and life. Its promote the production of eco- scale, machine-based farming. friendly, high-quality farm products and improve convenience for farmers and fishermen by supplying clean water. enhance the global competitiveness of Korea's agriculture in the increasingly globalizing world. KRC improves the quality of life for residents in farming, mountainous and fishing villages through customized support projects aimed at spreading happiness among villagers. KRC revitalize corporate social responsibility programs to boost welfare for farmers and fishermen. also organizes seasonal festivals and other events to spread happiness among members of rural communities.

2) 한국관광공사 ; Korean Tourism Organization(KTO)

한국관광산업의 중심축인 한국관광공사는 21세기 점점 더 치열해지는 세계관광 각축전 속에서 한국관광산업이 확실한 차세대 국가성장 동력이 되도록 변화와 혁신을 거듭하고 모두가 행복한 관광을 만들어 나가는 국민 기업, 혁신의 중단 없는 추진을 통하여 한국관광의 새로운 성장을 구현한다.

깨끗하고 투명한 윤리경영으로 관광한국의 위상을 높이 사회적 책임을 다하고 적극적인 실천을 통해 국민으로부터 신뢰받는 1등 공기업, 한국 관광산업의 새로운 패러다임을 창출하고 대한민국을 다시 찾고 싶은 매력적인 나라로 만드는 국민기업으로서 관광산업의 중추적인 역할을 담당하는 기업이다.

점점 더 치열해지는 세계관광 경쟁 속에서 살아남고, 나아가 관광산업이 확실한 차세대 국가 성장 동력이 되도록 끊임없이 변화와 혁신을 거듭하고 있는 클린경영 공기업이다.

Photo 9-2 Korean Tourism Organization, credit, KTO

Since its inception in 1962, the driving focus of the Korean Tourism Organization (KTO) has been to create and support necessary tourism facilities and services such as hotels, travel agencies, and transportation infrastructures. As the company has developed, the KTO further expanded its endeavors to include international promotion, developing and modifying Korea's tourism industry infrastructure, and developing tourism complexes to better accommodate a larger numbers of tourists.

The KTO has been a key player in drawing more international visitors to Korea. In 1962, the first recorded number of international visitors to Korea was only 20,000, with numbers soaring to one million by 1978. In 1988, the number reached 2 million; in 1998 there was a recorded number of 4 million visitors to Korea. The number of visitors to Korea has doubled every 10 years, with the trend seeming to hold steady with 14 million recorded visitors as of 2014. Lately, the KTO has been focusing its efforts on developing tourism technology as well as combining Hallyu (the 'Korean Wave') and the tourism industry through Hallyu marketing.

3) 한화케미칼(주) ; Hanwha Chemical

삶의 가치를 높이는 기술기업, 한화케미칼은 한화케미칼은 1965년 설립된 후 국내 최초 PVC를 생산한데 이어 PO, CA등의 각종 산업의 기반이 되는 기초 석유화학 제품 생산을 통해 생활 속에서 다양한 형태로 존재하며 삶의 질 개선에 기여해 왔으며, 석유화학 뿐 아니라 미래를 위한 친환경 기술인 신사업에 이르기까지 삶의 가치를 높이는 미래형 기술을 바탕으로 지속가능한 미래를 만들기 위해 노력해온 기업이다.

또한 체계적인 에너지경영시스템 구축, 온실가스 배출감축 등 기후변화에 우수하게 대응하는 기업에게 주어지는 탄소에너지경영 국제인증(CTS)을 국내 화학업계 최초로 획득하는 등 친환경에너지, 차세대 첨단 소재 같은 미래 신사업을 발굴하여 녹색 성장을 위한 발판을 굳건히 하고 있으며, 아울러 모든 임직원이 참여하는 사회공헌 활동과 신뢰에 기반한 상생 협력 관계 구축, 적법하고 투명한 정도 경영을 추진하며 사회와 함께 하는 지속가능한 성장을 이루어 나가고 있는 세계적 기업이다.

Photo 9-3 Hanwha Chemical Corporation credit,HCC

Leading the Korean petrochemical industry, Hanwha Chemical, Since its establishment in 1965, Hanwha Chemical has led the Korean petrochemical industry through market-leading general-purpose plastics and inorganic chemical products.

As the first producer of PVC in Korea, Hanwha Chemical has succeeded in manufacturing a full array of primary petrochemical products, including Polyolefins, PVC, CA, and TDI. Based on its leadership in the petrochemical market, Hanwha Chemical is now securing its prominence among future-oriented, eco-friendly businesses, taking a leap forward as a echnology-driven company that creates value in life.

Hanwha Chemical is also improving its efforts for sustainable development by organizing social contribution activities participated by all employees, establishing cooperative relationships with business partners based on reliability, and by promoting legitimate and transparent management.

4) 포스코 ; POSCO

포스코는 철을 기반으로 신성장 동력을 육성해 새로운 가치를 제공함으로써 세계인으로부터 존경받는 기업, 'POSCO the Great' 라는 비전 아래 좋은 제품과 서비스, 기업 시민의식과 이해관계자와의 소통을 바탕으로 이윤 이상의 가치를 창출하여 인류 사회의 공존과 번영에 기여하는 기업이다.

포스코가 추구하는 브랜드 핵심 가치는 '신뢰', 포스코의 신뢰는 포스코 패밀리와 고객, 국민, 정부 등 이해관계자와 상생하고 협력하여 대한민국 산업의 근간을 이루게 한 힘, 포스코는 이러한 신뢰의 힘으로 끊임없이 혁신하여 미래의 산업을 이끌고 사람들의 생활을 풍요롭게 창조해 나가는 기업이다.

포스코는 신뢰와 소통, 혁신과 시너지가 어우러진 초일류 패밀리 경영시스템을 확립해 가고 있으며, 새로운 가치창출의 기반이 되는 '스마트 워크플레이스(Smart Workplace)'를 구현하고 있으며, 미래 성장 동력 확충을 위한 기술 발굴 시스템을 완비할 뿐만 아니라 고객의 성공을 이끄는 새로운 마케팅상을 실현, 아울러 상호 신뢰와 동반성장을 위한 나눔과 상생의 경영을 실천하고 있으며, 기업 시민으로서 사회적 책임을 성실히 수행하는 데 앞장서고 있다.

신뢰와 소통의 기업문화와 일과 삶이 조화되는 행복한 일터를 조성하여, 직원들이 주인의식과 창의력을 가진 지식 근로자로 성장하며 자신의 꿈을 실현할 수 있도록 적극적으로 지원, 단순히 기업의 이윤만을 추구하는 회사가 아닌, 기업을 둘러싼 모든 이해관계자와 함께 성장하고자 하는 글로벌 기업이다.

Photo 9-4 POSCO, credit, posco

The key value at the core of the POSCO brand is 'Trust', POSCO's trust lies in the power that formed the foundation of Korea's industrial growth based on cooperation between the POSCO family and stakeholders, including customers, citizens and government. Fundamental, POSCO, the backbone of Korea's economic development, POSCO planted the seeds of Korea's economic growth, and will further strengthen the foundation of industry and realization of the future in various sectors beyond the steel business.

Great Workplace, Implementing an advanced family management system for the future, POSCO is establishing a leading family management system in which trust and communication, innovation and synergy all work in harmony. POSCO realizes the vision of Smart Workplace which will act as the foundation for creating new value, in addition to implementing an example of new marketing, which leads to the success of customers and also completes a system that discovers technologies in order to expand new growth engines.

In addition, POSCO is conducting management based on sharing and coexistence for the goal of having mutual trust and shared growth, while taking the initiative in performing its social responsibilities as a corporate citizen. Great People, Pursuing the growth of both company and individual at the same time, At POSCO, the visions of both the company and staff are converging in the same direction. POSCO is actively supporting staff in order for them to grow into knowledge-centric workers who are able to have a sense of ownership and creativity, and realize their dreams by establishing and implementing 'My Vision'.

Further to this, they are pursuing their individual vision as well as receiving differentiated lifelong education, such as in-house MBA e-learning and the development of a mindset that facilitates a happy workplace where corporate culture based on trust and communication, work and life are in harmony. Talented people who wish to display their abilities on the world stage and achieve their dreams with the company will open up a new future of POSCO.

5) 유한양행 ; Yuhan Corporation

'기업에서 얻은 이익은 그 기업을 키워 준 사회에 환원하여야 한다'는 창업자의 기업이념을 실현하는 기업이 유한양행임, 기업의 존립 바탕인 국가에 성실하게 납세하는 것은 당연하지만 정치와 기업이 철저하게 분리되어 투명한 경영을 해야 한다'는 그의 신념이 유한양행의 기업이미지에 또 하나의 큰 보탬을 준다.

유일한이 평생 기업가로서 펼쳐온 국익 사상, 혁신을 바탕으로 한 합리적 실용주의, 낭비를 절대 허용치 않는 근검절약의 정신과 청지기 정신은 한국 사회 기업사의 보기드문 모범이 되고 있다.

생전에 유일한은 기업인으로서보다 교육사업가로서 더 자부심을 가졌다고 한다. 외국 출장 시에도 '유한양행 회장' 명함보다는 'Educator'라 씌여있는 명함을 즐겨 사용했다는 일화만 보더라도 교육에 대한 그의 애정과 태도를 엿볼 수 있다. 그리고 틈만 나면 우리나라가 부강해지려면 기술교육을 받은 사람이 늘어나야 한다고 강조했다고 한다.

1956년부터 1968년까지 유한 사우공제회, 보건장학회, 유공관리기금 등을 설립하였고 1970년에는 '한국사회 및 교육원조신탁기금'을 설립함으로써 교육뿐만 아니라 사회원조사업의 지속 가능한 발전을 꾀하였으며, 기관 설립 이듬해인 1971년 타계할 당시 개인소유주식 14만941주(발행주식 수의 20.6%) 모두를 이 기관에 기부하여 현재 유한재단의 기틀을 마련했다.

Photo 9-5 Yuhan corporation, credit, Yuhan corporation

"A company's profits should return to the society in which it thrives." the Yuhan corporation in 1926 with the belief that only healthy people could reclaim their sovereignty and he sought to solve widespread public health problems.

Over 80 years, the founding creed to make the best medicines and contribute to public health has been succeeded by us through our intense research and development activities and successful collaboration with multinational pharmaceutical companies.

Dr. New was more proud of being an educator than of his achievements as an entrepreneur. His business cards sometimes listed his title as "Educator" rather than "President of Yuhan Corporation." In the same way that he believed only a healthy people can truly be sovereign, he also believed that only a well-educated people can make their nation prosperous and strong.

Dr. New's philanthropy went far beyond his support of education. In 1970, he donated shares of Yuhan Corporation stock to establish the Korean Social and Educational Assistance Trust Fund, an organization created to promote the general welfare of the nation and provide additional educational support.

In 1971, in the last days of his life, Dr. New contributed 140,941 shares, his entire remaining ownership interest in Yuhan Corporation, to secure the financial future of the fund that in 1977 became the Yuhan Foundation.

Yuhan has been playing active role in global citizenship since its foundation in 1926. Even before global citizenship was conceptualized, Dr. New believed that was the duty and responsibility of business to develop itself for the prosperity of all society, and his own personal commitment to this was the donation of all of his personal property throughout his life up until his death.

6) 삼성전자 ; Samsung Electronics

1969년 수원에서 창립한 이래, 오늘날 삼성전자는 전 세계 200개가 넘는 자회사를 거느린 글로벌 IT 리더로 발전하였다. 삼성전자 제품에는 주력 제품인 스마트폰과 태블릿 같은 모바일 통신 제품은 물론, TV, 모니터, 냉장고, 세탁기와 같은 가전제품, 또한 D램과 비메모리 반도체 같은 핵심 전자 부품에 있어 신뢰받는 공급사, 삼성은 전 세계 고객들이 편리하고 더욱 스마트한 라이프 스타일을 즐길 수 있도록 수준 높은 제품과 서비스를 만들고 공급했다.

삼성은 과감한 혁신과 가치 창조를 지속적으로 추구하면서 글로벌 커뮤니티를 개선, 삼성전자의 미래 비전을 규정하는 기본 원칙은 "미래사회에 대한 영감, 새로운 미래 창조". 2020년까지 연간 매출액 4천억 달러, 브랜드 가치 세계 5위 이내를 달성, 이러한 목표를 이루기 위한 관리 이니셔티브로 3대 핵심 전략 요소, 즉 창조 경영, 파트너십 경영, 인재 경영을 수립했으며, 여기에 삼성의 문화, 사업 운영, 그리고 경영과 관련된 내용을 포함, 의료 건강 및 바이오 기술과 같은 새로운 비즈니스 영역을 개척하려는 삼성은 향후 마주하게 될 새로운 도전과 기회를 기꺼이 맞이할 준비, 삼성전자는 경쟁력을 강화하고 혁신의 역사를 이어나가기 위해 지금까지 이룬 성과의 토대 위에 새로운 능력과 전문성을 구축하고 있다.

Photo 9-6 Samsung Electronics, credit, Samsung Electronics

Since its founding in Suwon, Korea in 1969, Samsung Electronics has grown into a global information technology leader, managing more than 200 subsidiaries around the world. The company's offerings include home appliances such as TVs, monitors, refrigerators, and washing machines as well as key mobile telecommunications products like smartphones and tablets. Samsung also continues to be a trusted provider of key electronic components like DRAM and non-memory semiconductors.

Vision 2020, The underlying principle that defines our vision for the future of Samsung Electronics is "Inspire the World, Create the Future".

This vision is at the very core of our commitment to lead innovations in technology, products and solutions that inspire communities around the world to join our aspiration for creating a better world full of richer digital experiences. Its flagship company, Samsung Electronics, leads the global market in high-tech electronics manufacturing and digital media.

Through innovative, reliable products and services, talented people, a responsible approach to business and global citizenship, and collaboration with our partners and customers, Samsung is taking the world in imaginative new directions. They looks for creative and collaborative visionaries to run our companies. By attracting talented managers and evolving our organization's culture to support them.

Its award-winning products include innovations that minimize the impact on our natural resources and help consumers reduce their carbon footprint. They also provide convenient ways for consumers to recycle their old electronics. Samsung vows to protect the environment by continuing to manufacture eco-conscious products and helping you to recycle them responsibly.

7) 현대자동차 ; Hyundai Motor

창의적 사고와 끝없는 도전을 통해 새로운 미래를 창조함으로써 인류사회의 꿈을 실현, 현대자동차의 모던 프리미엄이 전하는 선물은 자동차로 만나는 새롭고 놀라운 생활, 전 세계가 사랑하는 브랜드 현대자동차는 감각을 충족하는 체험으로, 가슴을 울리는 예술과 문화로 특별한 감성을 전달하고 친밀한 교감을 나누면서 고객의 삶을 더 풍요롭게 가꾸어 보다 다채롭고 흥미로운 방법으로 현대자동차의 모던 프리미엄을 창출, 현대자동차는 모든 고객들에게 프리미엄 감성을 제공한다.

제공하는 프리미엄은 소수만이 누리는 '특권' 이 아니라 모든 고객들이 우리의 제품과 새로운 기술을 통해 함께 누리는 '특별함', 고객에게 '특별함' 을 제공하는 방법은 다양, 제품의 높은 품질과 완벽한 디테일을 통해 품격 있는 감성을 전한다. 또한, 서비스의 편리함과 세심함을 통해 감동을 선사, 다가올 미래에 모두가 누릴 수 있는 새로운 이동수단을 끊임없이 연구함으로써, '사람' 을 가장 먼저 배려하는 이동생활(mobility)의 결정체가 될 것, 모든 고객들에게 프리미엄 감성을 제공한다는 사명을 실현하기 위해 창업정신으로부터 내려오는 도전과 열정을 바탕으로 고객의 곁에서 노력, 현대자동차는 고객 삶의 성실한 동반자로서, 가장 사랑받는 브랜드이다.

Photo 9-7 Hyundai Motor, credit, Hyundai Motor

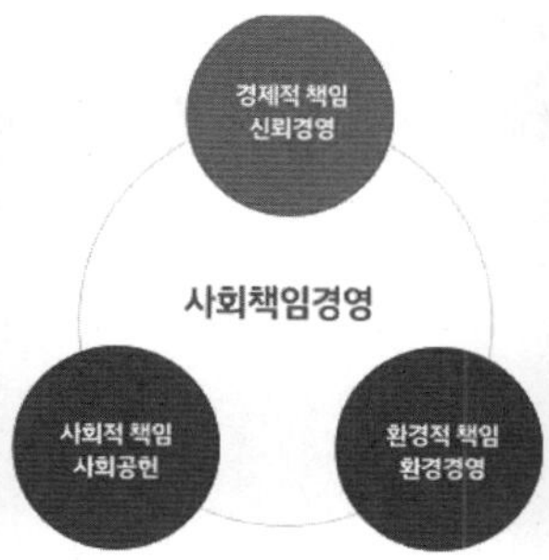

The technological advancements will not only allow Hyundai Motor to meet the safety and environmental regulations but allow us to begin a new era for the automotive industry. We will develop more green cars such as hybrids, electric vehicles and hydrogen fuel cells.

Hyundai Motor will continue to strengthen its market presence and to build on its reputation as an industry leader. They are aiming to achieve global sales of five million units, for the first time in the history of Hyundai Motor and, firmly establish our position in the global market.

In addition to the development of products for the future, the on-going effort to improve our customer's experience in sales and services will strengthen Hyundai Motor's appeal as a brand.

In such a time of change and uncertainty, it is crucial to build a unique set of strengths in order to overcome the challenges that lie ahead and to achieve sustained growth. In addition to developing its capacity as a global automobile manufacturer by achieving qualitative growth, Hyundai Motor will continue to invest in R&D in order to become a leader in technological innovation.

They will continue to expand the scope of our global CSR activities and strive to achieve win-win growth with our suppliers in order to tackle the challenges that arise and to make the world a better place for all.

Management Philosophy, Hyundai Motor Company's most fundamental reason for being, and the foundation for its continued existence. Core Values, Guiding principles for employee behavior and decision making that are essential to realizing our management philosophy and vision.

8) 광명동굴–근대 산업유산

과거 산업경관, 산업현장을 이색적인 문화경관으로 전환한 유형으로써, 대한민국 최고의 동굴테마파크인 광명동굴은 금, 은, 동을 채광하였던 황금광산에 문화와 예술을 융합한 다양한 볼거리로 가득한 신비의 공간이다.

와인을 체험할 수 있는 와인동굴, 동굴아쿠아월드, 황금폭포, 황금길, 황금궁전, 공포체험관, 동굴지하세계와 지하호수, 국내 최대의 용 조형물과 LED 빛의 공간 등 20여 개의 관람시설은 물론 주말에는 빛의 향연인 블랙라이트 퍼포먼스 공연이 개최되고 있으며, 주변을 산책하며 생활 속의 복잡함을 깨끗이 씻을 수 있는 힐링의 장소이다.

Photo 9-8 Gwangmyeong Cave, credit, Gwangmyeong city

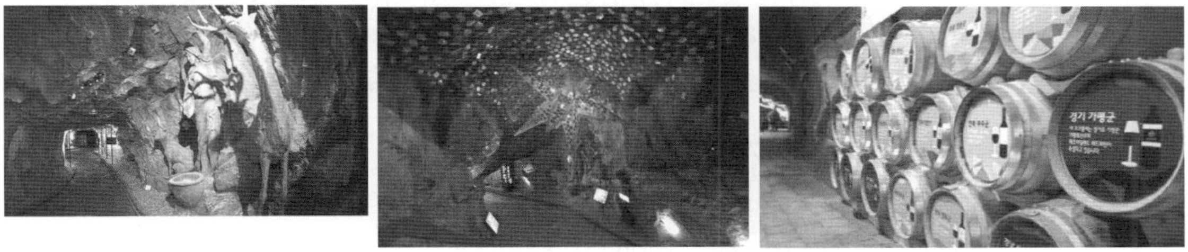

Beyond imagination, Gwangmyeong Cave, When you think of a "cave," you might imagine a natural cave. But Gwangmyeong Cave is the only man-made one in the capital area. The cave was developed in 1912 during the Japanese colony. Up until 1931, gold, silver, bronze, iron, brass were exploited to manufacture weapons during the Greater East Asia War and became the greatest metal mine of in the capital area as a center of Korea economic construction after liberation from Japan.

Gwangmyeong Cave (formerly named as Siheung Mine) which was shut down in 1972 is a place where people were drafted to work by force and abused during the Japanese Colonial Rule and the trace of modern industrialization still remains. It was abandoned for 40 years, from 1972 to 2011, with the strong smell of salted shrimps. In 2011, after being purchased by Gwangmyeong City, it has been transformed into a place where people can relax and enjoy cultural and art experiences.

It is considered the best cave theme park in Korea with combination of industrial heritage and cultural value, and accomplished the miracle of an abandoned mine. a Sustainable Economy Model, Since it opened with an admission charge in April 2014, Gwangmyeong Cave received over 1 million of tourists in just 10 months, earned 4 billion won in revenue, created 200 jobs and became a successful creative economic exemplar in Korea contributing to mutually beneficial growth from both a city and rural perspective, and a reinvigoration of the regional economy. In 2016, the 「Lascaux International Exhibition at Gwangmyng Cave」 and the 「Gwangmyeong Cave International Fantasy Contest and Fantasy Film Festival」, attracting 1.5 million of tourists, earned 8.5 billion won in revenue, and created 415 jobs with new attractions.

9) 보성녹차밭 대한다원–전통 · 향토 산업

지역산업, 지역문화와 결합되어 전통 제조방식의 체험이 가능한 유형으로써, 전남 보성 녹차 밭은 150만평 규모의 차밭이며, 한국 유일의 차(茶)관광농원임, 국내에서 가장 오래된 차밭을 배경으로 농원이며, 지리적으로 볼때 한반도 끝자락에 위치해 있어 바다와 가깝고, 기온이 온화하면서 습도와 온도가 차 재배에 아주 적당한 조건을 갖추고 있다.

대한다업관광농원이 이곳에 차 재배를 시작한 것은 1957년부터, 제주도를 제외하고는 내륙에서 가장 큰 규모이고, 차의 품격도 국내 제일을 자랑하며, 보성읍 봉산리 일대가 내려다보이는 산록에 자리 잡은 농원은 무려 991,740m^2(30만평)이나 되는 드넓은 평원을 형성하여 농원 건물과 함께 그림같은 경관을 보여주고, 농원으로 들어가는 입구에는 전신주 크기의 아름드리 삼나무들이 서있어 신선감이 있으며 현재 연간 녹차 120톤 이상을 생산한다.

대한다업(주)는 봉산리에 있는 보성다원 제 1다원과 회천리에 있는 제 2다원이 있으며, 제1다원은 국내 유일 차 관광농원으로 지정운영, 연간 관광객수도 100만 명이 넘고 있으며, 각종 CF촬영과 영화촬영지로도 유명하며, 영화 “선물”의 촬영 장소였으며

2003년 7월에는 KBS드라마 '여름향기'가 촬영됨. 현대인의 건강과 미용에 특효라는 과학적 입증으로 차 농가들이 점차 늘어가고 있으며, 매년 5월 12일 "다향제"라는 이름의 차 문화 행사를 국내에서 처음 개최하고, 풍작을 기원하는 다신제와 차잎 따기, 차 만들기, 차 아가씨 선발 등의 행사를 실시한다.

Photo 9-9 Boseong tea plantation(茶園), credit, Boseong-Gun.

The pride of the valuable town Boseong is its tea plantation(茶園), The terraced tea plantation covers the entire mountain like a green and fresh ocean.

It looks like a silk wave, green carpet or well-groomed garden trees. The largest tea producing area in Korea, Boseong has a terraced tea plantation on a mountainous area and its tea flavor and taste never fall behind wild tea as a quality product.

Boseong has a wild tea plantation of wider than 3ha, and, therefore, it can be called a tea plantation county other than the ones created after the Korea Liberation from the Japanese Colonial rule.

Boseong has held the Boseong Green Tea Festival every 10th of May since 1985 in order to verify the application of green tea through

Dasinje(茶神祭), tea-picking, tea-making and development of the nation's one and only seawater green tea spa.

Boseong enhances values of tea through the development of tea-based food and commercialization of tea-fed beef and pork. Boseong's green tea plantation became a popular tourist attraction thanks to its appearance in commercial films and dramas.

Good quality tea has a good taste, while low quality tea is good for one's health. Drinking tea clears the mind and is good for hearing, eyesight, digestion, and hangovers.

It also helps people sleep less, be less thirsty, and less tired. The fresh, green tea plantation makes you feel like having a cup of tea in a calm place full of the aroma of tea. When the characteristics of a processed product produced at a specific location, for example its reputation, quality, etc. Boseong green tea is cultivated in an eco-friendly manner to fit consumer tastes. It is produced with the world's best tea processing technology to guarantee its special flavor and aroma. Boseong green tea is a specialty of Boseong County and is produced and processed under certification as Korea's NO.1 KPGI(Korea Protected Geographical Indication) product.

10) 현대중공업-The Hyundai Heavy Industries

광대한 산업경관 및 중공업 제조공정을 체험할 수 있는 유형의 현대중공업은 1972년 조용한 어촌마을에서 창조와 개척 정신으로 조선 사업을 시작하여 세계에서 가장 많은 선박을 건조하는 조선회사로 성장, 한국을 세계1위의 조선대국이 되는데 크게 공헌하였다.

현대중공업은 조선사업을 통해 축적된 기술로 해양, 플랜트, 엔진기계, 전기전자시스템, 건설장비 사업에도 진출하여 세계적인 종합중공업 회사로 성장, 국가경제발전에 기여하였으며, 현대중공업은 창조와 개척정신으로 조선 사업을 시작한 이래 세계에서 가장 많은 선박을 건조하며 건실한 성장을 지속했다.

조선사업을 통해 축적한 기술을 바탕으로 해양플랜트, 엔진기계 사업에 진출하여 세계적인 종합중공업 기업으로 성장하였으며 조선부문 세계 1위, 대형엔진부문 세계 1위의 실적을 기록하는 등 글로벌 선도기업으로서 위상을 공고히 하고 있다.

Photo 9-10 Hyundai Heavy Industries, credit, HHI

Since its establishment in 1972, Hyundai Heavy Industries has grown into the world's leading heavy industries company by successfully diversifying from shipbuilding into offshore and engineering, industrial plant and engineering, engine and machinery, electro electric systems, construction equipment, and green energy businesses. The world's No.1 shipbuilding, Hyundai Shipbuilding Division, the world's number one shipbuilder, leads the global shipbuilding industry with a 15% share of the market. They are proud to note that we have not only played a pivotal role in our own nation's economic development but also have become a responsible global corporate citizen contributing to the sustainable development of the world economy.

HHI's approach to sustainability is always evolving and moving forward. We have expanded the meaning of sustainability to also include social and environmental sustainability. Vision of sustainability is rooted in Hyundai founder Chung Ju-yung's 'Hyundai Spirit'; Creative Wisdom, Positive Thinking, Unwavering Drive. HHI has prevailed over adversity with Hyundai Spirit. Creative Wisdom, Positive Thinking, and Unwavering Drive have developed our core values and vision. On the firm foundation of Hyundai Spirit, Hyundai Heavy has emerged as the world's biggest shipbuilder and an integrated heavy industries company with divisions specializing in offshore & engineering, industrial plant & engineering and engine & machinery. The Company also focuses on sharpening employees' work ethic in an effort to create a rule and principle-abiding corporate culture. As a socially responsible corporation, Hyundai Heavy has been active in promoting community activities such as charities, outreach programmes, and cultural programmes.

Tourism Guide Quiz

1. Can you tell me about five leading export items?
2. Can you briefly explain about sophisticated information society in korea?
3. Introduce Korea Rural Community Corporation briefly.
4. Can you explain the function of the KTO?
5. Introduce Yuhan corporation briefly.

수행 Tips : The ability to raise 성수동 수제화거리- 장수기업 · 산업테마거리

오리지널리티(originality)를 확보한 산업스토리, 산업원형을 중심으로 한 산업관광(industrial tourism)유형으로 1970년대부터 모여든 수제화 업체가 하나의 골목을 만들고 역사를 만들어 스타일 찾아가는 핫플레이스(Hot Place)가 있다.서울특별시 성동구 성수동 성수역 지하철역부터 뚝섬역 주변 수제화 타운 거리가 그곳이다. 현재 350여개 수제화(handmade shoes) 생산업체와 100여 개 중간 가공, 원부자재 업체가 있으며 독특한 분위기의 카페(cafe)도 속속 문을 열고 있다.

빈티지(vintage)한 매력으로 데이트명소, 사진 찍기 좋은 곳으로 떠오르고 있으며, 지자체에서는 구두 산업의 중심지인 성수동을 '수제 화 산업 지역 특화' 로 집중 육성하여 구두 산업을 넘어 문화 · 관광의 상징 사업으로 한 단계 발전시켜 지역경제 활성화를 도모하고자 하고 있다.

지역 특화산업인 수제화 산업을 디자인 및 마케팅 트랜드로 선도하여 고부가가치 산업으로 육성하고, 고급제화 인력 양성으로 구두 제작 기술의 고도화, 수제화를 중심으로 한 스토리텔링 관광코스를 개발하여 문화 · 관광 산업으로 발전시키고자 하고 있다.

이에 성수 구두테마 역 설치 · 운영하고 있으며 성수 수제화 공동판매장 설치 · 운영하고 있으며 구두테마공원 조성, 공방교육 운영, 수제화 전시 갤러리 및 카페 운영, 성수 디자인 팩토리 및 이슈 마켓 건립 운영, 수제화 특화거리 조성, 취 · 창업 연계 맞춤형 교육 프로그램 운영하고 있다.

- Happiness and misery are not fated but self-sought.-

Unit 10

Jeju Island : TOP 10 Things to do in Jeju

Domestic Tour Guide English

Unit **10**

Jeju Island : TOP 10 Things to do in Jeju

Fly just an hour and a half from the capital city of Seoul and you will arrive at South Korea's resort island, Jeju Island or Jeju. With breathtaking natural wonders and hundreds of unique attractions, it is no wonder that Jeju Island always comes out on top of the list as the best travel destination in Korea.

To help you get the best out of Jeju Island, we've compiled a bucket list of 10 best things to do in Jeju – try a bit of everything!

Get in touch with nature in Jeju Island. When it comes to nature, Jeju Island has it all. Named as 7 New Wonders of Nature in 2011, the island offers pristine beaches, waterfalls, oreums (volcanic cones), lava tube caves and many more awe-inspiring natural wonders that are absolutely bucket list-worthy. To help you decide which spots should top your list, we've picked our favorite ten.

1) 한라산 ; Hallasan Mountain

한반도의 최남단에 위치하고 있으며, 해발 1,950m로 남한에서 가장 높으며, 다양한 식생 분포를 이뤄 학술적 가치가 매우 높고 동식물의 보고이고, 1966년 10월 12일 천연기념물 제182호인 한라산천연보호구역으로 지정보호되고 있으며, 가을의 만산홍엽은 빼놓을 수 없는 경관이며, 유독 눈 속에 잠긴 설경의 한라는 절경 중의 절경으로 알려져 있다.

신생대 제4기의 젊은 화산섬인 한라산은 지금으로부터 2만5천년 전까지 화산분화 활동을 하였으며, 한라산 주변에는 360여 개의 오름들이 분포되어 있어 특이한 경관을 창출하고 있으며, 제주섬 중앙에 우뚝 솟은 한라산의 웅장한 자태는 자애로우면서도 강인한 기상을 가슴에 품고 있는 듯하고, 철 따라 어김없이 바뀌는 형형색색의 자연경관은 찾는 이로 하여금 절로 탄성을 자아내게 함.1970년 3월 24일 국립공원으로 지정되었고, 2002년 12월에는 UNESCO 생물권 보전지역으로 지정되었다.

특히 태고의 신비를 그대로 간직한 한라산과 아름다운 땅 제주는 신이 우리에게 선물한 최고의 보물이자 세계인이 함께 가꾸어야 할 소중한 유산으로 인정받아 2007년 6월 27일 제주 화산섬과 용암동굴이 우리나라 최초의 유네스코 세계자연유산으로 등재되었고, 2010년 10월 4일 세계지질공원으로 인증받았다.

Photo 10-1 Hallasan Mountain, credit, Jeju Special Self-Governing Province

A dormant volcano at the center of the island with crater lake on the top, surrounded by a national park with 368 parasitic volcanoes.

As one of Korea's 3 spirit mountains, Hallasan Mountain is located on the southernmost part of the Korean Peninsula, and lays claim to the title of South Korea's tallest mountain with the height of 1,950m above sea level.

Home to all sorts of vegetation, the mountain possesses immense scientific value and is a veritable treasure trove of animals and plants, leading to the designation of Hallasan Mountain Natural Reserve as Natural Monument 182 on October 12, 1966.

In fall, when everything is blanketed by a colorful display of flowers, the mountain covered with the red color of the fall foliage is truly a sight to behold, while the snow-covered mountain in the winter stands out as the view to surpass all views.

A young volcanic mountain from the Quarternary Period of the Cenozoic Era, Hallasan Mountain was believed to have erupted 25,000 years ago, and the 360 or so volcanic cones surrounding the mountain present a unique view. Furthermore, the majestic figure of Hallasan Mountain rising from the middle of the mountain makes it appear as if it is carrying itself with a benevolent yet tenacious spirit.

This celebrated mountain possesses a view of nature that is constantly changing forms and colors according to the season, and this scenery is guaranteed to elicit gasps and exclamations from all who come across it.

The mountain was designated as a National Park on March 24, 1970 and a UNESCO Biosphere Reserve in December 2002. Furthermore, the beautiful land of Jeju and Hallasan Mountain, which preserved the mystery of ancient times and connected Jeju to Jungmun with its western core, were acknowledged as god-given gifts and an unparalleled treasure that must be maintained by the people of the world, leading to the designation of the Jeju Volcanic Island and Lava Tubes as Korea's first UNESCO World Natural Heritage Site on June 27, 2007 as well as being recognized as Global Geopark on October 4, 2010.

2) 성산일출봉 ; Seongsan Ilchulbong(Sunrise Peak, UNESCO World Natural Heritage)

성산일출봉은 천연기념물 제 420호로서 2007년 세계자연유산 등재, 2010년 세계지질공원 대표명소로 인증되었으며, 해 뜨는 오름으로 불리는 성산일출봉은 해발 180m로 약 5천 년 전 얕은 수심의 해저에서 수성화산 분출에 의해 형성된 전형적인 응회구이다. 예부터 이곳 성산일출봉 정상에서 바라보는 일출광경은 영주 10경(제주의 경승지) 중에서 으뜸이라 한다.

넘실거리는 푸른 바다 저편 수평선에서 이글거리며 솟아오르는 일출은 온 바다를 물들이고 보는 이로 하여금 저절로 감탄케 한다. 지방기념물로 관리하다 2000년 7월 19일 천연기념물로 지정되었으며, 빼어난 경관과 지질학적 가치를 인정받아 2007년 7월 2일 UNESCO 세계자연유산에 등재되었으며, 2010년 10월 UNESCO 세계지질공원에 인증되었을 뿐만 아니라, 2011년도 대한민국 자연생태관광 으뜸명소, 2012년 12월 한국관광 기네스 12선에도 선정되었다.

Photo 10-2 Seongsan Ilchulbong , credit,Jeju Special Self-Governing Province

Seongsan Ilchulbong has long been considered one of the best scenic destinations in Korea, An 182m volcanic cone famous for spectacular sunrises. Seongsan Ilchulbong Peak, which is 180m above sea level, erupted underwater in the ocean about 5,000 years ago, which makes it a very rare case among the many craters in Jejudo Island.

Though people used to farm in the area, it is now a natural habitat for 200 types of vegetation such as silvergrass, vine, Pseudosasa japonica, and giant angelica as well as a natural habitat for a variety of wild animals.

It was designated a Natural Monument on July 19, 2000. It was recognized for its outstanding landscape and geological value by UNESCO on July 2, 2007, when it was added to the World Heritage List. And in October 2010, it was named a Global Geopark site.

3) 이호 테우 해수욕장 ; Iho Taewoo Beach

공항에서 가장 가까운 제주바다, 제주올레 17코스가 경유하는 이호테우해수욕장은 용담해안도로와 하귀-애월해안도로 중간에 자리하고 있다. 제주공항은 물론 제주시내와 가장 가까이 있는 해수욕장이며, 이호동의 '이호'와 통나무를 엮어 만들어 고기를 잡을 때 썼던 배를 일컫는 '테우'에서 그 이름이 유래됐다.

이곳은 모래가 검은 편이며 찜질하기에도 좋고, 백사장 경사가 완만하고 파도가 세지 않아 아이들이 놀기 좋은 곳이다. 비행기를 보며 해수욕을 즐길 수도 있고, 방파제에서 낚시를 즐길 수 있으며, 또, 매년 7, 8월 중에는 제주 고유의 어로문화를 복원한 '이호테우축제'가 열리며 멸치잡이 재현, 테우노젓기대회, 테우만들기, 원담고기잡이 등 전통 어촌문화체험들을 해 볼 수 있다. 밤이 되면 조랑말을 형상화해 만든 빨간색, 하얀색의 '쌍둥이 말 등대'에 불이 켜지고, 낮보다 아름다운 밤을 만들어준다. 야영하기에 좋은 솔숲, 아름다운 일몰과 야경으로 제주도민들의 사랑을 받고 있다.

Photo 10-3 Iho Taewoo Beach, credit, Jeju Special Self-Governing Province

The closest Beach to downtown Jeju city famous for iconic horse-shaped lighthouses.

Admission is free, and it is the closest beach from downtown Jeju-si. The beach is composed of black sand and pebbles. Like Samyang Black Sand Beach, it is a great place for a day in the sand.

They are two lighthouses that are red and white, built in the shape of the Jeju pony. This lighthouse goes well with the ocean in the background and is a popular tourist area, and became Iho's landmark.

4) 만장굴 : Manjanggul Lava Tube(UNESCO World Natural Heritage)

대자연의 신비, 세계적인 규모의 화산 용암의 침하운동으로 생성된 천연동굴이자 유네스코 지정 세계문화유산으로 등록된 곳, 만장굴은 총 길이가 약 7.4km이며, 부분적으로 다층구조를 지니는 용암동굴이다.

특히 주 통로는 폭이 18m, 높이가 23m에 이르는 세계적으로도 큰 규모의 동굴이다. 전 세계에는 많은 용암동굴이 분포하지만 만장굴과 같이 수십만 년 전에 형성된 동굴로서 내부의 형태와 지형이 잘 보존되어 있는 용암동굴은 드물어서 학술적, 보전적 가치가 매우 크다.

Photo 10-4 Manjanggul Lava Tube(UNESCO World Natural Heritage), credit, Jeju Special Self-Governing Province

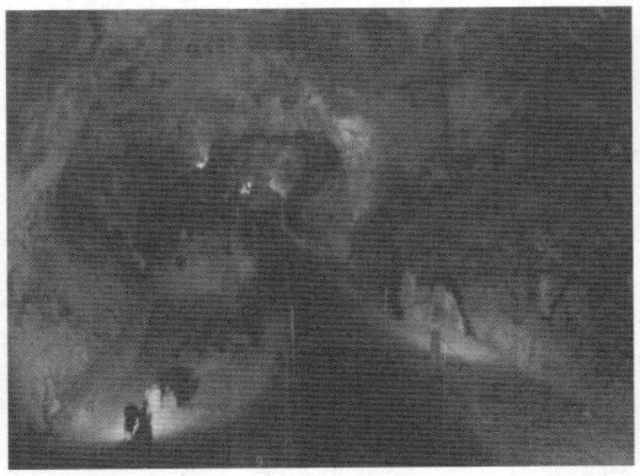

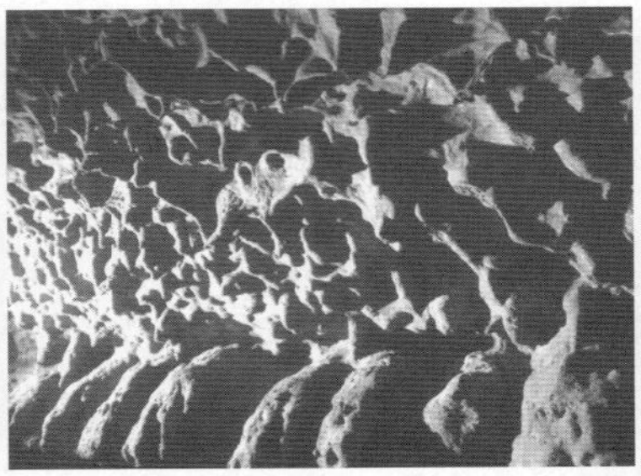

만장굴은 동굴 중간 부분의 천장이 함몰되어 3개의 입구가 형성되어 있는데, 현재 일반인이 출입할 수 있는 입구는 제2입구이며, 1km만 탐방이 가능하며, 만장굴 내에는 용암종유, 용암석순, 용암유석, 용암유선, 용암선반, 용암표석 등의 다양한 용암동굴생성물이 발달하며, 특히 개방구간 끝에서 볼 수 있는 약 7.6m 높이의 용암석주는 세계에서 가장 큰 규모로 알려져 있다.

A Natural Lava Tube Which Formed When Underground Lava Flowed Toward the Sea, the longest lava tube on Jeju with the largest recorded lava column in the world inside the cave.

The total length of Manjanggul Lava Tube is about 7.4km. It is a lava tube that is partially multilayered. The main tunnel' s width is 18m and its height is 23m.

It is one of the largest lava tubes in the world. There are many lava tubes in the world, but Manjanggul Lava Tube has a significant meaning in that it was formed thousands of years ago, and it is very well preserved. Therefore, it is very valuable to researchers and scientists.

Due to the sinking of the ceiling, there are 3 entrances. The one that tourists can use is the second entrance and they are only allowed to go as far as 1km into it. There are various cave formations in Lava Tunnel in Manjanggul Lava Tube, such as stalactites, stalagmites, flowstones, lava tubes, lava shelves, and lava rafts.

In particular, the lava column that is located at the end of the tourist area is about 7.6m high and is known as the highest lava column in the world.

5) **주상절리대**(중문대포해안) : **Jusangjeolli Cliffs**(Oceans Views at Daepo)

깎아지르는 듯한 절벽의 아름다움과 제주의 바다를 동시에 볼 수 있는 곳, 주상절리는 마치 예리한 조각칼로 섬세하게 깎아낸 듯한 4~6각형 형태의 기둥으로, 현무암질 용암류에 나타나는 수직절리를 말하며, 두꺼운 용암이 화구로부터 흘러나와 급격히 식으면서 발생하는 수축작용의 결과로 형성되었다. 마치 계단을 쌓은 듯 겹겹이 서 있는 육모꼴의 돌기둥이 병풍처럼 둘러쳐져 있어 자연의 신비로움을 만끽할 수 있다.

그리고 그 기둥들에 부딪히는 파도 또한 마음을 뺏기는 볼거리인데, 파도가 심하게 일 때는 높이 20m 이상 치솟는 '쇼'가 펼쳐지기도 해서 그곳을 찾는 사람들은 언제나 넋을 잃고 구경하곤 하며, 중문 · 대포해안 주상절리대는 높이가 30~40m, 폭이 약 1km 정도로 우리나라 최대 규모를 자랑하며, 제주도 천연기념물 제443호로 지정돼 있다.

Photo 10-5 Jusangjeolli Cliffs(Oceans Views at Daepo), credit,Jeju Special Self-Governing Province

The Classic Jeju-style Cliffs and Oceans Views at Daepo, unique volcanic rock formations that look like rectangular pillars near Jungmun Beach.

The columnar joints near the coast in the eastern Jungmun Tourist Complex, where the waves breaks and dark red hexagonal stones make up tall layers, is considered a gift of nature and was designated as Natural Monument No. 443.

If you stand in front of the joints you can see the waves hitting the stones and breaking into white bubbles, which feels as if they carry the sad stories of stone carvers, and the scenery is incredible as when the waves are turbulent they reach a height of about 20m.

The place is becoming ever more popular with tourists as they walk around and look at the incredible scenery along with the fresh scent of the sea.

6) 우도(해양도립공원) : Udo Maritime Park

소가 누워있는 형상을 하고 있는 제주의 가장 큰 섬, 우도는 일찍부터 소섬 또는 쉐섬으로 불리다가 한자로 우도(牛島)라 표기하였으며, 제주도 북동쪽 약 3.8km 지점에 위치하고 있다.

섬의 길이는 3.8km이며, 둘레는 17km, 우도는 완만한 경사와 옥토, 풍부한 어장, 우도팔경 등 천혜의 자연조건을 갖춘 관광지로써 매년 40~50만 명의 관광객이 찾아들고 있다.

우도 팔경과 같이 자연 절경 이외도 바다낚시, 자전거 하이킹, 잠수함과 유람선 등을 통해 여행의 재미를 더해주며, 관광객들은 주로 산호 해변, 우도봉, 검멀레 해변을 주로 찾고 있다.

Photo 10-6 Udo Maritime Park, credit,Jeju Special Self-Governing Province

At the far east of Jejudo Island, located 3.8km northeast from Seongsanpo Port, is Udo Island, which got its name because it looks like a cow lying down or a cow with its head up. If you see it from Jongdal-ri, Gujwa-eup, Bukjeju-gun, you can see an island which looks like a cow's body, from head to tail. With its unique shape, you can tell that it is Udo Island at a glance.

Udo Island is a blessed tourist site with natural environments such as plain rich soil, diverse fishing grounds, and the 8 Scenic Sights of Udo Island. Above all, you can experience Jejudo Island's unique and traditional culture such as female divers, Stonewall Walkway, and stone tombs, making you feel like you're in a smaller version of Jejudo Island.

Tourists can also enjoy various activities such as fishing, mountain biking, bus tour, boat tour, and submarine tour. On top of Udobong Peak, which is 132m high, you can see the entire island beneath you, and you can see the view of Jejudo Island, including Seongsan Ilchulbong Peak, with the clear blue ocean as the background.

Udo Island became even more famous because it was the filming site for the movie "A Love Story" featuring Lee Jeong-jae and Gianna Jun. If you walk along Udo Sanho Beach, where the movie was filmed, the spectacular view of the snow white sand and the blue ocean will have you wondering if you've stepped into the movie itself.

Udo Island became even more famous as a marine tourist site as it offers submarine tours where you can enjoy the view of an underwater world. It only takes 15 minutes by boat from Seongsanpo Port and the boats can carry cars so it is very convenient to visit.

7) 천지연폭포(Cheonjiyeon Falls)

하늘과 땅이 만나서 이룬 연못이라 하여 이름 붙여진 폭포 · 서귀포시 서홍동 · 천연기념물 제163호 · 천연기념물 제27호 · 올레6코스, 자연을 느끼며 산책할 수 있는 천지연 폭포이며, 천지연이라는 이름은 하늘과 땅이 만나 이루어진 연못이라는 것에 유래하며, 길이가 22m, 못의 깊이가 20m로, 위로도 아래로도 길이가 굉장하고, 이곳은 열대어의 일종인 무태장어가 서식하는 것으로도 유명하다.

그 외에도 오리와 잉어가 서식하고 있고, 폭포로 가는 길은 산책로로 꾸며져 있으며, 구실잣밤나무, 동백나무 등 난대성 식물이 숲을 이루고 있고, 잘 다듬어진 현무암으로 길이 평탄하게 만들어져 있다.

나오는 길에는 기원의 다리와 삼복상을 볼 수 있으며, 다리를 건너며 삼복을 나타내는 동물상에 동전을 던지고, 소원을 빌 수 있고, 산책로 끝자락에 위치한 폭포는 웅장한 소리를 내며 절벽 아래로 떨어지며, 오후 10시까지 야간개장을 하는데, 밤에 보는 폭포의 모습도 장관이다.

Photo 10-7 Cheonjiyeon Falls, credit, Jeju Special Self-Governing Province

Cheonjiyeon Falls, Named to Mean 'The Sky Connected With the Land'

At Cheonjiyeon Falls, white water falls from the rock cliff and make a thundering sound. It gets its name because it means "sky connected with land." It is 22m high and 12m wide, and the view and the sound that the waters create when they fall is magnificent.

Not only Elaeocarpus, which is designated as Natural Monument 163, but also a variety of temperate plants such as brambles, Psilotum nudum Griseb., Siebold's chinquapin, Shiny xylosma, and camellias grow in the valley near Cheonjiyeon Falls.

It is also famous for the Natural Habitat for Giant Mottled Eels (Natural Monument 27), which are nocturnal. Recently, a picture that captured a reflection of a rock that looks like a face is gaining lot of attention.

The rock itself does not look too unique, but when the surface of water reflects the rock, the rock and the reflection look like a face. When seen from the left, it looks like the face of an adult, but when viewed from the right, it looks like the face of a baby.

A representative of the General Services Office for Tourist Attractions said, "you wouldn't think that it looks like a face when you look at the rock only, but just like decalcomania, if you look at the reflection and the rock together, it magically looks like a human's face. The face is clearer in the afternoon, when the sun starts sinking in the west, than in the morning."

8) 마라도(마라해양도립공원) : Marado Island(Mara Ocean Park)

푸르른 초원이 아름다운 마라해양도립공원, 난대성 해양 동식물이 풍부하고 주변 경관이 아름다워 2000년 7월 천연기념물 제423호로 지정, 보호되고 있으며, 국토 최남단인 섬 · 서귀포시 대정읍 마라리 한국 최남단의 섬으로 대정읍 모슬포항에서 남쪽으로 11km 해상에 위치한 제주도에서 배를 타고 들어갈 수 있는 섬, 고구마 형태를 띠고 있으며, 해안은 오랜 해풍의 영향으로 기암절벽을 이루고 있으며, 나무 한 그루도 보이지 않는 넓은 초원이 특징이나 예전에는 산림이 울창하였다고 한다.

모슬포항과 산수이수동선착장에서 정기여객선과 관광유람선이 수차례씩 왕복 운항하고 있으며, 마라도를 들어서게 되면 넓은 초원에 푸르른 잔디가 가득하고, 초원의 군데군데에는 작은 건물들이 서있다.

가을에 이곳을 방문하게 되면 억새로 가득한 모습을 볼 수 있는데 이 또한 마라도만의 매력이며, 섬 전체가 가파르지 않은 언덕으로 되어 있어 부담 없이 거닐 수 있기 때문 나이가 많은 분들과 같이 오기에도 좋으며, 섬 한 바퀴를 도는 데 1~2시간 정도면 충분하다. 작고 소박한 섬이다 마라도가 품고 있는 매력은 한 번 그곳을 방문하게 되면 잊지 못할 추억이 되는 곳이다.

Photo 10-8 Marado Island, credit, Jeju Special Self-Governing Province

There are many beautiful things to see on Marado Island, such as steep coastal cliffs, strangely shaped rocks, a sea channel that is called "Namdaemun", and the sea cave. It is also worth seeing Cheonyeodang Shrine (or Halmangdang Shrine), which is a shrine that

prays for the safety of the divers, the Lighthouse of Marado Island, and Mara Branch School.

The residents of the island provide 16 rooms for tourists or anglers that visit the island. Janggunbawi Rock, which residents consider sacred because a patron saint descends on it, and Cheonyeodang Shrine, which has a legend of Aegieopgae, can also be found on the island. It only takes about an hour to tour the island.

When you reach Janggunseok Rock near the Lighthouse of Marado Island, you can see the southernmost point monument. Designated and Protected as Natural Monument 423 in July 2000 Due to Its Wildlife and Beautiful View. It is the starting point and the ending point of Korea. On the island, you can see the southernmost point monument and it only takes 90 minutes to walk along the coast.

9) 에코랜드 테마파크(Eco Land Theme Park)

곶자왈 원시림의 테마공원, 기차를 타고 숲을 여행하는 에코랜드, 에코랜드는 1800년대 증기기관차인 볼드윈 기종을 모델로 약 4.5km 거리의 곶자왈을 체험하는 테마파크이며, 곶자왈은 제주도 방언으로, 화산이 분출할 때 용암이 덩어리로 쪼개져 요철 지형이 만들어지면서 형성된 독특한 숲을 일컫는다. 보온과 보습 효과가 높아 다양한 식물이 공존하며, 가지가 하늘로 뻗어있어 곶자왈만의 생명력과 신비로움을 관람할 수 있다.

에코랜드는 각기 다른 테마를 가진 역들로 나뉘어 있는데, 메인역은 편의시설을 이용할 수 있고,에코브리지역은 규모가 큰 호수와 수상데크가 있으며, 레이크사이드역에는 풍차와 목초지가 주는 이국적인 풍경을 감상할 수 있으며, 피크닉가든역은 어린이들이 뛰놀 수 있는 키즈타운과 곶자왈 숲길인 에코로드를 볼 수 있고, 라벤더, 그린티&로즈가든역에는 허브, 장미, 녹차가 어우러진 유럽식 정원을 볼 수 있음. 에코랜드는 사계절 내내 다른 분위기를 띄고 있는데, 봄과 여름에는 푸른 녹음과 따뜻한 햇살을, 가을에는 알록달록 피어난 코스모스와 억새 물결을, 그리고 겨울에는 새하얀 설경을 볼 수 있다.

Photo 10-9 Eco Land Theme Park, credit,Jeju Special Self-Governing Province

Travel by Train in the Virgin Forest of Hallasan Mountain, Eco Land Theme Park is a place where you can enjoy approx. 991,735㎡ of Gotjawal virgin forest in the Lincoln Locomotive handmade in England using Baldwin as the model, which is the steam locomotive of 1800's.

Gotjawal in Gyorae, where Eco Land is located, not only contains large amounts of underground water, but has high heat conservation and moisturizing effect, so it is a forest of mystery where the nature from both northern and southern limit line co-exist.

You can enjoy the greatness of nature, which has covered the rocks of volcano, and covers up even the sky to make it to be the haven of animals and plants. During your ride of 4.5km, you can experience various insects, animals and plants all living in Gotjawal, the forest of mystery, and learn the unlimited benefit which the nature gives us.

10) 새별오름 : Saebyeol Oreum Volcanic Cone

서쪽에 위치해 있으며 억새가 예쁜 오름, 남봉을 정점으로 남서, 북서, 북동 방향으로 등성이가 있으며, 등성이마다 봉우리가 있으며, 서쪽은 삼태기 모양으로 넓게 열려 있고, 북쪽은 우묵하게 파여 있으며, 마치 별표처럼 둥그런 표창 같은 5개의 봉우리가 존재한다.

전체적으로 풀밭을 이루나 북쪽 사면에 일부 잡목이 형성되어 있고, 서북쪽 사면에 공동묘지가 조성되어 있으며, 매년 정월대보름을 전후하여 제주도를 대표하는 축제인 제주들불축제가 열리는 곳이다.

Photo 10-10 Saebyeol Oreum Volcanic Cone, credit,Jeju Special Self-Governing Province

With the southern peak as its summit, the volcanic cone had ridges to the southwest, northwest, and northeast. The western side is open widely in the shape of a Samtaegi (straw basket) to the north. There are 5 peaks that resemble a round asterisk.

The volcanic cone is generally covered in grass, though the northern slope is partially covered in scrubs, and there is a cemetery on the northwestern slope. The volcanic cone gets its name from the fact that it stands along with the morning star under the evening sky.

With so many destinations to visit in Jeju Island, you won't be able to visit and see all of them in one day (especially if you are traveling by foot or public transportation). If this is your first-time in Jeju Island, you will definitely be blown away by hundreds of museums scattered all over the island. In fact, Jeju's museums are one of the main reasons to visit the island.

Tourism Guide Quiz

1. Introduce Jeju Island briefly.
2. Recommend one of the best attractions in Jeju Island.
3. Pick one of the best places you have ever traveled in Jeju Island and explain the reason(s) for your choice.
4. Explain Seongsan Ilchulbong in Jeju Island?
5. Can you introduce the Manjanggul Lava Tube.

수행 Tips : The ability to raise 남이섬에서 느끼는 새로운 관광바람

한국관광 연구원의 관광지식정보시스템 관광통계에 따르면 남이섬을 찾은 동남아 관광객은 년간 약 80만 명으로 이 지역 외래 관광객의 35%에 달하고 있다.

한국을 찾는 대표적인 동남아 국가들은 태국, 말레이시아, 인도네시아, 대만, 홍콩, 싱가포르, 필리핀, 베트남, 캄보디아, 라오스 등인데 남이섬을 즐겨 찾고 있는 배경에는 남이섬이 그 동안 한발 앞서 추진해 온 동남아 국가들과의 진정성 어린 문화교감을 들 수 있다.

남이섬은 지난 2011년부터 연간 37만 명이 내한하는 태국인 관광객을 위해 태국 어 관광안내 리플릿을 비치하고 있으며, 아세안(ASEAN, 동남아시아국가연합) 지역의 대표적 공용 언어인 말레이 · 인도네시아어로 제작된 관광안내 리플릿을 국내 주요 관광지 중 최초로 도입했다.

3억 명 이상이 쓰고 있는 세계 5위권의 주요 언어인 말레이 · 인도네시아어는 말레이시아, 인도네시아, 브루나이, 싱가포르 등지에서 사용되고 있으며, 우리나라 관광업계에서는 놓칠 수 없는 주요 관광 홍보 대상 지역어이기도 하다.

또한 남이섬은 아세안을 위시한 여러 동남아 국가들과의 문화예술 교류도 활발히 진행해 오고 있다. 남이섬과 말레이시아 '랑카위 섬' 우호결연을 시작으로 전시, 공연, 학술대회 등 다방면의 교류를 지속적으로 실천하고 있다. 이에 힘입어 태국 영화, 인도네시아 드라마, 말레이시아 영화와 버라이어티쇼, 베트남 국영방송의 해외탐방코너 등 많은 프로그램들이 남이섬에서 촬영되면서 인기를 얻고 있다.

남이섬도 그들의 문화와 관습을 배우기 위해 해마다 60여 명의 직원들을 싱가포르, 말레이시아, 필리핀 등 동남아시아 일대로 연수를 보내고 있으며, 그들을 더 잘 알기 위한 학습의 결과와 노력이 관광객 증가로 연결되고 있는 것이다. 현 추세라면 남이섬을 찾는 동남아 관광객은 지속적으로 증가할 것으로 예상 할 수 있으며, 지난 십여 년 동안 아세안을 중심으로 동남아 관광시장으로부터 불어오는 관광 열풍의 선두주자로 성장 할 수 있다고 사료된다.

설렘을 안고 찾아와 추억을 가져가는, 사람 내음 나는 남이섬이 새로운 관광 바람, 남풍(南風)을 불어오게 하고 있는 것이다. 이리하여 아세안의 오피니언리더들인 필리핀 하원의장, 태국 국회의장, 베트남 국세청장, 인도네시아 무슬림협회 총재 등 주요 인사들이 남이섬을 찾아 한국의 문화와 자연을 느끼고 돌아가는 건 이제 익숙한 광경이 됐다. 한국을 찾는 관광객의 시장 다변화 차원에서 깊이 고려해야 될 때에 각 지자체 및 관광홍보 · 마케팅 담당자들에게 시사 하는 바가 크다.

– Where there is a will, there is a way. –

Index

【I】

【J】

【K】

【L】

【M】

저자 및 감수자 소개

저자 | **김 도 영**(Do-Young Kim)

김도영 교수는 경희대학교 일반대학원 관광학과에서 관광학 박사학위를 취득하였다. 관광산업계에서 관광영어통역사를 취득 후 실무현장에서 업무를 담당하였고, 국제여행부 팀장업무를 수행하였다. 경희대학교 호텔관광대학 관광영어통역과 겸임교수로 재직하면서 관광영어를 강의하였으며 현재는 한양여자대학교 호텔관광(학)과에서 교수로 재직 중이다.

■ **자격증** 관광통역안내사, 국외여행안내사, TESOL, CHA, CCIM

■ **저서 및 논문**

- The impact of tour quality and tourist satisfaction on tourist loyalty: The case of Chinese tourists in Korea, Tourism Management 32,1115-1124.
- The Effect of the Perception of Influenza A(H1N1) on International Travel Decision-making Process of Group Tourists, Journal of Tourism Sciences,35(7)189-209
- A Study on the model of medical tourism in korea, Journal of Tourism & Leisure Research, 23(3),203-223. 외 관광학 논문 20편
- 국외여행안내 실무론, 현학 사, 2104 외 3권

■ **주요경력**

(사)한국관광레저학회 부회장(현), 한국컨벤션학회 부회장(현), (사)한국해양기업협회 부회장(현), (사)한국호텔외식경영학회 이사, 한국관광연구학회이사, (사)한국일반여행업협회 이사, (주)POSCO, (주)한진관광 국제여행부 팀장, ㈜이에스 리조트 이사, (주)하나투어리스트 이사, 서울특별시 미래 도시육성사업단 연구위원, 교육인적자원부 관광교과도서 심의위원, 한국산업 인력공단 관광통역안내사 출제위원, 2012여수 EXPO세계박람회 수요예측조사자문위원

감수자 | **최 유 진**(Yoo-Jin Choi)

최유진 교수는 한양대학교 대학원 영문학과에서 한양대 영문학 박사학위를 취득 후 현재 한양여자대학교 호텔관광(학)에서 관광영어, 객실관리영어, 국내영어안내 영어 등을 강의하고 있다.

■ **저서 및 논문** 관광 영어 외

■ **주요경력**

18세기영문학회 연구이사, 영미문학페미니즘학회 섭외이사, 미래영어문학회 편집이사, 19세기영어권문학회 편집이사, 21세기영어문학회 편집이사

감수자 | **제임스 로라드 포스컷**(James, Ronald Forscut)

제임스 로라드 포스컷 교수는 University of Caterbury 정치 과학, 철학을 전공하고 현재 한양여자대학교 호텔관광(학)에서 원어민 교수로 재직 중이며 토익스피킹, 호텔커뮤니케이션 영어 등을 강의하고 있다.

■ **주요경력 및 자격증** IELTS평가위원, TESOL Certificate, CTBE Certificate

국내여행안내영어
Domestic Tour Guide English

2017년 8월 20일 초 판 인쇄
2017년 8월 31일 초 판 발행

저 자 김 도 영
감수자 최유진 · 제임스 로라드 포스컷
발행인 한 인 환
발행처 도서출판 **기 문 사**
등 록 1978. 8. 9. NO. 6-0637
주 소 서울시 동대문구 안암로 50-1(용두동) 홍신빌딩 3층
전 화 02) 2265-7214/922-8662~8663
팩 스 02) 922-8772

homepage : www.kimoonsa.co.kr
e-mail : book@kimoonsa.co.kr

ISBN : 978-89-7723-758-2 93740

정가 : 19,000원